MANCHESTER UNITED OFFICIAL YEARBOOK 2000

Compiled and Edited by Cliff Butler
Assisted by Ivan Ponting

Contributors
MARTIN EDWARDS
SIR ALEX FERGUSON
BARRY MOORHOUSE
CLIFF BUTLER
IVAN PONTING

Thanks to
ARTHUR ALBISTON, NEIL BAILEY, RUTH BAYLEY, ADAM BOSTOCK, DAVE BUSHELL, VINNIE CAMPBELL,
LEE CHAPMAN, DIANE CLIFFORD, JOHN COOKE, TONY COTON, MIKE COX, JIMMY CURRAN, SIMON DAVIES,
MARK DEMPSEY, MARK EDWARDS, SHARON FAULKNER, JULIAN FLANDERS, LES KERSHAW, TREVOR LEA,
EDDIE LEACH, STEPHANIE McCAIG, CAROLE McDONALD, PAUL McGUINNESS, TOMMY MARTIN, STUART
MATHIESON, DAVID MEEK, ROSS MILLARD, ALBERT MORGAN, DEREK NASSARI, DEBBIE NEWALL, CLARE
NICHOLAS, TOMMY O'NEIL, NICKY PARIS, MICK PRIEST, MATT PROCTOR, DAVID PUGH, KEN RAMSDEN, ARTHUR
ROBERTS, CARLY ROGERS, DAVE ROUSE, DAVID RYAN, JIMMY RYAN, JIM SANDFORD, ANDY SMITH, TOM
STATHAM, TIM TAYLOR, DANNY WEBBER, TONY WHELAN, DAVID WILLIAMS, ALAN WOODS, STUART
WORTHINGTON, ALEC WYLIE, ANNE WYLIE AND EVERYONE WHO SUPPLIED INFORMATION THROUGHOUT
THE 1999-2000 SEASON

THANKS ALSO TO ALL THE CLUBS WHO KINDLY GRANTED PERMISSION IN ALLOWING THEIR OFFICIAL
CLUB CRESTS TO BE REPRODUCED IN THIS PUBLICATION

Photographs
JOHN & MATTHEW PETERS, EXCEPT P146(T) ACTION IMAGES

Design and editorial
DESIGNSECTION FROME

First published in 2000 by
MANCHESTER UNITED BOOKS
an imprint of **ANDRE DEUTSCH**
76 Dean Street, London W1V 5HA

in association with
MANCHESTER UNITED FOOTBALL CLUB PLC
OLD TRAFFORD MANCHESTER M16 0RA

ISBN
0-233-99783-0

Printed and bound in the UK by
BUTLER & TANNER LTD. FROME AND LONDON

CONTENTS

MANCHESTER UNITED FOOTBALL CLUB PLC

Directors
C.M. EDWARDS (Chairman)
J.M. EDELSON
SIR BOBBY CHARLTON CBE
E.M. WATKINS LI.M.
R.L. OLIVE
P.F. KENYON
D.A. GILL

Chief Executive
C. MARTIN EDWARDS

Manager
SIR ALEX FERGUSON CBE

Secretary
KENNETH R. MERRETT

Honours

EUROPEAN CHAMPION CLUBS' CUP – Winners: 1968 · 1999

EUROPEAN CUP WINNERS' CUP – Winners: 1991

FA PREMIER LEAGUE – Champions: 1993 · 1994 · 1996 · 1997 · 1999 · 2000

FOOTBALL LEAGUE DIVISION ONE – Champions: 1908 · 1911 · 1952 · 1956 · 1957 · 1965 · 1967

FA CHALLENGE CUP – Winners: 1909 · 1948 · 1963 · 1977 · 1983 · 1985 · 1990 · 1994 · 1996 · 1999

FOOTBALL LEAGUE CUP – Winners: 1992

INTER-CONTINENTAL CUP – Winners: 1999

UEFA SUPER CUP – Winners: 1991

FA CHARITY SHIELD – Winners: 1908 · 1911 · 1952 · 1956 · 1957 · 1983 · 1993 · 1994 · 1996 · 1997
Joint Holders: 1965 · 1967 · 1977 · 1990

CLUB TELEPHONE NUMBERS	
Main Switchboard	0161-868 8000
Textphone for Deaf/Impaired Hearing	0161-868 8668
Ticket and Match Information	0161-868 8020
Commercial Department	0161-868 8200
Megastore	0161-868 8567
Mail Order Hotline	0161-868-7000
United Review Subscriptions	0161-868 7000
Magazine Subscriptions	01458 271132
Development Association	0161-868 8600
Membership and Supporters' Club	0161-868 8450
Conference and Catering	0161-868 8300
Museum and Tour Centre	0161-868 8631
United in the Community	0161-708 9451
United Radio (Matchdays Only)	0161-868 8888
Red Café	0161-868 8303
Club Call	09068 121161*
Web Site	www.ManUtd.com
MUTV	0870 8486888

* Calls cost 60p per minute at all times

CHAIRMAN'S MESSAGE

It gives me great pleasure to once again welcome you all to the pages of the Official Manchester United Yearbook. Last season saw the number of pages increased to include new features and expand the coverage of the club's playing activities from first team to academy. This improved format was very well received and has been retained this time round to provide an unrivalled account of the highs, lows and drama of last season.

A year ago we were reflecting on an amazing season in which we had collected the UEFA Champions League, FA Carling Premiership and the FA Cup. That was an almost impossible achievement to follow, but I am delighted that one of that amazing triple-trophy haul remains on display at Old Trafford.

The retention of the FA Carling Premiership saw the season end on a fabulous high note with the team finishing a record 18 points clear of runners-up Arsenal. And we enjoyed yet another marvellous season of football in the UEFA Champions League. I felt that we were more capable of going all the way to the final again, but Real were very impressive in a thrilling quarter-final at Old Trafford and fully deserving of their place in the semi-final.

Our involvement in the inaugural FIFA Club World Championship in Brazil may not have brought the preferred outcome, but I believe it an excellent way for the club to broaden its horizons. Sir Alex Ferguson, the players and staff are to congratulated on another highly successful season which saw records tumble as we moved towards our 13th championship. It was, of course, our sixth Premiership title in eight seasons, which in itself is a quite incredible feat. I must also mention the reserves who defeated Oldham Athletic to retain the Manchester Senior Cup for a second successive season.

Then there were quite a few individual honours as well, most notably Sir Alex's 7th 'Manager of the Year' award and skipper Roy Keane being chosen as Player of the Year by both the Football Writers' Association and the Professional Footballers' Association. And it wasn't only the manager and players who got amongst the record-breakers. Our fantastic supporters also chipped in with a remarkable show of dedication and loyalty, which led to the 32-year-old record for average home crowds being broken.

All in all I am delighted to be able to say that it was another magnificent season.

C. Martin Edwards

Manager's Message

Despite the disappointment of going out of the UEFA Champions League at the quarter-final stage, I think we can still look back on the Millennium season with a good deal of satisfaction. Winning the title for the sixth time in eight years is no mean achievement and a feat of which we are rightly proud.

The players' ambition and appetite has never been in doubt as far as I am concerned and I'm sure you will agree that they proved beyond a shadow of doubt that they are ready for any challenge that may come their way. Some people have suggested that it could become more difficult to motivate the lads following so much recent success. It could, but it hasn't and that is definitely not a problem, in fact that is the least of my worries as they are as keen to succeed today as they have ever been. Their faces following the Champions League defeat against Real Madrid at Old Trafford was enough to convince me that their hunger remains completely intact. It is a long time since I have seen them so despondent and I know they just can't wait to return to the competition next season. It was a terrible blow losing to Real, because I was convinced that we were more than capable of retaining the trophy. But I cannot deny that the Spanish club deserved their success on the night for they took the chances, which came their way and in the end we left ourselves too much to do.

On a more cheerful note, I was delighted with our performance when defeating Palmeiras in Tokyo to win the Inter-Continental Cup. It was the first time in history that this trophy had been won by a British club. I was fortunate to be at the Stade de France in Paris for the final and I have to say that Real won more easily than I thought they would. And whilst I expected them to win I also tipped Valencia to have more of a say but in the end it was quite an easy ride for the new champions.

I enjoyed the UEFA Champions League final, it was a fitting occasion to complete another season of European club football, but I didn't like watching another club collect that marvelous trophy. It just increased my determination to see it return to Old Trafford at the earliest opportunity. That brings me nicely to next season and the fresh challenges, which await us all. The FA Carling Premiership remains our priority, whilst we will also be trying our best to attain success again in the Champions League and FA Cup.

It promises to be another extraordinary season and with Old Trafford extended even further to accommodate almost 68,000 fans there should be an atmosphere to match.

AUGUST

SUNDAY 8	v EVERTON	A
WEDNESDAY 11	v SHEFFIELD WEDNESDAY	H
SATURDAY 14	v LEEDS UNITED	H
SUNDAY 22	v ARSENAL	A
WEDNESDAY 25	v COVENTRY CITY	A
MONDAY 30	v NEWCASTLE UNITED	H

EVERTON   1

STAM (o.g.) 87

13. Paul GERRARD	
14. David WEIR	
21. Mitch WARD	
4. Richard GOUGH	
5. Dave WATSON	
6. David UNSWORTH	
7. John COLLINS	
8. Nick BARMBY	
9. Kevin CAMPBELL	
10. Don HUTCHISON	
11. Scot GEMMILL	
SUBSTITUTES	
3. Michael BALL	
12. Mark PEMBRIDGE	
16. Danny CADAMARTERI (21) 70	
18. Terry PHELAN (10) 85	
35. Steve SIMONSEN	

MATCH REPORT

Until a flukey late Everton equaliser took the gloss off their day, United could be generally satisfied with their return to Premiership business after the summer recess.

Indeed, before Barmby's header cannoned off Stam's head to leave Bosnich helpless in the 87th minute, only twice had the Toffees threatened to thwart his ambition of a clean sheet in his first League outing as a Red Devil for more than eight years.

The visitors, meanwhile, had fashioned a succession of splendid scoring opportunities, being frustrated by a combination of their own profligacy and a magnificent goalkeeping display by Gerrard.

United lost little time in finding their customary, crisp-passing rhythm, and after only three minutes Keane's clever dink sent Scholes clear, only for the charging custodian to block the shot. It looked ominous for Everton and soon their fans' apprehension was justified when a Watson misjudgment allowed Cole to slip a delightful pass to Yorke who netted gleefully with a low drive which Gerrard touched but could not repel.

Then the Tobagan nearly doubled his tally with a snap shot and the Reds began to purr, only to receive a jolt – and a let-

Dwight Yorke receives congratulations from his team-mates after scoring United's first League goal of the season

1 MANCHESTER UNITED

7 YORKE

Ole Gunnar Solskjaer slots the ball around the outstretched leg of Everton's Richard Gough, but his shot was saved by Paul Gerrard

off – on 27 minutes when Ward crossed, Bosnich remained rooted to his line and Hutchison's header was deflected against a post.

There was further dramatic incident either side of the interval. First Gerrard saved brilliantly from Yorke, then Bosnich parried a Hutchison shot with Phil Neville and Berg blocking the follow-up efforts from Barmby and Campbell on the line.

Come the last half-hour the Reds took command and chances proliferated. Solskjaer might have notched a hat-trick, while Keane and Cole both went close. Even after Stam's unlucky intervention there was time enough for Butt to try and secure the points for United, but his cross-shot missed by inches.

MANCHESTER UNITED 4

1. Mark BOSNICH

12. Phil NEVILLE

3. Denis IRWIN

16. Roy KEANE

21. Henning BERG

6. Jaap STAM

7. David BECKHAM

18. Paul SCHOLES

9. Andy COLE

19. Dwight YORKE

11. Ryan GIGGS

SUBSTITUTES

8. Nicky BUTT (7) 57

10. Teddy SHERINGHAM (19) h-t

13. John CURTIS

17. Raimond VAN DER GOUW

20. Ole Gunnar SOLSKJAER (11) 57

SCHOLES 9
YORKE 35
COLE 54
SOLSKJAER 84

MATCH REPORT

Jaap Stam climbs above the Wednesday defence to head goalwards

No Premiership match is a doddle, but the Reds' comprehensive tanning of a distinctly wan Sheffield Wednesday came pretty close. Displaying all the class and assurance which had characterised their Treble triumph, the hosts netted twice in each half and easily could have doubled their tally.

The rout commenced when Giggs, in lively form on his return from injury, danced down the left flank before crossing for Scholes to swivel and dispatch an arcing left-foot volley from 12 yards.

0 SHEFFIELD WEDNESDAY

28. Pavel SRNICEK	
2. Peter ATHERTON	
3. Andy HINCHCLIFFE	
19. Jon NEWSOME	
5. Emerson THOME	
6. Des WALKER	
7. Danny SONNER	
16. Niclas ALEXANDERSSON	
9. Gerald SIBON	
23. Gilles DE BILDE	
14. Petter RUDI	

SUBSTITUTES

1. Kevin PRESSMAN
8. Benito CARBONE (9) 59
12. Richard CRESSWELL (23) 77
21. Lee BRISCOE (7) 63
22. Stephen HASLAM

Shortly afterwards, hero almost became villain when the little redhead's misdirected back-pass was intercepted by Alexandersson, who squandered a gilded opportunity.

Thereafter United dominated, with Yorke hitting a post and Berg blasting over from the rebound. The red tide continued to flow, and Wednesday's defences were breached again through Yorke's jack-knife header from another beautiful Giggs centre.

With his side firmly in control, Sir Alex Ferguson was able to withdraw the Tobagan at half-time, but his replacement, Sheringham, soon added to Wednesday's woe with a shot which was deflected into the net by Cole. Effectively that was it, though twice substitute Carbone might have reduced the arrears, but each time he miscued miserably with only Bosnich to beat.

In truth, United's ascendancy was never seriously threatened, and the crowd rose to a rousing run from Stam, then a shot from Solskjaer hit both post and bar. It was left to the Norwegian to round off the entertainment by converting a Sheringham effort which had rebounded from the woodwork.

Solskjaer eyes the ball carefully before unleashing a shot at the Wednesday goal

MANCHESTER UNITED 2

YORKE 77, 80

1. Mark BOSNICH
12. Phil NEVILLE
3. Denis IRWIN
16. Roy KEANE
21. Henning BERG
6. Jaap STAM
7. David BECKHAM
18. Paul SCHOLES
9. Andy COLE
19. Dwight YORKE
11. Ryan GIGGS

SUBSTITUTES

8. Nicky BUTT (18) 69
10. Teddy SHERINGHAM (19) 81
13. John CURTIS
17. Raimond VAN DER GOUW (1) 22
20. Ole Gunnar SOLSKJAER

MATCH REPORT

Jaap Stam makes sure that there's no way through for Leeds United's new striker Darren Huckerby

0 LEEDS UNITED

1. Nigel MARTYN	
18. Danny MILLS	
3. Ian HARTE	
22. Michael DUBERRY	
5. Lucas RADEBE	
6. Jonathan WOODGATE	
23. David BATTY	
8. Michael BRIDGES	
12. Darren HUCKERBY	
10. Harry KEWELL	
11. Lee BOWYER	

SUBSTITUTES

4. Alf-Inge HAALAND	
7. David HOPKIN (8) 19	
13. Paul ROBINSON	
19. Eirik BAKKE (10) 84	
21. Martin HIDEN (3) 75	

Until two late flashes of characteristic opportunism from Yorke there had been little to choose between these two sides. Indeed, although the hosts had fashioned marginally more clear scoring chances, it was the visitors who had gone closest to registering when the excellent Kewell struck a post after 65 minutes.

The powerful marksman was a thorn in the Reds' flesh throughout, especially in the first period when his direct running and any one of a trio of long-range howitzers might have broken the deadlock. The tempo did not relent after the interval but a goalless draw seemed likely following Kewell's miss after Radebe had broken up a United attack, then sent the Australian through one-on-one with van der Gouw, who was on for the injured Bosnich. The ball rapped the near upright and rebounded to safety, leaving Kewell on his knees in frustration.

United retaliated quickly and Phil Neville broke free on the right and crossed for Yorke to convert with an athletic, glancing effort from near the penalty spot. Three minutes later, with Leeds still reeling, the Reds won a free-kick on the left and Beckham's arcing delivery was met by Yorke at the near post. Even then the Yorkshiremen might have set up a grandstand finish had van der Gouw not saved superbly from Bowyer.

Dwight Yorke watches to make sure his effort is goalbound. Martin Hiden fears the worst

ARSENAL 1

LJUNGBERG 41

13. Alex MANNINGER

2. Lee DIXON

16. SILVINHO

4. Patrick VIEIRA

5. Martin KEOWN

20. Matthew UPSON

15. Ray PARLOUR

8. Fredrik LJUNGBERG

25. Nwankwu KANU

10. Dennis BERGKAMP

14. Thierry HENRY

SUBSTITUTES

7. Nelson VIVAS

9. Davor SUKER (14) 77

11. Marc OVERMARS (25) 71

18. Gilles GRIMANDI

24. John LUKIC

MATCH REPORT

United emerged triumphant from an enthralling late climax to a pulsatingly open encounter, thus inflicting on Arsenal their first home Premiership defeat for 20 months.

In broad terms, the first half was graced by fabulously fluent football, the second studded with dramatic incident, while the entire contest was suffused with passionate attrition,

David Beckham glides a free-kick through the Arsenal wall; Vieira, Kanu, Henry, Bergkamp, Ljungberg and Parlour take evasive action

2 MANCHESTER UNITED

59, 88 KEANE

17. Raimond VAN DER GOUW

12. Phil NEVILLE

3. Denis IRWIN

16. Roy KEANE

21. Henning BERG

6. Jaap STAM

7. David BECKHAM

18. Paul SCHOLES

9. Andy COLE

19. Dwight YORKE

11. Ryan GIGGS

SUBSTITUTES

8. Nicky BUTT (18) 61

10. Teddy SHERINGHAM (9) 77

13. John CURTIS

20. Ole Gunnar SOLSKJAER

31. Nick CULKIN (17) 90

exemplified by the clashes of Keane and Vieira. For all that, the stars were stand-in goalkeepers van der Gouw and Manninger, both of whom were magnificent.

For the first half-hour the visitors held sway. Cole nodded firmly against the bar from a Beckham free-kick, then the same supplier freed Giggs with a sublime through-pass, only for the Welshman to shoot wide. Meanwhile Henry shot into van der Gouw's midriff before a stunningly sudden long-distance drive from Kanu brought a flying parry from the Dutchman.

Thereafter Manninger saved superbly from Cole, Yorke and Berg, before Ljungberg put Arsenal in front after being played in by Bergkamp, who then tested van der Gouw from close range.

On 55 minutes the Gunners almost doubled their lead when Upson volleyed a corner against a post.

Then a Yorke header was ruled out for offside before United equalised when Keane played the ball into the box and Cole returned it to the charging Irishman, who netted with ease. End-to-end action ensued but a draw seemed certain until a Giggs shot was deflected to Keane, who scored adroitly from six yards.

Still there were thrills in store. In the fifth minute of added time, an Upson header was clutched on the line by van der Gouw, only for Keown to bundle both ball and keeper into the net. The strike was disallowed, the Dutchman was stretchered off, substitute Culkin took the free-kick and the final whistle sounded.

David Beckham salutes his two-goal skipper

COVENTRY CITY 1

ALOISI 80

1. Marcus HEDMAN
2. Marc EDWORTHY
17. Gary BREEN
4. Paul WILLIAMS
5. Richard SHAW
16. Stephen FROGGATT
7. Robbie KEANE
8. Noel WHELAN
18. Youssef CHIPPO
10. Gary McALLISTER
11. Moustapha HADJI

SUBSTITUTES

6. Muhamed KONJIC (17) 84
9. John ALOISI (11) 71
12. Paul TELFER (8) 34
21. Gavin STRACHAN
23. Raffaele NUZZO

MATCH REPORT

The margin of victory was narrow but the gulf between the teams managed by Sir Alex Ferguson and his former protégé, Gordon Strachan, was truly vast. United played their slickest football of the campaign to date, creating a plethora of scoring opportunities and it was astonishing that only two of them resulted in goals.

The first half featured a catalogue of near misses by the Red Devils. First Yorke shimmied past a defender and rapped an upright from 22 yards, then Giggs got behind the Sky Blues' rearguard only to pull a low shot marginally beyond the far post. Other opportunities went begging before a sumptuous move involving Beckham, Yorke and Sheringham resulted in the Tobagan scooping wide.

The second period began in similar vein, but the enforced removal of the injured Butt for Scholes changed the pattern. Beckham crossed from the right, Yorke flicked the ball across the area where it was met gleefully by the substitute, whose fierce 16-yard half-volley rocketed into the roof of Coventry's net via the boot of Breen.

If there was a slight element of good fortune about that goal, there was none about the next. The by now unstoppable Scholes took possession deep on the left, then sidestepped an opponent before delivering a breathtaking 50-yard pass to Beckham on the opposite flank. The ball was controlled instantly, then dispatched in a tantalising arc to Yorke, who netted with an unstoppable header.

2 MANCHESTER UNITED

63 SCHOLES
75 YORKE

17. Raimond VAN DER GOUW
12. Phil NEVILLE
3. Denis IRWIN
16. Roy KEANE
21. Henning BERG
6. Jaap STAM
7. David BECKHAM
8. Nicky BUTT
19. Dwight YORKE
10. Teddy SHERINGHAM
11. Ryan GIGGS

SUBSTITUTES

9. Andy COLE
13. John CURTIS (12) 79
18. Paul SCHOLES (8) 61
20. Ole Gunnar SOLSKJAER (10) 74
31. Nick CULKIN

Near the end Robbie Keane split the visitors' defence and Aloisi shook off the attentions of Stam to score with a neat shot from 15 yards. It was a fine goal but the final scoreline furnished scant indication of United's overall dominance.

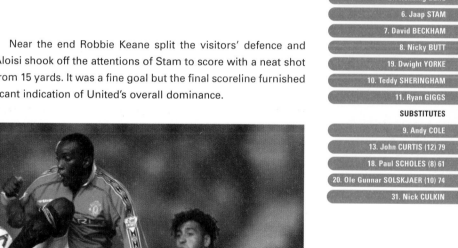

Dwight Yorke shows a clean pair of heels to Coventry's Richard Shaw

MANCHESTER UNITED 5

17. Raimond VAN DER GOUW

2. Gary NEVILLE

12. Phil NEVILLE

18. Paul SCHOLES

21. Henning BERG

6. Jaap STAM

7. David BECKHAM

8. Nicky BUTT

9. Andy COLE

19. Dwight YORKE

11 Ryan GIGGS

SUBSTITUTES

10. Teddy SHERINGHAM (7) 75

14. Jordi CRUYFF

23. Michael CLEGG (2) 81

25. Quinton FORTUNE (18) 70

31. Nick CULKIN

COLE 14, 46, 65, 71
GIGGS 81

MATCH REPORT

Henning Berg and Nicky Butt stifle yet another Newcastle attack

The managerless Magpies were routed with almost embarrassing ease and, ironically but rather inevitably, their tormentor-in-chief was one-time Tyneside idol Andy Cole. He netted four times and took his tally to eight goals in nine outings against his former employers.

Emphatically, though, this was not a one-man show. The Red Devils were in particularly assured collective form with their passing, especially that of David Beckham, a joy to behold.

1 NEWCASTLE UNITED

31 BERG (o.g.)

32. Tommy WRIGHT
2. Warren BARTON
18. Aaron HUGHES
34. Nikolaos DABIZAS
5. Alain GOMA
15. Nolberto SOLANO
7. Kieron DYER
37. Robert LEE
9. Alan SHEARER
20. Duncan FERGUSON
11. Gary SPEED
SUBSTITUTES
10. Silvio MARIC
13. Stephen HARPER
19. Jamie McCLEN (37) 70
27. David BEHARALL (15) 75
28. Paul ROBINSON (20) 80

Indeed, it is difficult to recall a performance of more sustained majesty from the England midfielder, who even went close to scoring from the halfway line.

Manchester United went ahead following a bout of typically inspirational one-touch football: Yorke to Cole to Scholes to Cole, then a slightly scuffed shot deceived Newcastle keeper Wright.

However, the visitors were not toothless and Dyer brought a smart save from van der Gouw before facilitating an unexpected equaliser when his curling cross was sliced into his own net by Berg. The hosts' response was swift, with Scholes heading over, then finding the net only for his strike to be ruled out for an earlier infringement.

After the interval, Newcastle maintained parity in both goals and manpower for only 40 seconds. A long ball from Scholes was seized upon by Cole, who shrugged off Dabizas before sidestepping Wright and converting. The Greek claimed a foul, protesting so strenuously that he was dismissed for using abusive language, a setback from which his side never recovered.

Thereafter it was exhibition stuff from the Red Devils. Cole completed his hat-trick when he latched on to a beautifully curved through-ball from Giggs. Gary Neville provided the pass for the marksman's clinically dispatched fourth, then to cap a fine display Giggs seized on a rebound to steer nonchalantly beyond Wright from 10 yards.

Andy Cole is a study in concentration as he shoots the Reds into a decisive lead

AUGUST IN REVIEW

SUNDAY 8	v EVERTON	A	1-1
WEDNESDAY 11	v SHEFFIELD WEDNESDAY	H	4-0
SATURDAY 14	v LEEDS UNITED	H	2-0
SUNDAY 22	v ARSENAL	A	2-1
WEDNESDAY 25	v COVENTRY CITY	A	2-1
MONDAY 30	v NEWCASTLE UNITED	H	5-1

PLAYER IN THE FRAME

Andy Cole

To all those who follow the exploits of Andy Cole it remained difficult to comprehend why he was not a regular international. The mystery deepened following his four-goal display against his former club, Newcastle United, which emphasised vividly the continuing advances in his overall game. Having matured, Andy has emerged as a serial creator of chances, as well as a deadly finisher.

FA CARLING PREMIERSHIP

		P	W	D	L	F	A	Pts
UP TO AND INCLUDING	MANCHESTER UNITED	5	4	1	0	11	3	13
WEDNESDAY 25 AUGUST 1999	Aston Villa	5	3	1	1	7	3	10
	Arsenal	5	3	1	1	7	4	10
	Tottenham Hotspur	4	3	0	1	8	5	9
	Middlesbrough	5	3	0	2	7	7	9
	Chelsea	3	2	1	0	7	2	7
	Everton	5	2	1	2	11	8	7
	Leicester City	5	2	1	2	8	6	7
	West Ham United	3	2	1	0	5	3	7
	Leeds United	5	2	1	2	6	5	7
	Sunderland	5	2	1	2	5	7	7
	Liverpool	4	2	0	2	4	4	6
	Watford	5	2	0	3	4	6	6
	Southampton	4	2	0	2	6	9	6
	Wimbledon	5	1	2	2	9	13	5
	Coventry City	5	1	1	3	4	5	4
	Bradford City	4	1	1	2	2	4	4
	Derby County	5	1	1	3	4	7	4
	Newcastle United	5	0	1	4	7	13	1
	Sheffield Wednesday	5	0	1	4	3	11	1

SEPTEMBER

SATURDAY 11	v LIVERPOOL	A
TUESDAY 14	v NK CROATIA ZAGREB	H
SATURDAY 18	v WIMBLEDON	H
WEDNESDAY 22	v SK STURM GRAZ	A
SATURDAY 25	v SOUTHAMPTON	H
WEDNESDAY 29	v OLYMPIQUE MARSEILLE	H

LIVERPOOL 2

1. Sander WESTERVELD
28. Steven GERRARD
21. Dominic MATTEO
4. Rigobert SONG
12. Sami HYYPIA
23. Jamie CARRAGHER
25. David THOMPSON
15. Patrick BERGER
9. Robbie FOWLER
22. Titi CAMARA
11. Jamie REDKNAPP

SUBSTITUTES

5. Steve STAUNTON
7. Vladimir SMICER (25) h-t
10. Michael OWEN (22) 64
14. Veggard HEGGEM (28) 64
19. Brad FRIEDEL

HYYPIA 23
BERGER 69

MATCH REPORT

For those who like their football red and raw, Liverpool versus Manchester United will always fit the bill. This encounter was no classic, being too frenetic for purists, but for sheer tumultuous passion it was unrivalled by anything else in the season to date.

In broad terms, the visitors controlled the first period, their poise and polish altogether too much for the hosts. But after the interval the Liverpudlians regrouped effectively, pounding the Red Devils' rearguard so relentlessly that they might have prevailed, but for a starring debut by goalkeeper Taibi.

The drama commenced early when Giggs' cross was put into his own net by Carragher. Thereafter the Liverpool defence looked woefully vulnerable and it was breached again when Cole rose to nod home from a Beckham free-kick.

At this point Anfield fell silent, but the home fans were revived by a towering blunder from Taibi, who flapped at a high free-kick and allowed Hyypia to reduce the arrears with a simple header.

More mistakes followed. First the referee failed to spot either a clear handball by Butt in one penalty area or a blatant tug on Giggs' shirt by Thompson

David Beckham challenges Liverpool's Dominic Matteo for the ball

3 MANCHESTER UNITED

4 CARRAGHER (o.g.)
18 COLE
45 CARRAGHER (o.g.)

26. Massimo TAIBI
12. Phil NEVILLE
27. Mikael SILVESTRE
18. Paul SCHOLES
21. Henning BERG
6. Jaap STAM
7. David BECKHAM
8. Nicky BUTT
9. Andy COLE
19. Dwight YORKE
11. Ryan GIGGS

SUBSTITUTES

10. Teddy SHERINGHAM
17. Raimond VAN DER GOUW
20. Ole Gunnar SOLSKJAER
23. Michael CLEGG (12) 84
30. Ronnie WALLWORK (8) 40

Andy Cole rises to head United into a 2–0 lead after 18 minutes

in the other. Then Berg was allowed a free header from another Beckham set-piece and in the resultant scramble Carragher scored another own-goal.

Immediately after the break Cole nearly settled matters from a centre by Giggs, but then Liverpool roared forward, only to be frustrated by Taibi, who made fabulous saves from Smicer and Fowler (twice). As the temperature rose, Matteo's superb through-ball set up Berger for the best goal of the game, and Cole was dismissed for a second bookable offence on 72 minutes.

However, United's defence held reassuringly firm, with new boy Silvestre – whom the Anfielders had coveted for themselves – making an outstanding contribution.

MANCHESTER UNITED 0

17. Raimond VAN DER GOUW
23. Michael CLEGG
12. Phil NEVILLE
18. Paul SCHOLES
21. Henning BERG
6. Jaap STAM
7. David BECKHAM
33. Mark WILSON
9. Andy COLE
19. Dwight YORKE
11. Ryan GIGGS

SUBSTITUTES

1. Mark BOSNICH
3. Denis IRWIN
10. Teddy SHERINGHAM (33) 60
13. John CURTIS
14. Jordi CRUYFF
25. Quinton FORTUNE (23) 76
34. Jonathan GREENING

MATCH REPORT

Manchester United's defence of their European crown began in disappointingly low-key mode against skilful and determined opponents. True, the Reds' efforts at a breakthrough reached their customary late crescendo, with Yorke chipping deftly against the Croatians' bar, Berg missing narrowly with a diving header and Sheringham's four-yard shot being blocked by goalkeeper Ladic in the dying seconds of injury time. That said, it was not a convincing all-round performance by the home team which, it should be stressed, was seriously depleted by injuries.

The visitors were marshalled shrewdly by their manager Ossie Ardiles who, in stark contrast to the cavalier style he employed during his days in charge of Tottenham Hotspur, packed his midfield with five workaholics.

Zagreb silenced the Old Trafford crowd by shading the early possession, their passing crisp and their movement imaginative, and though United improved as the first half wore on, a blocked drive by Cole and a miscued shot from Yorke were the nearest they came to penetration. Indeed, it was telling that the most eye-catching figure in a red shirt was the relentlessly dominant Stam, who was skipper in the absence of Keane.

The Reds upped the tempo in the second period and enjoyed their most potent spell. Cole came close to breaking the deadlock but his fierce shot was repelled by Ladic, then Stam headed wide from the resultant corner. However, Zagreb regrouped, counter-attacking briskly at times but never shooting accurately enough to bother the under-occupied van der Gouw.

0 NK Croatia Zagreb

1. Dazen LADIC
2. Mario TOKIC
17. Mario CVITANOVIC
15. Daniel SARIC
5. Goran JURIC
20. Stjepan TOMAS
22. Igor BISCAN
24. Krunoslav JURCIC
16. Josip SIMIC
10. Edin MUJCIN
11. Tomislav RUKAVINA

SUBSTITUTES

4. Goce SEDLOSKI
7. Nermin SABIC
14. Mihael MIKIC (16) 67
21. Josko JELICIC
23. Vladimir VASILJ
25. Tomislav SOKOTA (11) 88
30. Niljenko MUMLEK (10) 69

United's final push eventually produced a show of fervour from the stands, and Teddy Sheringham almost won it with the last kick of the match. But frustration reigned and it was left to the highly vocal – and largely bare-chested – Croatian contingent to celebrate at the end.

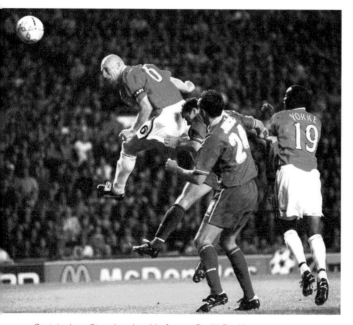

Captain Jaap Stam heads wide from a David Beckham corner

MANCHESTER UNITED 1

CRUYFF 74

26. Massimo TAIBI

27. Mikael SILVESTRE

3. Denis IRWIN

18. Paul SCHOLES

21. Henning BERG

6. Jaap STAM

12. Phil NEVILLE

20. Ole Gunnar SOLSKJAER

19. Dwight YORKE

10. Teddy SHERINGHAM

11. Ryan GIGGS

SUBSTITUTES

1. Mark BOSNICH

9. Andy COLE (20) 68

14. Jordi CRUYFF (11) 30

30. Ronnie WALLWORK

33. Mark WILSON

MATCH REPORT

Though United created their customary flurry of openings – all but one of which were spurned – no objective observer of this absorbing tussle could deny Wimbledon the right to their hard-earned point. Indeed, but for three brilliant interventions by Massimo Taibi, Egil Olsen's well-drilled team would have secured an unexpected victory.

In truth, the Red Devils never approached optimum form, no doubt being undermined by the combination of a marathon injury list and their European exertions. They were hindered further by the Dons' policy of massing behind the ball at every hint of danger, a strategem which was wholly understandable after they had taken an early lead.

That breakthrough came when Cort wriggled past Silvestre on the left and delivered a low cross to Badir, who netted crisply from 15 yards. On three other occasions, though, the Italian keeper proved United's saviour and averted a Cort hat-trick. Early in each half he denied the leggy Londoner, first from a narrow angle, then from

Teddy Sheringham tussles for the ball with Wimbledon's Jason Euell

1 WIMBLEDON

16 BADIR

Jordi Cruyff dances his way through the Dons' defence to equalise

1. Neil SULLIVAN
2. Kenny CUNNINGHAM
29. Trond ANDERSEN
4. Andy ROBERTS
5. Dean BLACKWELL
6. Ben THATCHER
7. Carl CORT
19. Walid BADIR
9. John HARTSON
10. Jason EUELL
11. Marcus GAYLE

SUBSTITUTES

3. Alan KIMBLE
8. Robbie EARLE
15. Carl LEABURN
21. Duncan JUPP (7) 80
23. Kelvin DAVIES

point-blank range. Finally, when Cort was through in the dying seconds, Taibi advanced boldly and knocked the ball away.

Against that there were plenty of opportunities for Sheringham, Yorke, Scholes and Cruyff – who had replaced the hobbling Giggs – but none of them were converted and deep in the second period the hosts' unbeaten record seemed in peril.

Cue Jordi's first goal for 11 months, and it was a fine one, the Dutchman exchanging passes with Scholes before skipping past Sullivan and slipping the ball into the unattended net. Thereafter Scholes (twice) and Cole almost supplied a winner, but it was Cort who might have had the last word.

SK STURM GRAZ 0

1. Kazimierz SIDORCZUK

12. Gilbert PRILASNIG

3. Gunther NEUKIRCHNER

14. Jan-Pieter MARTENS

5. Franco FODA

6. Roman MAHLICH

7. Gerald STRAFNER

8. Markus SCHUPP

21. Tomislav KOCIJAN

10. Ivica VASTIC

16. Ferdinand FELDHOFER

SUBSTITUTES

2. Michael BOCHTLER

9. Hannes REINMAYR (6) 75

11. Gyorgy KORSOS (16) 72

19. Imre SZABICS

22. Josef SCHICKLGRUBER

27. Georgios KUTSUPIAS (12) 71

28. Marko PANTELIC

MATCH REPORT

Dwight Yorke's downward header gives United a 2–0 lead away from home after just 31 minutes

This was a curious encounter. The score suggests a comfortable ride for United but that was not the case, with Sturm Graz fashioning more goal opportunities than their illustrious visitors. Suffice to say that the two most prominent figures were Reds' keeper van der Gouw and the home play-maker Vastic.

United started confidently. But then Graz clicked into gear

3 MANCHESTER UNITED

16 KEANE
31 YORKE
33 COLE

| 17. Raimond VAN DER GOUW |
| 12. Phil NEVILLE |
| 3. Denis IRWIN |
| 16. Roy KEANE |
| 21. Henning BERG |
| 6. Jaap STAM |
| 7. David BECKHAM |
| 18. Paul SCHOLES |
| 9. Andy COLE |
| 19. Dwight YORKE |
| 14. Jordi CRUYFF |
| **SUBSTITUTES** |
| 1. Mark BOSNICH |
| 10. Teddy SHERINGHAM (14) 68 |
| 20. Ole Gunnar SOLSKJAER (9) 76 |
| 23. Michael CLEGG |
| 25. Quinton FORTUNE |
| 33. Mark WILSON (16) 62 |
| 34. Jonathan GREENING |

and it was against the run of play when the Reds went ahead, a Beckham free-kick rebounding to Keane, whose swerving 30-yard thunderbolt found the net via the crossbar.

Undaunted, the hosts swept forward brightly, only to be rocked by a double blow which effectively decided the outcome. First Beckham's corner was met by Yorke's downward header and keeper Sidorczuk let the ball creep under his hands. Then Yorke swivelled away from his marker and found Cole, who nipped past Feldhofer before netting with clinical aplomb.

Sturm Graz reacted with both fortitude and enterprise and after 38 minutes Vastic brought a spectacular flying save from van der Gouw, who was then called on to repel a savage drive from Mahlich.

After the break the Austrians continued to attack and Vastic wasted two wonderful chances, the first when he skied his shot with only van der Gouw to beat, the second when he scuffed a 54th-minute penalty – awarded for a foul by Phil Neville on Kocijan – straight at the Dutchman.

Thereafter United were never in danger of capitulating but, in all honesty, they were flattered by the final scoreline.

Andy Cole celebrates United's third goal in 33 minutes

MANCHESTER UNITED 3

26. Massimo TAIBI

27. Mikael SILVESTRE

3. Denis IRWIN

18. Paul SCHOLES

21. Henning BERG

6. Jaap STAM

7. David BECKHAM

8. Nicky BUTT

19. Dwight YORKE

10. Teddy SHERINGHAM

20. Ole Gunnar SOLSKJAER

SUBSTITUTES

1. Mark BOSNICH

12. Phil NEVILLE

14. Jordi CRUYFF

25. Quinton FORTUNE

33. Mark WILSON

SHERINGHAM 34
YORKE 38, 64

MATCH REPORT

Here was a feast of breathtaking entertainment in which United approached their scintillating best, only for individual errors to allow Southampton a share of the points.

As an attacking force the Reds simply dazzled, but were poor at the back, while the Saints conducted a feisty rearguard action and showed sharp enterprise on the break.

Stars? Well, Beckham was outstanding and Yorke netted twice while every Southampton player excelled, though special praise should be reserved for Paul Jones, the acrobat between their posts, who played a large part in this match, several of his saves defying belief.

Unexpectedly, the Saints registered first when Hughes, the former and still much-loved Old Trafford idol, found Pahars, who nutmegged Stam before netting coolly from 15 yards.

That was the signal for United to mount a siege and Berg had headed against an upright before Beckham's low cross was converted smartly at the near post by Sheringham. Three minutes later Jones made two blinding parries from the Londoner before Sheringham regained possession and dinked a delicate cross for Yorke to nod home.

Later the Reds were denied by two goal-line clearances from Dodd, but then Southampton levelled when Taibi allowed a weak 20-yarder from Le Tissier to squirm embarrassingly through his guard.

Non-stop drama ensued with United spurning chance after chance before Yorke restored the lead with an instant 14-yarder

3 SOUTHAMPTON

17 PAHARS
51, 73 LE TISSIER

1. Paul JONES
2. Jason DODD
15. Francis BENALI
32. Trond SOLTVEDT
5. Claus LUNDEKVAM
6. Dean RICHARDS
14. Stuart RIPLEY
8. Matthew OAKLEY
9. Mark HUGHES
17. Marian PAHARS
30. Hassan KACHLOUL

SUBSTITUTES

4. Chris MARSDEN (5) 69
7. Matthew LE TISSIER (32) h-t
13. Neil MOSS
16. James BEATTIE (17) 90
24. Patrick COLLETER

Dwight Yorke and Paul Jones, Southampton's goalkeeper, came out honours even after this breathtaking encounter

from Butt's pass. Then Hughes twanged Taibi's crossbar with a 25-yard volley before Silvestre was caught in possession by Pahars, who set up Le Tissier's second equaliser.

Thereafter United pressed ceaselessly, only for Beattie to elude Stam in injury time. Taibi saved with his legs, thus earning a measure of redemption for his earlier clanger.

MANCHESTER UNITED 2

COLE 79
SCHOLES 83

17. Raimond VAN DER GOUW
12. Phil NEVILLE
3. Denis IRWIN
18. Paul SCHOLES
21. Henning BERG
6. Jaap STAM
7. David BECKHAM
8. Nicky BUTT
9. Andy COLE
19. Dwight YORKE
20. Ole Gunnar SOLSKJAER

SUBSTITUTES

1. Mark BOSNICH
10. Teddy SHERINGHAM (21) 77
14. Jordi CRUYFF
23. Michael CLEGG (9) 86
25. Quinton FORTUNE (20) 72
33. Mark WILSON
34. Jonathan GREENING

MATCH REPORT

It wasn't quite as dramatic as *that* night in Barcelona, though the comparison was irresistible. A goal down with time running out, once again United bounced back to claim a late victory.

This time the saviours were the often underestimated Cole and the indomitable Scholes. Cole equalised with an exquisitely executed overhead shot after Stam had nodded back a swirling Beckham free-kick, then Scholes latched on to a neat nod from Yorke before scuffling and stumbling through several challenges which brought him to his knees, but still managing to scoop home the winner from approximately 12 inches.

The double strike spared the blushes of the normally reliable Berg, whose blunder had gifted Marseille their goal from their only meaningful attack of the first half.

Andy Cole equalises with a spectacular overhead kick...

1 OLYMPIQUE MARSEILLE

41 BAKAYOKO

1. Stephane PORATO
2. Patrick BLONDEAU
3. Sebastien PEREZ
4. Pierre ISSA
24. Yannick FISCHER
23. William GALLAS
26. Peter LUCCIN
8. Frederic BRANDO
22. Ibrahima BAKAYOKO
12. Stephane DALMAT
11. Fabrizio RAVANELLI
SUBSTITUTES
7. Robert PIRES (11) 62
10. Ivan DE LA PENA (26) 77
14. Djamet BELMADI (4) 82
16. Stephane TREVISAN
17. Seydou KEITA
19. Kaba DIAWARA
28. Loris REINA

... and Paul Scholes wraps up the win seven minutes from time

Earlier the Reds had enjoyed overwhelming territorial advantage only to be frustrated as Porato saved from Solskjaer and Butt, and Cole steered narrowly wide. The Tobagan himself missed an even more clear-cut opportunity, shooting against the keeper's body from point-blank range.

United started the second half at a high tempo with both Cole and Solskjaer going close with cross-shots, but then the poised visitors, retreating behind the ball and defending in depth, established what seemed likely to be decisive control.

There was no panic from Sir Alex Ferguson's men, though, and with specialist substitute Sheringham unsettling the composure of the French side, the hosts' perseverance paid off in sensational style. In the end, United just about deserved it.

September in Review

SATURDAY 11	v LIVERPOOL	A	3-2
TUESDAY 14	v NK CROATIA ZAGREB	H	0-0
SATURDAY 18	v WIMBLEDON	H	1-1
WEDNESDAY 22	v SK STURM GRAZ	A	3-0
SATURDAY 25	v SOUTHAMPTON	H	3-3
WEDNESDAY 29	v OLYMPIQUE MARSEILLE	H	2-1

PLAYER IN THE FRAME

Jordi Cruyff

Emerged from virtual oblivion on the outer edges of Sir Alex Feguson's squad to contribute a late equaliser at home to Wimbledon. Jordi, whose outwardly casual style masks a burning desire to excel, gave one of his more convincing all-round displays, thus underlining his usefulness in the Old Trafford set-up. What he craved was a settled first-team sequence, but that was not to be.

FA CARLING PREMIERSHIP

	P	W	D	L	F	A	Pts
MANCHESTER UNITED	9	6	3	0	23	10	21
Leeds United	9	6	1	2	17	11	19
Arsenal	9	6	1	2	12	7	19
Sunderland	9	5	2	2	14	8	17
Chelsea	7	5	1	1	10	3	16
Aston Villa	9	5	1	3	11	9	16
Leicester City	9	4	2	3	14	11	14
Tottenham Hotspur	8	4	2	2	14	11	14
Everton	8	4	1	3	14	9	13
West Ham United	7	4	1	2	9	5	13
Middlesbrough	9	4	0	5	10	13	12
Liverpool	7	3	1	3	10	9	10
Southampton	8	3	1	4	13	16	10
Watford	9	3	0	6	5	9	9
Coventry City	9	2	2	5	11	13	8
Wimbledon	9	1	5	3	13	18	8
Bradford City	8	2	2	4	4	9	8
Derby County	9	2	2	5	7	15	8
Newcastle United	9	1	1	7	18	22	4
Sheffield Wednesday	9	0	1	8	3	24	1

UP TO AND INCLUDING
SUNDAY 26TH SEPTEMBER 1999

OCTOBER

SUNDAY 3	v CHELSEA	A
WEDNESDAY 13	v ASTON VILLA	A
SATURDAY 16	v WATFORD	H
TUESDAY 19	v OLYMPIQUE MARSEILLE	A
SATURDAY 23	v TOTTENHAM HOTSPUR	A
WEDNESDAY 27	v NK CROATIA ZAGREB	A
SATURDAY 30	v ASTON VILLA	H

CHELSEA 5

POYET 1, 55
SUTTON 16
BERG (o.g.) 59
MORRIS 82

1. Ed DE GOEY
2. Dan PETRESCU
3. Celestine BABAYARO
4. Jes HOGH
5. Frank LEBOEUF
17. Albert FERRER
7. Didier DESCHAMPS
8. Gustavo POYET
9. Chris SUTTON
25. Gianfranco ZOLA
11. Dennis WISE

SUBSTITUTES

14. Graeme LE SAUX (2) 78
19. Tore Andre FLO (25) 69
20. Jody MORRIS (11) 66
21. Bernard LAMBOURDE
23. Carlo CUDICINI

MATCH REPORT

After 45 competitive games without defeat, it was meltdown day for Manchester United at Stamford Bridge. It all began to go horribly wrong after just 28 seconds when Taibi dropped another colossal clanger, charging wildly towards a cross from Petrescu and failing to reach it, thus allowing Poyet to outjump Irwin and glance the ball into the unguarded net.

Strong arm tactics as Andy Cole tangles with Chelsea's Frank Leboeuf

0 MANCHESTER UNITED

26. Massimo TAIBI
27. Mikael SILVESTRE
3. Denis IRWIN
18. Paul SCHOLES
21. Henning BERG
6. Jaap STAM
7. David BECKHAM
8. Nicky BUTT
9. Andy COLE
19. Dwight YORKE
12. Phil NEVILLE

SUBSTITUTES

10. Teddy SHERINGHAM (18) 66
17. Raimond VAN DER GOUW
20. Ole Gunnar SOLSKJAER (9) 66
23. Michael CLEGG
33. Mark WILSON (7) 66

Thereafter Chelsea buzzed menacingly and soon their pressure paid off when Ferrer's deep centre was met by Sutton's brilliant looping header, this time giving the Italian keeper no chance.

Still, United are renowned for their resilience and there was no need for panic, but after 23 minutes Butt lost his head and, effectively, the game for his side. True, he was the victim of a nasty foul – and perhaps a few choice words – from Wise, but there was no excuse for the retaliatory knee with which he floored the Chelsea skipper. It was a moment of unutterable senselessness and the referee had no choice but to send him off.

Ironically the visitors, who reorganised with Yorke in midfield and Cole on his own up front, looked more cohesive with ten men and Scholes forced a sharp save from de Goey with a fierce 20-yarder.

However, Chelsea passed with characteristic fluency and controlled the remainder of the game, scoring three more goals. First Babayaro was given too much space following a free-kick and the ball ran to Leboeuf, whose shot was parried by Taibi but only to Poyet, who netted with ease. Then Zola's cross was turned into his own net by Berg and, the final indignity, Le Saux found the unmarked Morris, who shot under Taibi from 15 yards.

A chastening experience for United, then, and they could have no excuses.

Paul Scholes outjumps Chelsea's Celestine Babayaro to head clear

ASTON VILLA 3

JOACHIM 18
TAYLOR 49
STONE 90

39. Peter ENCKELMAN
24. Mark DELANEY
15. Gareth BARRY
34. Colin CALDERWOOD
5. Ugo EHIOGU
6. George BOATENG
7. Ian TAYLOR
17. Lee HENDRIE
9. Dion DUBLIN
12. Julian JOACHIM
11. Alan THOMPSON

SUBSTITUTES

2. Steve WATSON (5) h-t
10. Paul MERSON
13. Michael OAKES
22. Darius VASSELL (12) 57
26. Steve STONE (11) 75

MATCH REPORT

As an opportunity for the latest wave of young Red Devils to gain big-match experience, this was a worthwhile exercise; but as a meaningful contest between two of the nation's leading clubs, it was a dead loss.

Sir Alex Ferguson failed to name one Premiership regular in his starting line-up. True, Solskjaer, Bosnich and Cruyff are familiar names and Clegg and Curtis have tasted a modicum of senior action, but the rest were rookies, pure and simple. Indeed four players – O'Shea, Chadwick, Healy and Wellens – were handed their top-level debuts on a night when Villa were allowed to cruise comfortably into the next round of the competition.

In the circumstances, this United side did well to limit their full-strength opponents to three goals, though it must be stressed that Villa were never remotely stretched. The hosts started in dominant mode and took the lead after 18 minutes when Joachim bent a shot beyond the reach of his former team-mate, Bosnich.

Thereafter, the Australian keeper showed excellent form, though he was powerless to prevent Villa doubling their lead when Taylor scored following a long throw from Delaney.

That might have been the signal for a rout, but Bosnich brilliantly deflected a shot from Hendrie over the bar, then Vassell's shot rapped the United woodwork, before Stone registered the third goal in stoppage time.

For visiting fans, it was encouraging to see flashes of skill from Chadwick and Greening, and the defence deserved collective praise for sticking to their unenviable task.

0   MANCHESTER UNITED

1. Mark BOSNICH
23. Michael CLEGG
28. Danny HIGGINBOTHAM
30. Ronnie WALLWORK
37. John O'SHEA
13. John CURTIS
14. Jordi CRUYFF
42. Michael TWISS
20. Ole Gunnar SOLSKJAER
34. Jonathan GREENING
39. Luke CHADWICK

SUBSTITUTES

29. Alex NOTMAN
31. Nick CULKIN
38. David HEALY (28) 66
40. Lee ROCHE
41. Richard WELLENS (42) 74

Luke Chadwick takes on Villa's Ugo Ehiogu

Ole Gunnar Solskjaer tries to find a way through the solid Villa defence

MANCHESTER UNITED 4

1. Mark BOSNICH
2. Phil NEVILLE
3. Denis IRWIN
18. Paul SCHOLES
27. Mikael SILVESTRE
6. Jaap STAM
7. David BECKHAM
8. Nicky BUTT
9. Andy COLE
19. Dwight YORKE
11. Ryan GIGGS

SUBSTITUTES

16. Roy KEANE (6) 55
17. Raimond VAN DER GOUW
20. Ole Gunnar SOLSKJAER (9) 67
30. Ronnie WALLWORK
34. Jonathan GREENING (11) 71

YORKE 40
COLE 42, 50
IRWIN (penalty) 45

MATCH REPORT

A devastating sequence of four goals in 10 minutes either side of the interval returned United to winning ways after their recent stutters. Significantly, too, they displayed all the poise and certainty which elevated them to treble glory in 1998-99, the imperious manner of their performance being almost as welcome as the three points it earned.

Andy Cole meets David Beckham's cross and makes it 4–0

1 WATFORD

68 JOHNSON

1. Alec CHAMBERLAIN
16. Nigel GIBBS
3. Peter KENNEDY
4. Robert PAGE
5. Steve PALMER
6. Paul ROBINSON
7. Michel NGONGE
8. Micah HYDE
14. Nordin WOOTER
10. Richard JOHNSON
32. Mark WILLIAMS

SUBSTITUTES

11. Nick WRIGHT (8) h-t
13. Chris DAY
17. Tommy SMITH (5) 83
19. Clint EASTON
35. Charlie MILLER (7) 61

Both fluency and urgency were evident in their opening burst and though plucky Watford laboured prodigiously, they could not prevent their hosts creating a succession of chances. Accordingly Yorke (twice) and Cole went close, then Giggs finished feebly.

At the other end, Wooter buzzed dangerously and was the focal point of several raids, but with the central defensive partnership of Stam and Silvestre looking ever more majestic, there seemed minimal likelihood of defensive embarrassment.

The avalanche which buried the Hornets' hopes began when Butt crossed from the right and Yorke executed a fabulous overhead kick, which Watford keeper Chamberlain reached but could not repel. The lead was doubled when a sweet Giggs delivery from the left was met by a diving header from Cole, then Kennedy floored the rampant Beckham in the box and Irwin put the outcome beyond reasonable doubt with a firmly-struck penalty.

Another overhead, this time from Cole following a Beckham centre, made it four and, with Keane welcomed back for a gentle run-out after injury, United shifted into cruise control.

There was deserved consolation for the visitors when Johnson netted with an unstoppable shot, then Wooter headed against the bar, but another goal for Watford would have distorted the scoreline. Later Graham Taylor – whose side finished with ten men after Williams was dismissed for a wild 89th-minute lunge at Greening – admitted as much, adding: 'We've had our bottoms smacked today.'

OLYMPIQUE MARSEILLE 1

GALLAS 69

1. Stephane PORATO
2. Patrick BLONDEAU
3. Sebastien PEREZ
4. Pierre ISSA
23. William GALLAS
6. Eduardo BERRIZZO
7. Robert PIRES
8. Frederic BRANDO
26. Peter LUCCIN
12. Stephane DALMAT
11. Fabrizio RAVANELLI

SUBSTITUTES

9. Florian MAURICE (11) 74
10. Ivan DE LA PENA (8) 64
14. Djamel BELMADI
16. Stephane TREVISAN
19. Kaba DIAWARA
22. Ibrahima BAKAYOKO
28. Loris REINA (12) 88

MATCH REPORT

On a pudding of a pitch in the rain-soaked south of France, United slithered to their first Champions League reverse since losing at home to Juventus, some 22 months and 19 matches earlier.

Content to play on the counter for long stretches of a dour, joyless game, they capitulated to the slickest move of the night, when centre-back Gallas exchanged a lightning one-two with the splendid Dalmat, then dispatched a fierce shot past Bosnich with the outside of his right foot.

Thereafter the hitherto restrained Reds attacked relentlessly, but could not find the net until the third minute of added time, when Solskjaer headed home Beckham's inswinging free-kick from the left, only for Stam to be ruled marginally offside.

Despite their low-key gameplan, the visitors had been the first to threaten a breakthrough when Yorke's header from another Beckham delivery left goalkeeper Porato stranded, only to cannon to safety off defender Berizzo.

This proved to be a misleadingly exciting incident and nearly half an hour of stalemate followed before Ravanelli released Pires, whose shot brought a fine diving save from Bosnich. Shortly after the 'White Feather' menaced again,

Andy Cole shoots but fails to hit the target

0 MANCHESTER UNITED

| 1. Mark BOSNICH |
| 12. Phil NEVILLE |
| 3. Denis IRWIN |
| 16. Roy KEANE |
| 21. Henning BERG |
| 6. Jaap STAM |
| 7. David BECKHAM |
| 18. Paul SCHOLES |
| 9. Andy COLE |
| 19. Dwight YORKE |
| 11. Ryan GIGGS |
| **SUBSTITUTES** |
| 8. Nicky BUTT |
| 14. Jordi CRUYFF |
| 17. Raimomd VAN DER GOUW |
| 20. Ole Gunnar SOLSKJAER (21) 83 |
| 23. Michael CLEGG |
| 28. Danny HIGGINBOTHAM |
| 34. Jonathan GREENING |

Roy Keane's low cross-shot goes just wide of the Marseille goal

bending a free-kick narrowly wide of the post with the Australian beaten.

The second half was not much livelier than the first, with United's best chance falling to Keane, who was freed into space on the left by an exquisite pass from Cole. However, the skipper's low cross-shot was just off target.

At the other end, back-in-favour Bosnich pulled off a solid close-range block from Ravanelli, but was powerless to prevent the decisive incursion by Gallas.

The result cost United the leadership of their group to Marseille, but with two matches to come their destiny remained in their own hands.

TOTTENHAM HOTSPUR 3

1. Ian WALKER

2. Stephen CARR

3. Mauricio TARICCO

4. Steffen FREUND

5. Sol CAMPBELL

21. Luke YOUNG

18. Ruel FOX

8. Tim SHERWOOD

17. Oyvind LEONHARDSEN

10. Steffen IVERSEN

14. David GINOLA

SUBSTITUTES

12. Justin EDINBURGH

13. Espen BAARDSEN

15. Ramon VEGA (21) 77

20. Jose DOMINGUEZ

32. John PIERCY (18) 88

IVERSEN 37
SCHOLES (o.g.) 40
CARR 71

MATCH REPORT

Andy Cole jinks his way through Spurs' defence

United supplied the lion's share of coherent football in the face of commendably spirited opposition by George Graham's resurgent Spurs, and it could be argued that the scoreline was misleading. After all, the north Londoners' decisive strikes came via a handball, a bizarre own-goal and an unstoppable effort the like of which no custodian could have countered.

But all that is to ignore one unpalatable truth. The fact is that there was little sign of understanding between the Reds' keeper

1 MANCHESTER UNITED

24 GIGGS

1. Mark BOSNICH
12. Phil NEVILLE
3. Denis IRWIN
16. Roy KEANE
27. Mikael SILVESTRE
6. Jaap STAM
7. David BECKHAM
18. Paul SCHOLES
9. Andy COLE
19. Dwight YORKE
11. Ryan GIGGS

SUBSTITUTES

17. Raimond VAN DER GOUW
20. Ole Gunnar SOLSKJAER (7) 69
21. Henning BERG
28. Danny HIGGINBOTHAM
34. Jonathan GREENING (3) 83

and their back four, hardly surprising given that they had been unable to settle on a regular replacement for the departed Schmeichel and that a new defender, Silvestre, had been added.

The action flowed from end to end, though United had the edge and took the lead with a high quality goal. Cole threaded a through-ball to Giggs, who seemed well policed by Campbell and Young. But the Welshman twisted adroitly between the two centre-halves and gave Walker no chance with his precise finish.

Now, with Keane in masterful box-to-box form, the visitors looked likely to seize control, until uncertainty at the back turned the game on its head. First Sherwood nodded on a corner and the sprawling Iversen, unseen by the referee, handballed against a post before scrambling the rebound past Bosnich. Then, almost immediately, Ginola took possession from a short corner and his routine delivery was headed firmly into his own net by Scholes.

The second half, played in torrential rain, produced more end-to-end thrills before Carr contributed his contender for goal of the season, a savage 25-yard screamer from wide on the right.

For the first time in 290 Premiership games, United had scored first and lost.

Ryan Giggs chips one from the edge of the box

NK CROATIA ZAGREB 1

12. Tomislav BUTINA

2. Mario TOKIC

17. Mario CVITANOVIC

4. Goce SEDLOSKI

5. Goran JURIC

20. Stjepan TOMAS

15. Daniel SARIC

25. Tomislav SOKOTA

14. Mihael MIKIC

10. Edin MUJCIN

11. Tomislav RUKAVINA

SUBSTITUTES

3. Damir KRZNAR

6. Zoran PAVLOVIC

8. Robert PROSINECKI (5) 36

16. Josip SIMIC (14) 54

23. Vladimir VASILJ

26. Ardian KOZNIKU

30. Niljenko MUMLEK (17) 69

PROSINECKI 90

MATCH REPORT

Calmly, and for the most part comfortably, United ensured qualification for the next stage of European competition with a match to spare. Recent reverses had persuaded some observers to fear the worst, but yet again Sir Alex Ferguson's men performed with clinical efficiency when it really mattered, much to the frustration of a passionate home crowd.

In contrast to their stifling tactics at Old Trafford, the Croatians mounted several early attacks, then Mujcin went down in the Reds' penalty area under a challenge from Scholes, but the referee dismissed fanciful claims for a spot-kick.

Ironically it was a foul on Scholes at the other end which led to United going ahead, Beckham curling a high-velocity free-kick into the far bottom corner of Butina's net from just outside the left corner of the box.

The visitors cruised further towards their objective shortly after the break when a left-wing cross from Irwin was nodded out to Keane, whose 25-yard volley was marginally but decisively deflected by Tokic, past his own keeper.

Thereafter United coped easily with Zagreb's attacks until just before the end, when Saric centred and Prosinecki placed the ball coolly inside Bosnich's near post

Ryan Giggs shows off his close control skills

2 MANCHESTER UNITED

32 BECKHAM
49 KEANE

1 Mark BOSNICH
12 Phil NEVILLE
3 Denis IRWIN
16 Roy KEANE
21 Henning BERG
6 Jaap STAM
7 David BECKHAM
18 Paul SCHOLES
9 Andy COLE
19 Dwight YORKE
11 Ryan GIGGS

SUBSTITUTES

4 David MAY
14 Jordi CRUYFF (9) 79
17 Raimomd VAN DER GOUW
20 Ole Gunnar SOLSKJAER (19) 59
23 Michael CLEGG
28 Danny HIGGINBOTHAM
34 Jonathan GREENING (18) 68

Zagreb's keeper, Butina, punches clear as Jordi Cruyff tries to get in on goal

from 12 yards. But it was too late to matter to United.

A clean sheet would have been welcome, but the Reds were through and that was enough for their 600 travelling supporters to explode with glee at the final whistle.

MANCHESTER UNITED 3

1. Mark BOSNICH
12. Phil NEVILLE
3. Denis IRWIN
16. Roy KEANE
27. Mikael SILVESTRE
6. Jaap STAM
7. David BECKHAM
18. Paul SCHOLES
9. Andy COLE
19. Dwight YORKE
11. Ryan GIGGS

SUBSTITUTES

14. Jordi CRUYFF (11) 79
17. Raimond VAN DER GOUW
20. Ole Gunnar SOLSKJAER (19) 66
21. Henning BERG
33. Mark WILSON (9) 79

SCHOLES 30
COLE 45
KEANE 65

MATCH REPORT

Though the scoreline flattered United, it bore testimony to the tantalising creativity of David Beckham. All three goals came from his devilish dispatches from the right flank, and his efforts were rewarded with a trio of top-quality finishes.

The visitors began in bold, enterprising mode and Dublin and Boateng went close before Beckham began to make meaningful incursions. Indeed the fiery Dublin netted but Carbone was offside, and it was only this escape that appeared to prod the Reds into devastating reprisal.

First Beckham delivered a trademark curler which Scholes diverted beyond James with a sweet half-volley. There followed chances to increase the lead as attacks rained in on Villa, who were breached again when an overhit cross from Giggs was collected by Beckham. The man of the moment delivered it from the byline into the path of Cole, who netted from 12 yards.

Villa responded with a lively spell at the start of the second period, but the issue was settled in classic style when yet another Beckham centre was backheeled exquisitely by Scholes to Keane, whose drive beat James from 20 yards.

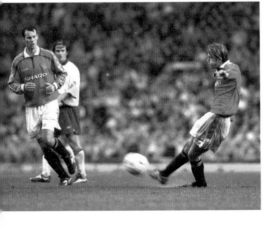

David Beckham provided pinpoint crosses for all three United goals

0 ASTON VILLA

1. David JAMES

24. Mark DELANEY

15. Gareth BARRY

4. Gareth SOUTHGATE

34. Colin CALDERWOOD

6. George BOATENG

7. Ian TAYLOR

17. Lee HENDRIE

9. Dion DUBLIN

18. Benito CARBONE

11. Alan THOMPSON

SUBSTITUTES

2. Steve WATSON

3. Alan WRIGHT (11) 73

10. Paul MERSON (18) 76

26. Steve STONE (6) 55

39. Peter ENCKELMAN

Gareth Southgate heads clear from Andy Cole and Dwight Yorke

OCTOBER IN REVIEW

SUNDAY 3	v CHELSEA	A	0-5
WEDNESDAY 13	v ASTON VILLA	A	0-3
SATURDAY 16	v WATFORD	H	4-1
TUESDAY 19	v OLYMPIQUE MARSEILLE	A	0-1
SATURDAY 23	v TOTTENHAM HOTSPUR	A	1-3
WEDNESDAY 27	v NK CROATIA ZAGREB	A	2-1
SATURDAY 30	v ASTON VILLA	H	3-0

PLAYER IN THE FRAME

Mark Bosnich

No sooner had the self-assured Australian began life as Peter Schmeichel's successor than he fell prey to injury and indifferent form. The arrival of Massimo Taibi and the ongoing solidity of Raimond van der Gouw might have demoralised less confident individuals, but Mark showed rare strength of character to reclaim his place.

FA CARLING PREMIERSHIP

		P	W	D	L	F	A	Pts
UP TO AND INCLUDING	Leeds United	12	8	2	2	25	16	26
MONDAY 25 OCTOBER 1999	Arsenal	12	8	1	3	20	12	25
	Sunderland	12	7	3	2	21	10	24
	MANCHESTER UNITED	12	7	3	2	28	19	24
	Tottenham Hotspur	11	6	2	3	20	15	20
	Leicester City	12	6	2	4	20	17	20
	Chelsea	10	6	1	3	17	7	19
	Everton	12	5	3	4	21	18	18
	Aston Villa	12	5	3	4	13	12	18
	Middlesbrough	12	6	0	6	16	16	18
	West Ham United	10	5	2	3	12	9	17
	Liverpool	11	4	3	4	12	11	15
	Coventry City	12	3	4	5	16	15	13
	Southampton	11	3	3	5	18	22	12
	Wimbledon	12	2	6	4	18	26	12
	Bradford City	11	3	2	6	9	17	11
	Newcastle United	12	3	1	8	23	27	10
	Watford	12	3	0	9	8	18	9
	Derby County	12	2	3	7	10	21	9
	Sheffield Wednesday	12	1	2	9	8	27	5

NOVEMBER

TUESDAY 2	v SK STURM GRAZ	H
SATURDAY 6	v LEICESTER CITY	H
SATURDAY 20	v DERBY COUNTY	A
TUESDAY 23	v AC FIORENTINA	A

MANCHESTER UNITED 2

1. Mark BOSNICH
2. Gary NEVILLE
3. Denis IRWIN
4. David MAY
21. Henning BERG
16. Roy KEANE
34. Jonathan GREENING
33. Mark WILSON
9. Andy COLE
20. Ole Gunnar SOLSKJAER
11. Ryan GIGGS

SUBSTITUTES

6. Jaap STAM
12. Phil NEVILLE (33) 53
14. Jordi CRUYFF (34) 65
17. Raimond VAN DER GOUW
19. Dwight YORKE
23. Michael CLEGG
28. Danny HIGGINBOTHAM (3) 76

SOLSKJAER 56
KEANE 65

MATCH REPORT

A scintillating strike by Ole Gunnar Solskjaer illuminated a distinctly low-key display by United, whose victory made sure of top slot in their group and a place among the seeds in the next stage.

There was no shortage of entertaining moments for the Old Trafford crowd, but this encounter with the Austrian champions lacked true urgency, much of the action unfolding at an incongruously gentle tempo.

Deprived of Beckham and Scholes through suspension, the Reds signalled their approach by resting Stam and Yorke, and they were lucky not to fall behind during the early exchanges. First Vastic struck a post with a low centre from near the corner flag, then the same player volleyed brilliantly against the other upright only for Kocijan to balloon the rebound over a gaping net.

In fairness, Cole might have scored twice in between those incidents, miscuing from close range following a majestic May header, then seeing a firm drive cleared off the line by Strafner after Schicklgruber had spilled a Gary Neville cross.

Andy Cole miscues from close range

1 SK STURM GRAZ

88 VASTIC (penalty)

22. Josef SCHICKLGRUBER

18. Markus SCHOPP

3. Gunther NEUKIRCHNER

14. Jan-Pieter MARTENS

12. Gilbert PRILASNIG

6. Roman MAHLICH

7. Gerald STRAFNER

17. Didier ANGIEBEAUD

21. Tomislav KOCIJAN

10. Ivica VASTIC

20. Mehrdad MINAVAND

SUBSTITUTES

1. Kazimierz SIDORCZUK

2. Michael BOCHTLER (21) 74

9. Hannes REINMAYR (14) 71

15. Georg BARDEL (17) 71

19. Imre SZABICS

23. Thomas GROBL

Ole Gunnar Solskjaer cracks the ball into the net to give United the lead

With Sturm positive in attack but defensively naive, more chances came United's way, and Solskjaer missed badly with a header before he made amends with a goal which deserved to grace a more memorable contest. Greening delivered from the right, a nodded clearance reached the edge of the box and the Norwegian met it with the most savage left-foot volley imaginable.

The Reds consolidated their supremacy when the lively May headed against the bar and the ball bounced out to Keane, who cracked it past Schicklgruber from ten yards.

Vastic halved the arrears from the penalty spot after being fouled by Giggs, after which Bosnich was required to make two competent saves as the Austrians sought an unlikely point.

MANCHESTER UNITED 2

COLE 30, 83

1. Mark BOSNICH
12. Phil NEVILLE
28. Danny HIGGINBOTHAM
16. Roy KEANE
27. Mikael SILVESTRE
6. Jaap STAM
18. Paul SCHOLES
20. Ole Gunnar SOLSKJAER
9. Andy COLE
19. Dwight YORKE
11. Ryan GIGGS

SUBSTITUTES

4. David MAY (28) 79
14. Jordi CRUYFF
17. Raimond VAN DER GOUW
21. Henning BERG (12) 83
34. Jonathan GREENING

MATCH REPORT

The Red Devils celebrated Sir Alex Ferguson's thirteenth anniversary as manager with a victory over the fifth-placed Foxes, thus returning to the top of the Premiership.

True, United's performance was more fragmentary than fluent, but plenty of scoring opportunities were created, and in Cole they had the undisputed man of the match.

Though his strike-rate had always been high, now he radiated a confidence which had not always been apparent, a mood exemplified by the extravagant manner of his opening goal.

Phil Neville, on the right flank, exchanged passes with Keane before chipping forward to Solskjaer, whose header reached Cole on the edge of the box but facing away from goal. In one lithe movement, the newly-recalled England marksman executed the perfect bicycle kick, the ball clipping the far post before nestling in the net behind the surprised Flowers.

Until then, Leicester had been holding their own, with Cottee missing one chance after Neville had appeared to be dazzled by the sun and Heskey failing to cap a surging run with a testing shot.

Now the hosts – for whom Higginbotham made a confident full

Paul Scholes battles for midfield dominance

0 LEICESTER CITY

1. Tim FLOWERS
24. Andrew IMPEY
3. Frank SINCLAIR
4. Gerry TAGGART
18. Matt ELLIOTT
6. Mustafa IZZET
7. Neil LENNON
14. Robbie SAVAGE
9. Emile HESKEY
27. Tony COTTEE
11. Steve GUPPY

SUBSTITUTES

5. Steve WALSH (27) 79
15. Phil GILCHRIST
22. Pegguy ARPHEXAD
29 Stefan OAKES
37. Theo ZAGORAKIS

Andy Cole dances past Frank Sinclair before scoring his second

League debut – began to threaten and after the interval Yorke (twice), Cole and Solskjaer all went close. Izzet responded by freeing Heskey, who danced past Bosnich, only for his acute-angled shot to be blocked on the line by Silvestre.

Appropriately, the final word rested with the quicksilver Cole. Reached by Yorke, he sidestepped a defender only for his shot to be cleared off the line by Lennon. However, the ball cannoned off an upright and fell once more to United's predatory number-nine, who netted from six yards.

DERBY COUNTY 1

DELAP 90

21. Mart POOM

2. Horacio CARBONARI

3. Stefan SCHNOOR

4. Darryl POWELL

5. Tony DORIGO

16. Jacob LAURSEN

7. Seth JOHNSON

8. Dean STURRIDGE

26. Marvin ROBINSON

10. Rory DELAP

22. Vass BORBOKIS

SUBSTITUTES

12. Malcolm CHRISTIE (22) 75

17. Spencer PRIOR

23. Paul BOERTIEN

24. Andy OAKES

28. Adam MURPHY (8) 75

MATCH REPORT

United prevailed more comfortably than the score suggests in a disjointed, sometimes unsavoury encounter with the lowly Rams.

Understandably enough, Jim Smith's below-strength side were unrelentingly aggressive as they continued the fight for their Premiership lives, especially after being reduced to ten men when Schnoor was sent off for a second bookable offence seven minutes before the interval.

In response, the Reds produced sufficient quality, know-how and determination to maintain their status as Premiership leaders but, perhaps preoccupied by the prospect of a Champions League expedition to Italy three days later, they never slipped into top gear.

The first half was frantic, arid and tetchy, culminating in the German defender's dismissal after he ploughed wildly into Yorke from behind. The referee had little choice but to brandish the red card, though whether he needed the frantic encouragement of Beckham and Gary Neville to do so remained open to debate.

The second period was marginally easier on the eye, with United pressing home their numerical superiority relentlessly and they took the lead when Beckham's cross from the right was headed out to Butt, whose powerful 16-yard half-volley

Gary Neville is first on the scene to congratulate Nicky Butt on his goal early in the second half

2 MANCHESTER UNITED

53 BUTT
84 COLE

17. Raimond VAN DER GOUW
2. Gary NEVILLE
12. Phil NEVILLE
16. Roy KEANE
27. Mikael SILVESTRE
6. Jaap STAM
7. David BECKHAM
8. Nicky BUTT
9. Andy COLE
19. Dwight YORKE
11. Ryan GIGGS

SUBSTITUTES

10. Teddy SHERINGHAM
18. Paul SCHOLES
20. Ole Gunnar SOLSKJAER (7) 87
21. Henning BERG (27) 78
26. Massimo TAIBI

took a slight but telling deflection on its way into the net. It was a deserved fillip for the midfielder, who had laboured tirelessly in his first senior outing since a hernia operation. Thereafter the visitors wore down their spirited opponents, but carelessness in front of goal limited their advantage until Giggs broke free on the left and centred for Cole to head home unhindered.

That should have been that, but in stoppage time van der Gouw dropped a clanger, missing a curling free-kick from Johnson and allowing Delap to nod into the unguarded net.

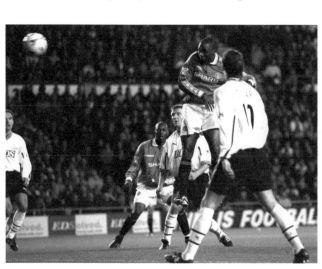

Andy Cole rises unchallenged to put United 2-0 up

AC FIORENTINA 2

1. Francesco TOLDO
2. Tomas REPKA
3. Moreno TORRICELLI
14. Sandro COIS
23. Alessandro PIERINI
6. Aldo FIRICANO
16. Angelo DI LIVIO
18. Abel BALBO
9. Gabriel BATISTUTA
10. Manuel RUI COSTA
17. Jorg HEINRICH

SUBSTITUTES

4. Daniele ADANI (23) 79
5. Pasquale PADALINO
11. Fabio ROSSITTO (16) 67
12. Guiseppe TAGLIALATELA
21. Mauro BRESSAN (18) 79
24. Christian AMOROSO
27. Andrea TAROZZI

BATISTUTA 24
BALBO 52

MATCH REPORT

Two elementary individual errors signalled a calamitous start to the second stage of the Red Devils' European title defence. The culprits were Roy Keane, of all people, and Henning Berg, though they should not shoulder the entire blame for this ominous reverse.

With Sir Alex Ferguson opting for an attacking formation, it was an open, end-to-end encounter, with Rui Costa and Scholes sparkling in midfield for their respective sides.

Indeed, the feisty little Mancunian almost engineered an early breakthrough with a raking pass to Giggs, only for the Welshman to mis-control the ball, and then Scholes fired narrowly wide from 20 yards after fine work from Yorke.

The Florentines were buzzing, though, and after Rui Costa had forced a splendid left-sided parry from Bosnich, Keane delivered the sloppiest of back-passes, horribly short of his astonished keeper. That arch-predator Batistuta was on to it in a flash and netted with an unstoppable curler from 20 yards.

United hit back at once, with Toldo making a smart save from Scholes, but the visitors were stretched on several occasions by the ceaseless movement of

Roy Keane threatens Francesco Toldo's goal

0 MANCHESTER UNITED

| 1. Mark BOSNICH |
| 2. Gary NEVILLE |
| 3. Denis IRWIN |
| 16. Roy KEANE |
| 21. Henning BERG |
| 6. Jaap STAM |
| 7. David BECKHAM |
| 18. Paul SCHOLES |
| 9. Andy COLE |
| 19. Dwight YORKE |
| 11. Ryan GIGGS |
| **SUBSTITUTES** |
| 8. Nicky BUTT |
| 10. Teddy SHERINGHAM (9) 63 |
| 12. Phil NEVILLE (21) 63 |
| 17. Raimond VAN DER GOUW |
| 20. Ole Gunnar SOLSKJAER (19) 63 |
| 25. Quinton FORTUNE |
| 28. Danny HIGGINBOTHAM |

Ryan Giggs, in full flight, hurdles Fiorentina's Moreno Torricelli

Batistuta and Balbo.

However, an equaliser almost materialised shortly before half-time when a Beckham free-kick was blocked by Toldo, then rebounded from Pierini and Repka before bouncing off the crossbar and behind to safety. That incident summed up the champions' fortunes.

Soon after the interval came Berg's aberration, when he was caught in possession by 'Batigol', who sent in Balbo to shoot through the guard of the wrong-footed Bosnich from 14 yards.

As time ebbed away, Scholes missed badly from close range and both Sheringham and Solskjaer miskicked when well placed. Thus ended a night of frustration.

NOVEMBER IN REVIEW

TUESDAY 2	v SK STURM GRAZ	H	2-1
SATURDAY 6	v LEICESTER CITY	H	2-0
SATURDAY 20	v DERBY COUNTY	A	2-1
TUESDAY 23	v AC FIORENTINA	A	0-2

PLAYER IN THE FRAME

Ryan Giggs

In the month of his 26th birthday, Ryan furnished exhilarating evidence that he was moving into his pomp. As searingly pacy and mesmerically skilful as ever, now the Welshman married those priceless natural gifts ever more consistently to an awareness of the pattern of play around him. Come the spring he was to be even more devastating, but his Inter-Continental Cup Man-of-the-Match award offered an appropriate late-autumn accolade.

FA CARLING PREMIERSHIP

		P	W	D	L	F	A	Pts
UP TO AND INCLUDING	Leeds United	16	11	2	3	29	19	35
SUNDAY 28 NOVEMBER 1999	MANCHESTER UNITED	15	10	3	2	35	20	33
	Arsenal	16	10	2	4	28	16	32
	Sunderland	16	9	4	3	27	16	31
	Leicester City	16	9	2	5	26	20	29
	Liverpool	16	8	3	5	20	13	27
	Tottenham Hotspur	15	8	2	5	25	20	26
	Chelsea	14	7	3	4	20	11	24
	West Ham United	15	7	3	5	17	14	24
	Middlesbrough	16	7	2	7	20	23	23
	Everton	16	5	6	5	24	22	21
	Coventry City	16	5	5	6	23	18	20
	Aston Villa	16	5	4	7	14	18	19
	Wimbledon	16	3	8	5	22	29	17
	Newcastle United	16	4	4	8	27	30	16
	Southampton	15	4	4	7	20	25	16
	Bradford City	15	3	3	9	12	24	12
	Derby County	16	3	3	10	15	28	12
	Watford	16	3	2	11	13	28	11
	Sheffield Wednesday	15	1	3	11	13	36	6

DECEMBER

SATURDAY 4	v EVERTON	H
WEDNESDAY 8	v VALENCIA CF	H
SATURDAY 18	v WEST HAM UNITED	A
SUNDAY 26	v BRADFORD CITY	H
TUESDAY 28	v SUNDERLAND	A

MANCHESTER UNITED 5

1. Mark BOSNICH	IRWIN (penalty) 27
2. Gary NEVILLE	SOLSKJAER 29, 43, 52, 58

1. Mark BOSNICH
2. Gary NEVILLE
3. Denis IRWIN
16. Roy KEANE
27. Mikael SILVESTRE
6. Jaap STAM
18. Paul SCHOLES
8. Nicky BUTT
20. Ole Gunnar SOLSKJAER
10. Teddy SHERINGHAM
11. Ryan GIGGS

SUBSTITUTES

7. David BECKHAM
9. Andy COLE (11) 64
12. Phil NEVILLE (27) 64
17. Raimond VAN DER GOUW (1) 8
19. Dwight YORKE

MATCH REPORT

If the Red Devils were jet-lagged following their midweek coronation as World Club Champions in Tokyo then someone should have told Ole Gunnar Solskjaer, whose four goals in half an hour destroyed Everton. At any other club, surely, the quicksilver Norwegian would be a first-team regular, yet here, with Christmas not far away, he was making only his sixth League start of the campaign.

United began fluently, spurning several inviting chances only to be stunned when Everton scored a simple goal, Jeffers turning in an Unsworth cross from close range.

Paul Scholes works his way through the Everton defence

1 EVERTON

7 JEFFERS

13. Paul GERRARD
15. Richard DUNNE
14. David WEIR
4. Richard GOUGH
19. Abel XAVIER
6. David UNSWORTH
7. John COLLINS
8. Nick BARMBY
9. Kevin CAMPBELL
17. Francis JEFFERS
12. Mark PEMBRIDGE
SUBSTITUTES
2. Alex CLELAND (8) 63
3. Michael BALL (15) 63
20. Philip JEVONS
24. Tony GRANT (12) 81
35. Steve SIMONSEN

The quicksilver Ole Gunnar Solskjaer scores the Reds' third goal

Immediately Bosnich was withdrawn with a hamstring injury and replaced by van der Gouw. Not long afterwards Dunne handled a cross from Keane and Irwin equalised with a textbook penalty, then Solskjaer took over. First he ran on to a perceptive through-ball from Scholes and stroked it past the splendid Gerrard.

Two minutes before the interval the same maker and taker combined in similar fashion to put United two in front, and the outcome was settled early in the second half when the Norwegian glanced in a precise header from an exquisite Irwin centre, then guided the ball under Gerrard from ten yards after the hapless Dunne had twice squandered possession.

United's easy victory restored them to the top of the League.

MANCHESTER UNITED 3

17. Raimond VAN DER GOUW	KEANE 38
2. Gary NEVILLE	SOLSKJAER 47
3. Denis IRWIN	SCHOLES 70
16. Roy KEANE	
12. Phil NEVILLE	
6. Jaap STAM	
7. David BECKHAM	
18. Paul SCHOLES	
9. Andy COLE	
20. Ole Gunnar SOLSKJAER	
11. Ryan GIGGS	

SUBSTITUTES

8. Nicky BUTT (18) 72
10. Teddy SHERINGHAM
14. Jordi CRUYFF
19. Dwight YORKE (9) 72
21. Henning BERG
28. Danny HIGGINBOTHAM
31. Nick CULKIN

MATCH REPORT

Truly this was a gala night for the English, European and newly-crowned world club champions. After surviving early pressure applied by the stylish Spaniards, United played beautifully to claim a three-goal victory which reflected the splendour of their performance.

David Beckham was at his most compellingly brilliant, creating the second and third goals, while man-of-the-moment Roy Keane – who had signed a new contract shortly before the game – opened the scoring with a sweetly-struck 20-yarder.

The Red Devils' other hero was Raimond van der Gouw, who pulled off two crucial saves to foil a slick first-minute raid inspired by the impressive Mendieta, then dived full-length to parry goal-bound efforts from Angloma and Lopez in the second period.

With Yorke ousted by the in-form Solskjaer, the home attack took time to settle but gradually the ingenuity of Beckham and Giggs wrested the initiative from their enterprising opponents as a delightfully open and fluent contest took shape.

Solskjaer and Giggs went close, Lopez tested van der Gouw's positioning with an audacious 40-yard chip and Beckham rapped Palop's bar with a trademark free-kick. United deserved a breakthrough and it came when a headed clearance dropped into the path of Keane and he volleyed unstoppably into the far corner of Valencia's net.

Angloma might have equalised shortly before the break but

David Beckham was at his most compellingly brilliant in the second half

0 VALENCIA CF

26. PALOP
2. Mauricio PELLEGRINO
3. Joachim BJORKLUND
20. Jocelyn ANGLOMA
5. Miroslav DJUKIC
6. MENDIETA
7. Claudio LOPEZ
8. FARINOS
9. OSCAR
21. MILLA
15. Amedeo CARBONI

SUBSTITUTES

4. CAMARASA
12. SORIA
13. BARTUAL
17. Juan SANCHEZ (9) 69
19. Goran VLAOVIC (7) 85
24. Daniel FAGIANI
30. CABEZAS

the Reds began the second half at a gallop, with Beckham's low cross being turned home neatly by Solskjaer at the near post.

Valencia responded with spirit and briefly United stuttered. Both Lopez and Oscar missed excellent chances to reduce the arrears, but then the Reds resumed their ascendancy. A third goal seemed inevitable and it arrived when Beckham delivered exquisitely from the right and Scholes' glancing header directed the ball inside the far post. It was a fitting climax to a glittering display.

Paul Scholes rises high to head United's third from David Beckham's cross

WEST HAM UNITED 2

DI CANIO 24, 53

1. Shaka HISLOP
18. Frank LAMPARD
20. Scott MINTO
13. Marc-Vivien FOE
15. Rio FERDINAND
6. Neil RUDDOCK
7. Marc KELLER
8. Trevor SINCLAIR
12. Paulo WANCHOPE
10. Paolo DI CANIO
11. Steve LOMAS

SUBSTITUTES

9. Paul KITSON
22. Craig FORREST
25. Stevland ANGUS
30. Javier MARGAS
38. Adam NEWTON

MATCH REPORT

Manchester United started in top gear, all but destroying West Ham with waves of scintillating attacks which yielded three early goals, but then allowed the plucky Hammers to claw their way back into contention. However, Sir Alex Ferguson's men reacted like true champions, dominating the latter stages and winning with plenty to spare.

The opening goal was a work of art. Keane sprayed a raking crossfield ball to the right, Beckham volleyed a first-time cross which laid bare the home defence and Yorke wrong-footed Hislop with a cute header from five yards.

The second strike was similarly slick, Giggs finding Yorke on the left with a delicious flick, the Tobagan returning the favour, leaving the Welshman to nudge cleverly past the keeper.

In truth, the third goal owed something to fortune, Giggs seizing on a rebound from Ruddock to beat the unsighted Hislop from 20 yards. Still, the margin did not flatter and a massacre seemed imminent.

Enter di Canio, who volleyed a knockdown from Ruddock underneath van der Gouw, and the hitherto one-sided contest assumed a more balanced perspective. Though United continued to make chances – Giggs, Scholes and Keane all went close – West Ham rallied bravely either side of the interval and were rewarded when their Italian star, sent free by Keller, rounded van der Gouw imperiously to further reduce the deficit.

David Beckham grimaces with effort as he drives at the West Ham defence

4 MANCHESTER UNITED

9, 63 YORKE
13, 20 GIGGS

17. Raimond VAN DER GOUW
2. Gary NEVILLE
3. Denis IRWIN
16. Roy KEANE
27. Mikael SILVESTRE
6. Jaap STAM
7. David BECKHAM
18. Paul SCHOLES
19. Dwight YORKE
10. Teddy SHERINGHAM
11. Ryan GIGGS

SUBSTITUTES

8. Nicky BUTT (7) 77
12. Phil NEVILLE (3) h-t
20. Ole Gunnar SOLSKJAER
21. Henning BERG
26. Massimo TAIBI

Dwight Yorke heads home David Beckham's cross to put United ahead after nine minutes

Soon the Hammers might have equalised, di Canio over-elaborating before chipping straight at the keeper. His profligacy was punished ruthlessly and immediately, Giggs crossing for Yorke to stab home the clincher.

Thereafter United dazzled, Beckham missing narrowly with two glorious efforts, Giggs almost claiming his hat-trick and a Butt strike being disallowed for offside. It had been a sumptuous display by a side nearing its best once again.

MANCHESTER UNITED 4

1. Mark BOSNICH
2. Gary NEVILLE
12. Phil NEVILLE
16. Roy KEANE
27. Mikael SILVESTRE
6. Jaap STAM
18. Paul SCHOLES
8. Nicky BUTT
20. Ole Gunnar SOLSKJAER
10. Teddy SHERINGHAM
25. Quinton FORTUNE

SUBSTITUTES

9. Andy COLE (10) 67
14. Jordi CRUYFF
19. Dwight YORKE (8) 67
26. Massimo TAIBI
30. Ronnie WALLWORK (6) 81

FORTUNE 75
YORKE 79
COLE 88
KEANE 89

MATCH REPORT

After being bogged down for 75 minutes on a muddy pitch the Red Devils overwhelmed the brave Bantams with an irresistible mixture of ferocity and precision. As the quagmire had deepened and wave after wave of United attacks had been repelled, the possibility had grown that Bradford might re-cross the Pennines with an heroically-gained point. However, the dam was breached and the resultant deluge of goals was brutally crushing.

Despite a safety-first 4-5-1 formation, the visitors began enterprisingly and former Old Trafford favourite Lee Sharpe created the first clear-cut opening, only for Mills' shot to be blocked. Then Redfearn sent a low effort narrowly wide of Bosnich's goal before the inevitable pressure began to build at the other end. Sheringham had a goal ruled out for offside and Fortune, on his full League debut, rapped the bar with a delectably curved left-foot free-kick.

The introduction of Cole and Yorke galvanised United and thereafter the breakthrough came quickly. Butt found Solskjaer, whose cross from the right was turned home from close range by the lively Fortune.

First start, first goal – a great moment for Quinton Fortune as he scores after 75 minutes

0 BRADFORD CITY

13. Matt CLARKE

18. Gunnar HALLE

3. Andy MYERS

4. Stuart McCALL

5. David WETHERALL

14. Andy O'BRIEN

7. Jamie LAWRENCE

15. Dean WINDASS

9. Lee MILLS

26. Neil REDFEARN

16. Lee SHARPE

SUBSTITUTES

6. Ashley WESTWOOD

8. Robbie BLAKE (3) 80

11. Peter BEAGRIE (7) 55

28. Dean SAUNDERS (26) 80

31. Aiden DAVISON

Mikael Silvestre keeps the ball away from Bradford's Lee Mills

The game was put beyond Bradford's reach when first Yorke and then Cole cut in from the left flank to beat the beleaguered Clarke. The job was completed by Keane, who intercepted a loose pass, then ploughed unstoppably past a Bradford challenge before shooting into the far corner of the net from 15 yards. All was well that ended well but, undeniably, Paul Jewell's side had given the champions a Boxing Day fright.

SUNDERLAND 2

1. Thomas SORENSEN	McCANN 2
2. Chris MAKIN	QUINN 12
3. Michael GRAY	
4. Kevin KILBANE	
5. Steve BOULD	
6. Paul BUTLER	
7. Nicky SUMMERBEE	
16. Alex RAE	
9. Niall QUINN	
21. Gavin McCANN	
20. Stefan SCHWARZ	

SUBSTITUTES

13. Andrew MARRIOTT

18. Darren WILLIAMS (16) 52

28. John OSTER

29. Eric ROY

31. Michael REDDY (4) 90

MATCH REPORT

Andy Cole leaps above the Sunderland defence to get on the end of a corner, but his effort was in vain

2 MANCHESTER UNITED

27 KEANE
87 BUTT

1. Mark BOSNICH
2. Gary NEVILLE
3. Denis IRWIN
16. Roy KEANE
27. Mikael SILVESTRE
6. Jaap STAM
7. David BECKHAM
8. Nicky BUTT
9. Andy COLE
19. Dwight YORKE
11. Ryan GIGGS

SUBSTITUTES

10. Teddy SHERINGHAM (3) 77
12. Phil NEVILLE (9) 89
17. Raimond VAN DER GOUW
20. Ole Gunnar SOLSKJAER (7) 84
21. Henning BERG

After making a calamitous start which left Sunderland two goals to the good after only 12 minutes, United dominated the remainder of a pulsating contest and escaped with a point, thanks to a controversial late goal from Butt.

The action had barely entered its second minute when a long ball from the left was glanced on by Niall Quinn to McCann, who took it adroitly on his chest and stabbed it past Bosnich. Sunderland continued to threaten and when Schwarz delivered a wickedly curling cross from the left, Quinn sneaked ahead of Silvestre and beat Bosnich with a first-time toe-poke.

As for United, Sorensen was not tested until a 30-yard half-volley from Keane thudded into his arms in the 24th minute, a strike which appeared to awaken the sluggish Red Devils and signalled the commencement of a long siege on the home goal.

Soon it bore fruit when a Beckham nudge found Cole, who swivelled and laid the ball into the path of the charging Keane, the United skipper shooting under Sorensen from 16 yards.

Now United attacked ceaselessly, with Yorke, Keane, Stam and Cole all going close before the break. Further relentless pressure continued throughout the second period, but the deadlock was not broken until United won a contentious free-kick on the right. The resulting half-clearance fell to Butt, who netted with a bobbling shot from 20 yards.

The attacking spirit of Roy Keane and Nicky Butt paid off when the latter scored the 87th-minute equaliser

December in Review

SATURDAY 4	v EVERTON	H	5-1
WEDNESDAY 8	v VALENCIA CF	H	3-0
SATURDAY 18	v WEST HAM UNITED	A	4-2
SUNDAY 26	v BRADFORD CITY	H	4-0
TUESDAY 28	v SUNDERLAND	A	2-2

PLAYER IN THE FRAME

Raimond van der Gouw

Raimond's performance in keeping a clean sheet in the home victory over Valencia confirmed what his many admirers had been declaring for months – that, despite his advancing years, the tall Dutchman was an accomplished keeper who had finally emerged from Peter Schmeichel's shadow. Earlier in the season he had played a brilliant part in the triumph at Highbury and it was fitting that, at last, he totalled enough appearances to earn a title medal.

FA Carling Premiership

UP TO AND INCLUDING
SUNDAY 26 DECEMBER 1999

	P	W	D	L	F	A	Pts
Leeds United	19	14	2	3	34	20	44
Manchester United	18	13	3	2	48	23	42
Sunderland	19	11	4	4	33	22	37
Arsenal	19	11	3	5	34	20	36
Liverpool	19	10	4	5	28	16	34
Tottenham Hotspur	18	9	3	6	30	22	30
Leicester City	19	9	2	8	27	26	29
Everton	19	7	6	6	33	28	27
Chelsea	17	8	3	6	23	18	27
Middlesbrough	19	8	3	8	23	26	27
West Ham United	18	7	5	6	21	20	26
Aston Villa	19	7	4	8	18	20	25
Coventry City	19	6	6	7	26	22	24
Wimbledon	19	4	10	5	30	32	22
Newcastle United	19	5	5	9	30	34	20
Southampton	18	4	5	9	21	29	17
Bradford City	18	4	4	10	15	29	16
Derby County	19	4	3	12	16	31	15
Watford	19	3	2	14	14	40	11
Sheffield Wednesday	18	2	3	13	16	42	9

JANUARY

THURSDAY 6	v RAYOS DEL NECAXA	A
SATURDAY 8	v VASCO DA GAMA	A
TUESDAY 11	v SOUTH MELBOURNE	A
MONDAY 24	v ARSENAL	H
SATURDAY 29	v MIDDLESBROUGH	H

RAYOS DEL NECAXA   1

1. Hugo PINEDA
2. Salvador CABRERA
3. Sergio ALMAGUER
20. Jose HIGAREDA
12. Hernan VIGNA
18. Jose MILIAN
7. Alex AGUINAGA
8. Luis PEREZ
9. Agustin DELGADO
10. Markus LOPEZ
19. Cristian MONTECINOS

SUBSTITUTES

4. Ignacio AMBRIZ (12) 80
5. Andres SCOTTI
6. Miguel ACOSTA (20) 83
11. Samuel TORRES
13. Carlos OCHOA
14. Israel VELASQUEZ
15. Octavio BECERRIL
16. David OLIVA
17. Alexandro ALVAREZ
21. Sergio VASQUEZ (19) 78
22. Jose GUADARRAMA
23. Jaime HERNANDEZ

MONTECINOS 14

MATCH REPORT

Ole Gunnar Solskjaer needed all his skills to avoid tough tackles like this

Not for the first time, Manchester United thrived on adversity to complete a dramatic late comeback. A goal down at half-time, labouring in intense heat and humidity, with Beckham sent off and Sir Alex Ferguson dismissed from the bench for disputing a decision, they appeared to have little chance. Yet somehow, displaying their now-familiar cocktail of spirit and ability, the Reds reversed the tide to claim a share of the spoils. Indeed, they came close to victory on a night of unremitting drama.

1 MANCHESTER UNITED

88 YORKE

1. Mark BOSNICH
2. Gary NEVILLE
3. Denis IRWIN
16. Roy KEANE
5. Mikael SILVESTRE
6. Jaap STAM
7. David BECKHAM
8. Nicky BUTT
9. Andy COLE
19. Dwight YORKE
11. Ryan GIGGS

SUBSTITUTES

4. Danny HIGGINBOTHAM
11. Teddy SHERINGHAM (9) 72
12. Phil NEVILLE (8) 72
13. Paul RACHUBKA
14. Jordi CRUYFF
15. Jonathan GREENING
17. Raimond VAN DER GOUW
14. Mark WILSON
20. Ole Gunnar SOLSKJAER (3) 72
21. Henning BERG
22. Quinton FORTUNE
23. Ronnie WALLWORK

The match began slowly but burst into life when Aguinaga fell to the ground, even though the chasing Stam had made no contact. Nevertheless a free-kick was awarded and Montecinos dispatched a left-foot curler into the net. To make matters worse Beckham was dismissed two minutes before the break.

In the second period, the Reds stabilised and were unlucky to concede a 57th-minute penalty when Silvestre was adjudged to have impeded Montecinos. However, justice was done when Bosnich saved Aguinaga's spot-kick. Now United pushed forward courageously. Sheringham nodded to Solskjaer, whose volleyed shot bobbled across goal, allowing Yorke to make instant amends by sweeping in the equaliser.

Andy Cole tussles with Necaxa's Jose Milian

VASCO DA GAMA 3

14. HELTON
2. JORGINHO
13. GILBERTO
4. MAURO GALVAO
5. AMARAL
6. FELIPE
17. JUNIOR BAIANO
8. JUNINHO
9. RAMON
10. EDMUNDO
11. ROMARIO
SUBSTITUTES
3. ODVAN
7. DONIZETE
14. TORRES
15. PAULO MIRANDA (2) 69
16. PEDRINHO
18. VALBER
19. VIOLA
20. MARCIO
21. NASA (9) 76
22. VALKMAR
23. Alex OLIVEIRA (8) 79

ROMARIO 24, 26
EDMUNDO 43

MATCH REPORT

Two horrendous errors, committed within the space of two minutes by the normally reliable Gary Neville, torpedoed United's world championship aspirations. First he under-hit a routine back-pass, Edmundo cutely found Romario, who netted from close range. Then, not realising that Romario was lurking on his shoulder, he attempted to chest a high ball back to Bosnich. The elusive marksman nipped in and rounded Bosnich

Dwight Yorke couldn't find a way through the tight Vasco defence

1 MANCHESTER UNITED

81 BUTT

1. Mark BOSNICH
2. Gary NEVILLE
3. Denis IRWIN
16. Roy KEANE
5. Mikael SILVESTRE
6. Jaap STAM
12. Phil NEVILLE
8. Nicky BUTT
20. Ole Gunnar SOLSKJAER
19. Dwight YORKE
11. Ryan GIGGS

SUBSTITUTES

4. Danny HIGGINBOTHAM
7. David BECKHAM (not eligible)
9. Andy COLE
10. Teddy SHERINGHAM (20) h-t
13. Paul RACHUBKA
14. Jordi CRUYFF (6) 71
15. Jonathan GREENING
17. Raimond VAN DER GOUW
18. Mark WILSON
21. Henning BERG
22. Quinton FORTUNE (11) 77
23. Ronnie WALLWORK

Even Roy Keane couldn't contain the attacking might of Vasco De Gama

before driving home from 12 yards. Now United strove to steady themselves, which they seemed to have achieved when they were undone by a dazzling example of world-class finishing, Edmundo executing a sumptuous reverse flick before sprinting beyond Silvestre and stabbing adroitly past Bosnich.

During a second half in which they exerted heavy pressure, United crafted a succession of openings, but a goal would not come. Finally, a Cruyff free-kick was nudged back by Keane and Butt scored. By then, sadly, it was too late.

SOUTH MELBOURNE   0

20. Chris JONES

2. Steve IOSIFIDIS

3. Fausto DE AMICIS

18. Robert LIPAROTI

5. Con BLATSIS

6. David CLARKSON

7. Steve PANOPOULOS

15. Goarn LOZANOVSKI

9. Paul TRIMBOLI

10. Michael CURCIJA

11. John ANASTASIADIS

SUBSTITUTES

1. Milan UDVARACZ

4. Nick ORLIC (not eligible)

8. Vaughan COVENY (11) 66

12. Richie ALAGICH

13. Adrian CUZZUPE

14. Anthony MAGNACCA

16. George GOUTZIOULIS (18) 31

17. Jim TSEKINIS (6) 71

19. Tas PSONIS

21. Radoslav CULIBRK

22. Mustafa MUSTAFAO

23. Chris ROCHE

MATCH REPORT

An unmistakable aura of anti-climax enveloped United's slow-moving encounter with Australia's finest, but there were some positive aspects to be gleaned from a contest which, at a casual glance, might have been mistaken for a practice match.

Certainly the first-half performance of Fortune, who looked bright and eager and scored two smart goals, was encouraging, as were the cool, competent displays of the young defenders Higginbotham and Wallwork, although it must be admitted that they were placed under little pressure. Wilson and Greening showed enterprise in midfield, too, so at least a new generation of Reds will have learned from the exercise. And Cruyff, afforded

Jordi Cruyff gets a run in the sun for the last championship game

2 MANCHESTER UNITED

8, 20 FORTUNE

17. Raimond VAN DER GOUW
12. Phil NEVILLE
23. Ronnie WALLWORK
4. Danny HIGGINBOTHAM
18. Mark WILSON
21. Henning BERG
15. Jonathan GREENING
14. Jordi CRUYFF
9. Andy COLE
20. Ole Gunnar SOLSKJAER
22. Quinton FORTUNE

SUBSTITUTES

1. Mark BOSNICH
2. Gary NEVILLE
3. Denis IRWIN
5. Mikael SILVESTRE
6. Jaap STAM
7. David BECKHAM (18) 77
8. Nicky BUTT
10. Teddy SHERINGHAM (not eligible)
11. Ryan GIGGS
13. Paul RACHUBKA (17) 83
16. Roy KEANE
19. Dwight YORKE

David Beckham shows his free-kicking ability to the world

a rare opportunity in central midfield, sprayed the ball around with elegant assurance.

United took the lead when Solskjaer cut in from the right and passed to Cole, whose back-heel set up Fortune's emphatic left-foot finish from 10 yards. The South African winger struck again 12 minutes later when he ran on to a delightful through-ball from Cole before clipping past the keeper.

Melbourne had few opportunities but were unlucky not to score after 75 minutes when Coveny's six-yard dink cleared van der Gouw and hit both posts before being cleared. So ended United's interest in the first Club World Championship.

MANCHESTER UNITED 1

SHERINGHAM 74

1. Mark BOSNICH

2. Gary NEVILLE

3. Denis IRWIN

16. Roy KEANE

27. Mikael SILVESTRE

6. Jaap STAM

7. David BECKHAM

8. Nicky BUTT

9. Andy COLE

19. Dwight YORKE

11. Ryan GIGGS

SUBSTITUTES

10. Teddy SHERINGHAM (9) 66

12. Phil NEVILLE (3) 88

17. Raimond VAN DER GOUW

20. Ole Gunnar SOLSKJAER

21. Henning BERG

MATCH REPORT

After nearly a month without Premiership action, the Red Devils looked rusty on their return from Rio, and, if the truth be told, they were outclassed by Arsenal for the first quarter of the match. Characteristically, though, they clawed their way back from the brink of defeat, eventually generating enough attacking rhythm to merit their share of the points.

The Gunners, depleted by the absence of five leading players but still fielding nine internationals, began in confident manner and Bosnich had already saved smartly from Henry's adroit near-post flick when Stam, apparently fazed by an irregular bounce, was caught in possession by Ljungberg, who netted with a precise low 20-yarder between the keeper's legs.

United might have had a 27th-minute penalty when Keown pulled back Giggs and Cole might have equalised following a Yorke header. But Arsenal remained the more potent force and it took a magnificent left-handed block from Bosnich to thwart Henry, who had been freed by Ljungberg.

The lethargic hosts responded shortly before the interval when Butt was foiled

Ryan Giggs wins a race for the ball with Arsenal's Lee Dixon

1 ARSENAL

12 LJUNGBERG

1. David SEAMAN	
2. Lee DIXON	
16. SILVINHO	
4. Patrick VIEIRA	
5. Martin KEOWN	
18. Gilles GRIMANDI	
15. Ray PARLOUR	
8. Fredrik LJUNGBERG	
14. Thierry HENRY	
17. Emmanuel PETIT	
23. Stephen HUGHES	
SUBSTITUTES	
3. Nigel WINTERBURN (16) 24	
12. Christopher WREH	
13. Alex MANNINGER	
19. Stefan MALZ (23) 70	
22. Oleg LUZHNY	

Teddy Sheringham earns a point for United 16 minutes from the end

by Seaman's dive and Giggs missed with the rebound, but it was midway through the second period before Sir Alex Ferguson's men began to convince.

Then power-drives from Butt and Keane were stopped by Keown and Grimandi, before the Gunners' hitherto-underworked rearguard cracked. Keane chipped to Giggs on the left and Seaman could only palm away the Welshman's cross. Beckham sidefooted the loose ball cleverly to Sheringham, whose recent introduction in place of Andy Cole for had proved mightily effective, and the substitute netted from four yards, one of the simplest goals he will ever score.

Thereafter United finished strongly but without creating a clear-cut chance to snatch a winner. On balance, a fair result.

MANCHESTER UNITED 1

BECKHAM 87

1. Mark BOSNICH

2. Gary NEVILLE

3. Denis IRWIN

16. Roy KEANE

27. Mikael SILVESTRE

6. Jaap STAM

7. David BECKHAM.

8. Nicky BUTT

19. Dwight YORKE

10. Teddy SHERINGHAM

11. Ryan GIGGS

SUBSTITUTES

9. Andy COLE (10) 80 .

12. Phil NEVILLE

17. Raimond VAN DER GOUW

18. Paul SCHOLES (2) 69

20. Ole Gunnar SOLSKJAER (3) 80

MATCH REPORT

After dominating most of a tense encounter, United found themselves staring into the jaws of defeat against Boro, then escaped with a late victory thanks to a soft goal from Beckham.

The visitors spent most of the first half on the back foot. The second period brought further pressure from United, and when Ziege was red-carded on 61 minutes a home victory seemed inevitable. However, 10 minutes later Juninho was floored by Stam. The referee awarded a penalty and Keane was booked for his over-zealous objections. But Bosnich responded brilliantly, diving to his right to palm away Juninho's firmly struck kick.

Mark Bosnich dives to save Juninho's well-struck 71st-minute penalty

0 MIDDLESBROUGH

1. Mark SCHWARZER
2. Curtis FLEMING
17. Christian ZIEGE
28. Colin COOPER
5. Gianluca FESTA
6. Gary PALLISTER
22. Mark SUMMERBELL
19. Hamilton RICARD
9. Paul INCE
23. JUNINHO
18. Andy CAMPBELL

SUBSTITUTES

13. Marlon BERESFORD
15. Neil MADDISON (18) 80
20. Alun ARMSTRONG
26. Anthony ORMEROD (19) h-t
29. Jason GAVIN (6) 20

Jaap Stam shows that he can attack as well as defend

Now United resumed the offensive, but it seemed they would be frustrated until Beckham curled a weak shot towards the near post. Schwarzer seemed to have the ball covered, but it squirmed through his grasp and over the line for the goal which restored Sir Alex Ferguson's team to the top of the table.

JANUARY IN REVIEW

THURSDAY 6	v RAYOS DEL NECAXA	A	1-1
SATURDAY 8	v VASCO DA GAMA	A	1-3
TUESDAY 11	v SOUTH MELBOURNE	A	2-0
MONDAY 24	v ARSENAL	H	1-1
SATURDAY 29	v MIDDLESBROUGH	H	1-0

PLAYER IN THE FRAME

Quinton Fortune

The amiable but ambitious South African emerged as the major plus of United's expedition to Rio de Janeiro for the Club World Championship. After appearing as a lively but late substitute for Ryan Giggs against Vasco da Gama, Quinton made an explosive impact when starting the encounter with South Melbourne, scoring two early goals and narrowly missing a hat-trick. Fortune smiled, and the world smiled with him!

FA CARLING PREMIERSHIP

	P	W	D	L	F	A	Pts
Leeds United	22	15	2	5	37	25	47
MANCHESTER UNITED	20	13	5	2	51	2	44
Arsenal	23	13	5	5	42	23	44
Liverpool	23	12	5	6	34	20	41
Sunderland	23	11	5	7	37	31	38
Chelsea	23	10	7	6	31	22	37
Tottenham Hotspur	23	10	5	8	34	27	35
West Ham United	22	8	8	6	28	25	32
Aston Villa	23	8	7	8	22	23	31
Leicester City	23	9	4	10	32	34	31
Everton	23	7	9	7	37	34	30
Coventry City	22	7	8	7	30	24	29
Wimbledon	23	6	10	7	34	37	28
Middlesbrough	21	8	4	9	24	30	28
Newcastle United	23	7	6	10	39	39	27
Derby County	23	6	5	12	23	33	23
Southampton	22	6	5	11	26	37	23
Bradford City	23	5	6	2	19	35	21
Sheffield Wednesday	22	4	4	4	20	46	16
Watford	23	4	2	17	21	50	14

UP TO AND INCLUDING
MONDAY 24 JANUARY 2000

FEBRUARY

SHEFFIELD WEDNESDAY 0

28. Pavel SRNICEK

2. Peter ATHERTON

3. Andy HINCHCLIFFE

4. Wim JONK

17. Ian NOLAN

6. Des WALKER

16. Niclas ALEXANDERSSON

22. Steven HASLAM

9. Gerald SIBON

23. Gilles DE BILDE

15. Philip SCOTT

SUBSTITUTES

1. Kevin PRESSMAN

12. Richard CRESSWELL (9) 83

14. Petter RUDI (15) 60

18. Simon DONNELLY (23) 70

37. Tom STANIFORTH

MATCH REPORT

There were two Manchester Uniteds on show at Hillsborough. In the first half there was a cagey, laborious outfit which showed scant enterprise or imagination and failed to muster a shot on target until the 33rd minute. But after the interval, with the fit-again Scholes replacing Butt, they were transformed into a free-flowing attacking unit which outplayed their gallant hosts more comprehensively than the scoreline suggests.

Lowly Wednesday, still smarting from their weekend FA Cup ejection by Gillingham, poured forward from the first whistle. They adopted a shoot-on-sight policy, the pick of their efforts being a 30-yarder from Jonk which warmed the hands of keeper Bosnich.

Having soaked up the Owls' pressure, United set about securing the victory that would stretch their Premiership lead to three points, attacking with a potency reminiscent of their Treble-winning form.

Sheringham came close to snatching the lead with a glancing header, only to be denied by the excellent Srnicek, then the Czech tipped Keane's rasping drive over the crossbar and a Yorke effort was cleared off the line by Hinchcliffe.

Dwight Yorke and Sheffield Wednesday captain Peter Atherton tussle for possession

1 MANCHESTER UNITED

74 SHERINGHAM

| 1. Mark BOSNICH |
| 2. Gary NEVILLE |
| 3. Denis IRWIN |
| 16. Roy KEANE |
| 27. Mikael SILVESTRE |
| 6. Jaap STAM |
| 7. David BECKHAM |
| 8. Nicky BUTT |
| 19. Dwight YORKE |
| 10. Teddy SHERINGHAM |
| 11. Ryan GIGGS |
| **SUBSTITUTES** |
| 9. Andy COLE |
| 12. Phil NEVILLE |
| 17. Raimond VAN DER GOUW |
| 18. Paul SCHOLES (8) h-t |
| 20. Ole Gunnar SOLSKJAER |

Dwight Yorke and Roy Keane apply pressure to the Wednesday goal

There were numerous other near-misses but just as the visiting fans began to fear a frustrating outcome, the Wednesday rearguard was finally breached. Silvestre began the move, which progressed smoothly through Yorke and Giggs before Sheringham dispatched a cleverly angled left-footer between the splayed legs of Srnicek from 15 yards.

It was a timely strike from the Londoner, currently locked in negotiations for a new contract at Old Trafford and much in demand from other clubs at home and abroad.

After their goal, the champions cruised comfortably through the dying stages of the game, never looking in the remotest danger of conceding an equaliser.

MANCHESTER UNITED 3

1. Mark BOSNICH
2. Gary NEVILLE
12. Phil NEVILLE
16. Roy KEANE
27. Mikael SILVESTRE
6. Jaap STAM
7. David BECKHAM
18. Paul SCHOLES
9. Andy COLE
10. Teddy SHERINGHAM
20. Ole Gunnar SOLSKJAER
SUBSTITUTES
3. Denis IRWIN
8. Nicky BUTT (20) 71
14. Jordi CRUYFF (10) 81
17. Raimond VAN DER GOUW
19. Dwight YORKE

COLE 40, 55

SCHOLES 77

MATCH REPORT

A goal of exquisite quality by Andy Cole and an inventive all-round display from Paul Scholes illuminated a curiously lacklustre United performance. But with Leeds and Arsenal both tasting defeat on the same day, it was enough for the Red Devils to move six points clear at the head of the Premiership pack.

Coventry played neat, purposeful football underpinned by prodigious industry, and it was difficult to credit that they were still looking for their first league win of the season away from Highfield Road. In the early stages, United struggled to pierce an efficient offside trap and much of their play was untidy and unconvincing, until Cole stepped in with a sequence of artistry of which Eric Cantona would have been proud. After scrapping for possession following a long throw by Gary Neville, the quicksilver marksman weaved past a challenge on the edge of the box before dispatching an inch-perfect chip over Hedman and into the net via the crossbar.

Still, though, the United machine did not purr, even after Cole had doubled the lead with a simple close-range header from Beckham's free-kick. Coventry refused to fold and after Eustace pierced

Andy Cole's team-mates rush to congratulate him on his spectacular strike

2 COVENTRY CITY

65, 90 ROUSSEL

the centre of the home defence with worrying ease, Roussel hammered a near-post drive past Bosnich.

The 25-yard daisy-cutter from Scholes which restored the two-goal margin owed something to luck though he did deserve it. However, Roussel's late response was equally merited, accurately reflecting the closeness of the contest.

1. Magnus HEDMAN
32. Tomas GUSTAFSSON
17. Gary BREEN
4. Paul WILLIAMS
5. Richard SHAW
14. Carlton PALMER
7. Robbie KEANE
12. Paul TELFER
31. Cedric ROUSSEL
10. Gary McALLISTER
16. Stephen FROGGATT
SUBSTITUTES
6. Muhammed KONJUI
15. Laurent DELORGE
21. Gavin STRACHAN
24. John EUSTACE (12) 11
26. Steve OGRIZOVIC

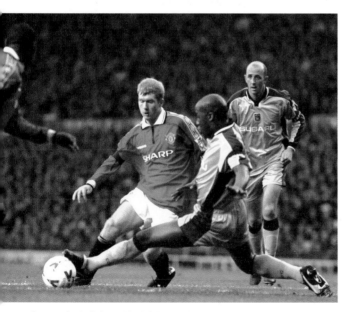

Scorers Andy Cole and Paul Scholes play a neat one-two

NEWCASTLE UNITED 3

13. Steve HARPER
2. Warren BARTON
18. Aaron HUGHES
39. Helder CRISTOVAO
34. Nikos DABIZAS
32. Kevin GALLACHER
7. Kieron DYER
37. Robert LEE
9. Alan SHEARER
20. Duncan FERGUSON
11. Gary SPEED
SUBSTITUTES
1. Shay GIVEN
4. Didier DOMI (32) 83
8. Diego GAVILAN (7) 83
14. Temuri KETSBAIA (20) 62
38. Jose ANTUNES

FERGUSON 26
SHEARER 76, 86

MATCH REPORT

Andy Cole gets a cross over for Beckham to shoot for goal

It was one of the blackest days of Manchester United's season to date. They suffered their first Premiership defeat since October, their lead at the top of the table was halved to three points and skipper Roy Keane was sent off.

In fact, it was the Irishman's 64th-minute dismissal which was the turning point in a turbulent encounter. Until then, though the Magpies deserved their one-goal lead, the destination of the points remained in the balance.

The Red Devils had begun in style, but paid heavily for missing two beautifully crafted openings. First Sheringham scooped Scholes' low cross over the bar, then Beckham half-volleyed high and wide after a neat hooked pass from Cole.

0 MANCHESTER UNITED

1. Mark BOSNICH

2. Gary NEVILLE

3. Denis IRWIN

16. Roy KEANE

27. Mikael SILVESTRE

6. Jaap STAM

7. David BECKHAM

18. Paul SCHOLES

9. Andy COLE

10. Teddy SHERINGHAM

11. Ryan GIGGS

SUBSTITUTES

8. Nicky BUTT (3) 69

12. Phil NEVILLE

17. Raimond VAN DER GOUW

20. Ole Gunnar SOLSKJAER (10) 75

21. Henning BERG

The Magpies responded in devastating fashion: Lee chipped forward to Shearer, who nodded to Ferguson on the edge of the box; the giant Scot allowed the ball to bounce, then swivelled and dispatched a searing left-foot volley past Bosnich.

Newcastle might have increased their lead when a Dyer centre was deflected on to a post by Stam, then Speed hammered wide of an empty net and Shearer nodded narrowly over.

However, the visitors steadied after the break and were grievously unlucky not to equalise when Beckham found Cole from the left and the former Gallowgate idol dinked cleverly over Harper. TV evidence suggested that the ball had crossed the line before the keeper clawed it back, but the referee waved play on.

Thereafter the Mancunians' day deteriorated rapidly. Keane was given his marching orders for a second bookable offence, several of his team-mates became increasingly argumentative and Shearer netted twice more, first with a low 25-yard curler, then with a 10-yard drive which capped a sweeping move.

In the end, Manchester United got what they deserved and were well beaten.

Ryan Giggs gives Warren Barton the runaround

LEEDS UNITED   0

1. Nigel MARTYN
2. Gary KELLY
3. Ian HARTE
20. Matthew JONES
5. Lucas RADEBE
6. Jonathan WOODGATE
16. Jason WILCOX
19. Eirik BAKKE
17. Alan SMITH
10. Harry KEWELL
11. Lee BOWYER

SUBSTITUTES

4. Alf-Inge HAALAND
7. David HOPKIN
12. Darren HUCKERBY
13. Paul ROBINSON
18. Danny MILLS

MATCH REPORT

A goal of predatory opportunism by Andy Cole and the generous assistance of the Elland Road woodwork saw a much-improved Manchester United through to a crucial victory against their closest Championship rivals.

It was a morning of intense drama, from the announcement that David Beckham was dropped, reportedly for disciplinary reasons, to the final whistle of a compellingly tight but sporting encounter between two well-matched sides.

The Red Devils began confidently, but most of the first-half goal threats emanated from the left foot of Harte, Leeds' dead-ball specialist. Three times his cunningly curled free-kicks brought smart saves from Bosnich, one of them an acrobatic plunge to his left at full stretch.

As the second period gathered momentum there remained a sense of two fine teams cancelling each other out, but then Scholes found Cole with a raking ball out of defence. The Reds' marksman cushioned the ball on his forehead, swivelled as he dinked it over Radebe, then bore down on goal while holding off the powerful

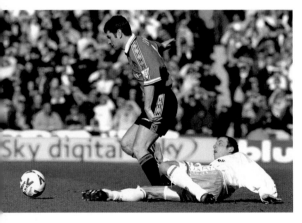

Denis Irwin rides a sliding tackle from Leeds' midfielder Lee Bowyer

1   MANCHESTER UNITED

52 COLE

1. Mark BOSNICH
2. Gary NEVILLE
3. Denis IRWIN
16. Roy KEANE
27. Mikael SILVESTRE
6. Jaap STAM
18. Paul SCHOLES
8. Nicky BUTT
9. Andy COLE
19. Dwight YORKE
11. Ryan GIGGS
SUBSTITUTES
10. Teddy SHERINGHAM (19) 30
12. Phil NEVILLE
14. Jordi CRUYFF
17. Raimond VAN DER GOUW
21. Henning BERG

Andy Cole gets set to shoot United into the lead after 52 minutes

South African. Martyn advanced but to no avail as Cole placed a clinical shot into the corner of the net.

Leeds then retaliated with spirit. Bakke headed against the Reds' crossbar, then a Kewell cross was deflected on to the same piece of wood by Keane. Scholes almost scored with a low volley from a Giggs cross, but the defining moment came after 81 minutes. A speculative shot from Wilcox was pushed out by Bosnich, Smith crashed the rebound against a post and Bowyer skied over the empty net from five yards. It was a debilitating miss from which Leeds never looked likely to recover.

WIMBLEDON 2

EUELL 2
CORT 63

1. Neil SULLIVAN
2. Kenny CUNNINGHAM
3. Alan KIMBLE
22. Chris WILLMOTT
30. Hermann HREIDARSSON
12. Neal ARDLEY
7. Carl CORT
29. Trond ANDERSEN
34. Andreas LUND
10. Jason EUELL
11. Marcus GAYLE

SUBSTITUTES

5. Dean BLACKWELL
8. Robbie EARLE
19. Walid BADIR (34) 88
20. Martin ANDRESEN (12) 74
23. Kelvin DAVIS

MATCH REPORT

Sloppiness at the heart of the Manchester United rearguard and an exceptional performance by Wimbledon goalkeeper Sullivan cost the champions two points in a contest which, for the most part, they dominated. That the Reds twice came from behind to claim a share of the spoils was due to the brilliance of Giggs, who created both equalisers with moments of sheer inspiration.

It took the Dons only 70 seconds to seize the initiative. Cunningham chipped into the box, Lund met the delivery with a cushioned header and Euell reacted more quickly than Stam to steer a high volley past Bosnich.

Shortly afterwards the leaden-footed Reds were almost undone again when the elusive Lund met a cross from the right and the United custodian turned a neatly-directed header against his post.

Now the visitors stirred and Sullivan saved bravely at the feet of Giggs and athletically from a Cruyff drive, but was powerless to prevent what followed. Giggs took possession in midfield and dispatched an exquisite airborne through-pass. On the other end of it was Cruyff, who volleyed home emphatically from 12 yards.

Jordi Cruyff celebrates his equalising goal

2 MANCHESTER UNITED

30 CRUYFF
80 COLE

1. Mark BOSNICH
2. Gary NEVILLE
12. Phil NEVILLE
14. Jordi CRUYFF
27. Mikael SILVESTRE
6. Jaap STAM
7. David BECKHAM
8. Nicky BUTT
9. Andy COLE
10. Teddy SHERINGHAM
11. Ryan GIGGS
SUBSTITUTES
3. Denis IRWIN
17. Raimond VAN DER GOUW
20. Ole Gunnar SOLSKJAER (14) 71
21. Henning BERG (12) 70
25. Quinton FORTUNE

Andy Cole crashes in United's second equaliser of the afternoon

The Reds upped the pace after the interval but were foiled repeatedly by Sullivan and then fell behind when Kimble was allowed to cross from the left and Cort glanced in a header.

Cue frenetic pressure on the Wimbledon goal, with Sullivan leaping to repel a Beckham free-kick, then blocking a Cole shot with his legs. The breakthrough came when Giggs picked up the ball from a Dons corner, then ran the length of the field and feinted to shoot before setting up Cole, who netted with a rasping cross-shot. Later Sullivan frustrated Cole again from point-blank range before leaving the pitch a hero.

FEBRUARY IN REVIEW

WEDNESDAY 2	v SHEFFIELD WEDNESDAY	A	1-0
SATURDAY 5	v COVENTRY CITY	H	3-2
SATURDAY 12	v NEWCASTLE UNITED	A	0-3
SUNDAY 20	v LEEDS UNITED	A	1-0
SATURDAY 26	v WIMBLEDON	A	2-2

PLAYER IN THE FRAME

David Beckham

David was admirably level-headed in the face of the largely puerile but inevitable media hysteria which followed what might charitably be described as a slight difference of opinion between the England midfielder and Sir Alex Ferguson. After being omitted from the side which beat Leeds, Beckham bounced back to display arguably the most glittering form of his career to date, thus silencing the snipers in emphatic manner.

FA CARLING PREMIERSHIP

UP TO AND INCLUDING
SATURDAY 26 FEBRUARY 2000

	P	W	D	L	F	A	Pts
MANCHESTER UNITED	26	17	6	3	59	33	57
Leeds United	26	16	3	7	39	29	51
Arsenal	26	14	5	7	46	27	47
Liverpool	25	14	5	6	38	21	47
Chelsea	26	13	7	6	37	24	46
Sunderland	26	11	7	8	42	37	40
Everton	26	10	9	7	46	35	39
Aston Villa	26	10	8	8	31	24	38
Tottenham Hotspur	26	11	5	10	35	29	38
Leicester City	25	10	5	10	35	36	35
West Ham United	25	9	8	8	34	35	35
Newcastle United	26	9	7	10	46	41	34
Coventry City	26	8	8	10	35	32	32
Middlesbrough	26	9	5	12	27	37	32
Wimbledon	26	6	11	9	37	45	29
Southampton	25	8	5	12	30	41	29
Derby County	26	6	7	13	28	39	25
Bradford City	26	6	7	13	26	42	25
Sheffield Wednesday	26	4	5	17	23	53	17
Watford	26	4	3	19	23	57	15

MARCH

WEDNESDAY 1	**v FC GIRONDINS BORDEAUX**	**H**
SATURDAY 4	**V LIVERPOOL**	**H**
TUESDAY 7	**v FC GIRONDINS BORDEAUX**	**A**
SATURDAY 11	**v DERBY COUNTY**	**H**
WEDNESDAY 15	**V AC FIORENTINA**	**H**
SATURDAY 18	**LEICESTER CITY**	**A**
TUESDAY 21	**VALENCIA CF**	**A**
SATURDAY 25	**BRADFORD CITY**	**A**

MANCHESTER UNITED 2

17. Raimond VAN DER GOUW

2. Gary NEVILLE

3. Denis IRWIN

16. Roy KEANE

27. Mikael SILVESTRE

6. Jaap STAM

7. David BECKHAM

8. Nicky BUTT

9. Andy COLE

10. Teddy SHERINGHAM

11. Ryan GIGGS

SUBSTITUTES

1. Mark BOSNICH

12. Phil NEVILLE (9) 81

14. Jordi CRUYFF

20. Ole Gunnar SOLSKJAER (11) 87

21. Henning BERG

25. Quinton FORTUNE (16) 87

30. Ronnie WALLWORK

GIGGS 41
SHERINGHAM 84

MATCH REPORT

Ryan Giggs embarks on his run that ended with the game's first goal

Two devastating goals, both immaculate in conception and deceptively simple in execution, failed to disguise a distinctly uneven United performance, but they were enough to strengthen significantly the Red Devils' prospects of qualifying for the Champions League knockout stage.

For lengthy passages of play the hosts failed to pass with their customary coherence while Bordeaux, though lacking in penetration and employing a riskily ambitious offside trap, moved the ball around with smooth assurance. However, United

0 FC GIRONDINS BORDEAUX

16. Ulrich RAME

14. Francois GRENET

24. Herve ALICARTE

15. Corentin MARTINS

5. Jerome BONNISSEL

21. Kodjo AFANOU

7. Michel PAVON

8. Johan MICOUD

9. Lilian LASLANDES

18. Lassina DIABATE

11. Sylvain WILTORD

SUBSTITUTES

1. Teddy RICHERT

4. Nisa SAVELJIC

6. Jean-Christophe ROUVIERE

10. Stephane ZIANI (15) 65

19. Marc ZANOTTI

20. Laurent BATLLES

27. Pascal FEINDOUNO

created more scoring opportunities and deserved their win.

After the French champions had started the sprightlier, the hosts hit back and Giggs miscued when well placed, then Beckham brilliantly bent a 25-yard free-kick against Rame's bar. Thereafter Cole went close with a volley before United took the lead during a five-minute purple patch before the interval. A long kick from van der Gouw – preferred in goal to Bosnich – was nodded by Sheringham to Cole. He found Beckham on the right wing and the England star's instant cross was turned in adroitly by Giggs from six yards: beautiful, simple, unstoppable.

However, most of the second period produced anxiety and anti-climax in equal measure. Bordeaux began to attack with belief and Alicarte had almost scored with two free headers before Laslandes broke free and set up a sitter which was missed by Wiltord.

The Reds stepped up the tempo and Beckham saw another free-kick parried by Rame, Cole missed from point-blank range and Keane had a one-on-one shot blocked.

Finally the comfort zone was reached when Sheringham passed to Giggs on the left and the mercurial Welshman burst between a posse of defenders before crossing sweetly for Teddy to head into an unguarded net.

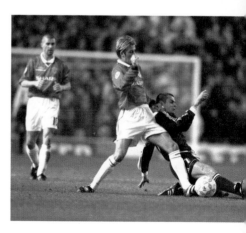

Tight defending sees David Beckham dispossessed

MANCHESTER UNITED 1

SOLSKJAER 45

17. Raimond VAN DER GOUW

2. Gary NEVILLE

3. Denis IRWIN

16. Roy KEANE

27. Mikael SILVESTRE

6. Jaap STAM

7. David BECKHAM

8. Nicky BUTT

20. Ole Gunnar SOLSKJAER

19. Dwight YORKE

11. Ryan GIGGS

SUBSTITUTES

1. Mark BOSNICH

9. Andy COLE (20) 80

10. Teddy SHERINGHAM (19) 85

12. Phil NEVILLE

21. Henning BERG

MATCH REPORT

Another demoralisingly late victory against Liverpool was no more than a seemingly routine sidefoot away. In the third minute of added time, with the scores level, Silvestre delivered a perfect low cross from the left flank. Sheringham had time, space and most of a yawning net to aim at, but somehow he thumped his shot against Carragher and a golden opportunity had been spurned.

However, a draw was the fairest outcome to an exciting game in front of the biggest crowd in Premiership history. United enjoyed more possession, as might be expected of table-topping champions on their own turf, but the visitors matched them in terms of chances created.

The first drama came when Gary Neville crossed from the right and Solskjaer rose unopposed, only to head unaccountably wide. Liverpool's reply was not long in coming and it was devastating, Berger lashing home a goal with a fulminating free-kick from 20 yards.

In the next few minutes, the Anfielders could have won the game. First Berger's free header from a Song cross was clawed away by van der Gouw, then Stam blocked a savage drive by Liverpool's Guinea international Camara.

But United steadied themselves and, with Hyypia off the field for stitches, Solskjaer took the opportunity to equalise with the final kick of the first half. Giggs crossed from the left and the quicksilver Norwegian outwitted two defenders before netting deftly from the corner of the six-yard box.

1 LIVERPOOL

27 BERGER

1. Sander WESTERVELD
2. Stephane HENCHOZ
21. Dominic MATTEO
14. Vegard HEGGEM
12. Sami HYYPIA
23. Jamie CARRAGHER
7. Vladimir SMICER
16. Dietmar HAMANN
18. Erik MEIJER
22. Titi CAMARA
15. Patrik BERGER

SUBSTITUTES

4. Rigobert SONG (14) 19
5. Steve STAUNTON
10. Michael OWEN (22) 77
24. Danny MURPHY (12) h-t
26. Jorgen NIELSEN

The second period saw Liverpool come out to defend stoutly and openings were scarce until the 64th minute when Giggs made a sublime pass that freed Solskjaer, whose shot was partially blocked by Westerweld, but the resolute defender Carragher was there to clear off the line.

Suddenly Liverpool retaliated and van der Gouw saved splendidly from Smicer, then Owen chipped over the keeper but marginally wide. Thereafter United attacked relentlessly but Sheringham's late miss ensured that the points were shared.

Ole Gunnar Solskjaer's shot curls past Sander Westerveld

FC GIRONDINS BORDEAUX 1

PAVON 9

16. Ulrich RAME
14. Francois GRENET
20. Laurent BATLLES
4. Nisa SAVELJIC
5. Jerome BONNISSEL
21. Kodjo AFANOU
7. Michel PAVON
8. Johan MICOUD
9. Lilian LASLANDES
10. Stephane ZIANI
11. Sylvain WILTORD

SUBSTITUTES

1. Teddy RICHERT
6. Jean-Christophe ROUVIERE (10) 60
18. Lassina DIABATE (20) 9
19. Marc ZANOTTI
22. Giuseppe COLUCCI
27. Pascal FEINDOUNO (11) 82

MATCH REPORT

Nicky Butt rides the challenges as the Reds pour forward

A typical example of supreme opportunism by the trusty Solskjaer saved the day but, in all honesty, United were fortunate to beat ten-man Bordeaux. After the hosts had started brightly they were boosted by an uncharacteristic clanger by the normally reliable van der Gouw, who shaped to catch Pavon's innocuous 25-yarder, only to palm the ball into his own net.

Bordeaux were jolted after 23 minutes when Laslandes was dismissed for a second bookable offence, a late challenge committed shortly after being carded for dissent. They did not buckle when Keane slotted in the equaliser, though, and Wiltord

2   MANCHESTER UNITED

33 KEANE
84 SOLSKJAER

17. Raimond VAN DER GOUW
2. Gary NEVILLE
3. Denis IRWIN
16. Roy KEANE
27. Mikael SILVESTRE
6. Jaap STAM
7. David BECKHAM
8. Nicky BUTT
9. Andy COLE
10. Teddy SHERINGHAM
11. Ryan GIGGS

SUBSTITUTES

1. Mark BOSNICH
12. Phil NEVILLE
14. Jordi CRUYFF
19. Dwight YORKE (10) 77
20. Ole Gunnar SOLSKJAER (3) 83
21. Henning BERG (9) 86
25. Quinton FORTUNE

shaved a post after nutmegging Stam just before the interval.

Enter Solskjaer, substitute sublime. Sixty seconds after taking the field, he slotted an immaculate low shot past Rame. Thus the holders inflicted on Bordeaux only their second home European defeat in nine years. A below-par performance had yielded a splendid result.

Ole Gunnar Solskjaer carefully delivers the shot for the winning goal

MANCHESTER UNITED 3

YORKE 13, 70, 72

1. Mark BOSNICH
2. Gary NEVILLE
12. Phil NEVILLE
16. Roy KEANE
27. Mikael SILVESTRE
21. Henning BERG
7. David BECKHAM
18. Paul SCHOLES
20. Ole Gunnar SOLSKJAER
19. Dwight YORKE
25. Quinton FORTUNE

SUBSTITUTES

8. Nicky BUTT (25) 71
10. Teddy SHERINGHAM
11. Ryan GIGGS
17. Raimond VAN DER GOUW
30. Ronnie WALLWORK (16) 76

MATCH REPORT

Dwight Yorke emerged from a worrying sequence of indifferent form with a match-winning hat-trick which restored the effervescent Tobagan's trademark grin.

However, to claim the points, United also needed heroics from Mark Bosnich, who made three blinding point-blank parries as Derby raiders repeatedly strode through a flimsy home defence. Indeed, the Reds' rearguard was caught slumbering after only 20 seconds and the Australian had to be at his sharpest to deny Christie from close range.

Soon Yorke put United in front in unusual manner, blocking

Dwight Yorke's leaps above the Derby defence to restore United's lead

1 DERBY COUNTY

66 STRUPAR

21. Mart POOM
2. Horacio CARBONARI
3. Stefan SCHNOOR
16. Jacob LAURSEN
5. Tony DORIGO
19. Steve ELLIOTT
7. Seth JOHNSON
29. Stefano ERANIO
12. Malcolm CHRISTIE
10. Rory DELAP
27. Giorgi KINKLADZE
SUBSTITUTES
8. Dean STURRIDGE (5) 74
17. Spencer PRIOR
18. Richard JACKSON
24. Andy OAKES
35. Branko STRUPAR (3) h-t

Poom's attempted clearance, then reaching the rebound ahead of the keeper and turning it into the unguarded net. The Estonian atoned after 28 minutes when he saved superbly from Scholes' spot-kick – Christie having been penalised for a shove on Neville – and then he frustrated efforts from Scholes and Solskjaer in quick succession.

With the Reds pouring forward at this point, another record-breaking Old Trafford crowd sat back in anticipation of a goal feast. Instead, in the second half they saw their team labour lethargically, a lapse which might have cost them dearly.

Once again the elusive Christie was through on goal only to be frustrated by Bosnich, and a shot by Carbonari was deflected narrowly wide. The urgently-needed wake-up call came in the form of a deserved Derby equaliser, turned home by Strupar after a lovely pass from the speedy Kinkladze.

Eventually United responded, transforming the contest with two goals in two minutes. First Fortune broke down the left before crossing for Yorke to net with a soaring header, then Keane freed the Tobagan to slot precisely past Poom. Still Bosnich was required to make another brilliant stop, this time from Strupar, and had Wallwork's late header not rebounded from Derby's post, the scoreline would have been cruelly misleading.

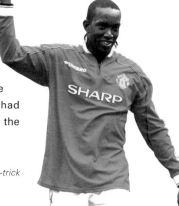

Dwight Yorke earned himself the match ball by scoring a hat-trick

MANCHESTER UNITED 3

1. Mark BOSNICH
2. Gary NEVILLE
3. Denis IRWIN
16. Roy KEANE
21. Henning BERG
6. Jaap STAM
7. David BECKHAM
18. Paul SCHOLES
9. Andy COLE
19. Dwight YORKE
11. Ryan GIGGS

SUBSTITUTES

8. Nicky BUTT
10. Teddy SHERINGHAM
12. Phil NEVILLE
17. Raimond VAN DER GOUW
20. Ole Gunnar SOLSKJAER
25. Quinton FORTUNE
27. Mikael SILVESTRE

COLE 20
KEANE 33
YORKE 70

MATCH REPORT

This was more like it. In a thunderous encounter of crackling intensity, Manchester United gave their best performance of the season to date, thus reaching the Champions League quarter-finals for the fourth successive year.

For the first 70 minutes, after which the Red Devils' third goal effectively put the game beyond the Italians' reach, the action was unremitting, the football from both sides was of the highest quality, and the brief summary which space permits does scant justice to the drama.

After an early double save by Bosnich from Rui Costa, United attacked with venom and Cole created three chances from the left flank, but Yorke was unable to convert the chances on two occasions and Rossitto edged out Beckham at the far post.

Still the hosts poured forward and a Keane piledriver had been blocked when Old Trafford was silenced by the sheer brilliance of Batistuta. Eluding Stam with imperious ease, the Argentinian unleashed a swerving 30-yarder of sudden, savage violence which hit the net while Bosnich was still in mid-air.

It was a truly memorable strike, but within four minutes United responded in

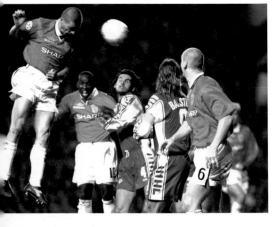

Roy Keane goes close with a powerful header

1 AC FIORENTINA

16 BATISTUTA

1. Francesco TOLDO	
2. Tomas REPKA	
3. Moreno TORRICELLI	
4. Daniele ADANI	
23. Alessandro PIERINI	
17. Jorg HEINRICH	
16. Angelo DI LIVIO	
8. Predrag MIJATOVIC	
9. Gabriel BATISTUTA	
10. Manuel RUI COSTA	
11. Fabio ROSSITTO	
SUBSTITUTES	
6. Aldo FIRICANO	
12. Giuseppe TAGLIALATELA	
15. Paul OKON	
20. Enrico CHIESA (8) 63	
21. Mauro BRESSAN	
24. Christian AMOROSO (16) 76	
27. Andrea TAROZZI (3) 76	

kind. With his back to goal, Cole controlled a Neville cross and swivelled to beat Toldo with a low 25-yard half-volley.

The England marksman had almost topped that with the subtlest of chips when the Reds went ahead, Beckham's steepling corner being headed against the bar by Berg, leaving Keane to dispatch a booming volley into the net via an upright.

A pulsating contest lurched further from Fiorentina's grasp when Rossitto was dismissed for fouling Yorke on 62 minutes and the Tobagan concluded the business with a precise downward header from a curling Giggs cross some eight minutes later.

With the match out of reach of Fiorentina it was exhibition time with the Welshman in mesmeric form, going close to adding what would have been a deserved fourth goal.

Dwight Yorke celebrates his 70th-minute goal

LEICESTER CITY 0

1. Tim FLOWERS
14. Robbie SAVAGE
3. Frank SINCLAIR
4. Gerry TAGGART
18. Matt ELLIOTT
6. Mustafa IZZET
7. Neil LENNON
8. Stan COLLYMORE
29. Stefan OAKES
10. Darren EADIE
11. Steve GUPPY

SUBSTITUTES

15. Phil GILCHRIST
20. Ian MARSHALL (10) 82
22. Pegguy ARPHEXAD
24. Andrew IMPEY
27. Tony COTTEE (29) 72

MATCH REPORT

The new-look David Beckham was on classic form

After scaling lofty peaks of excellence against Fiorentina, United confined themselves to mere foothills of competence at Filbert Street, but still proved an insurmountable obstacle to lacklustre Leicester. With the exception of David Beckham's drastic new hairdo, which produced feverish excitement among the massed ranks of photographers, this was a low-key affair.

Fielding the side which had dazzled the Italians, United began economically, with the Foxes enjoying the lion's share of early

2   MANCHESTER UNITED

33 BECKHAM
84 YORKE

1. Mark BOSNICH
2. Gary NEVILLE
3. Denis IRWIN
16. Roy KEANE
21. Henning BERG
6. Jaap STAM
7. David BECKHAM
18. Paul SCHOLES
9. Andy COLE
19. Dwight YORKE
11. Ryan GIGGS

SUBSTITUTES

8. Nicky BUTT (11) 86
10. Teddy SHERINGHAM (9) 83
12. Phil NEVILLE
17. Raimond VAN DER GOUW
20. Ole Gunnar SOLSKJAER

possession but rarely threatening to penetrate. Indeed, the opening half-hour produced little more excitement than a dinked through-ball from Oakes which forced Bosnich to sprint from his line and block Eadie's charge.

Then Giggs flexed his muscles, careering menacingly down the left, only to be halted by a crude challenge from Sinclair. Beckham exacted retribution in the best possible manner, bending a precise 25-yard free-kick over Leicester's disintegrating wall and just inside Flowers' near post.

Once in front, the Reds never looked remotely likely to surrender their lead and opted mainly for midfield solidity, restricting themselves to sporadic attacks. The most enterprising of these involved Giggs. First he found Irwin, who cut inside from the left to deliver a stinging volley which was parried by Flowers, then the Welshman combined sweetly with Sheringham to set up Yorke for United's second goal.

Leicester mustered few chances, and it seemed unlikely that Sir Alex Ferguson's men would face a less taxing 90 minutes in the two months that lay ahead.

Roy Keane – always in the thick of the action

VALENCIA CF 0

1. CANIZARES

2. Mauricio PELLEGRINO

14. GERARD

20. Jocelyn ANGLOMA

5. Miroslav DJUKIC

18. KILY GONZALEZ

7. Claudio LOPEZ

8. FARINOS

17. Juan SANCHEZ

10. ANGULO

15. Amedeo CARBONI

SUBSTITUTES

3. Joachim BJORKLUND

9. OSCAR

11. Adrian ILIE (17) 70

13. Jorge BARTUAL

19. Goran VLAOVIC

24. Daniel FAGIANI

31. GERARDO

MATCH REPORT

After two vividly contrasting halves of football – the first packed with swashbuckling incident, much of the second an arid stand-off – Manchester United emerged as convincing winners of their group. The Spaniards, who also qualified for the quarter-finals, began in opulently aggressive mode, entertaining royally as they fashioned a series of early openings.

However, they found Bosnich at his acrobatic best, the Australian pulling off spectacular saves from a Gerard header and a Gonzalez shot, while efforts by Angulo and Sanchez were narrowly off-target.

Having seen off this frenzied first wave of attacks, the Red Devils began to make inroads of their own, passing deliciously and setting up three clear scoring opportunities. First the lively Fortune delivered an exquisite cross from the left and Sheringham's powerful header from six yards was parried by Canizares. Then the veteran marksman turned creator, his curving dispatch being scuffed uncharacteristically into the keeper's hands by the stretching Solskjaer.

Shortly after that, the Norwegian's perceptive delivery found Scholes, whose low shot from the edge of the box was

Teddy Sheringham featured in the starting line-up

0 MANCHESTER UNITED

1. Mark BOSNICH
2. Gary NEVILLE
3. Denis IRWIN
16. Roy KEANE
21. Henning BERG
6. Jaap STAM
18. Paul SCHOLES
8. Nicky BUTT
20. Ole Gunnar SOLSKJAER
10. Teddy SHERINGHAM
25. Quinton FORTUNE

SUBSTITUTES

9. Andy COLE
12. Phil NEVILLE
14. Jordi CRUYFF (20) 67
17. Raimond VAN DER GOUW
19. Dwight YORKE
27. Mikael SILVESTRE
30. Ronnie WALLWORK

Nicky Butt rides the challenges as the red tide was rising

deflected inches wide of the stranded Canizares' post. Despite that burst of high endeavour by the visitors, the most explosive moment of the night was supplied by the hosts shortly before the interval, Angloma unleashing a 25-yard thunderbolt which cannoned off the inside of the far post and rebounded to safety.

After an hour, with a draw suiting both sides, the game died on its feet. It was a shame that what had begun as an open contest should degenerate into lengthy periods of safety-first passing. But, with the stakes so high, it was sadly inevitable.

BRADFORD CITY 0

13. Matt CLARKE

18. Gunnar HALLE

22. Wayne JACOBS

4. Stuart McCALL

5. David WETHERALL

14. Andrew O'BRIEN

7. Jamie LAWRENCE

15. Dean WINDASS

28. Dean SAUNDERS

33. Jorge CADETE

11. Peter BEAGRIE

SUBSTITUTES

6. Ashley WESTWOOD

8. Robbie BLAKE (33) 70

16. Lee SHARPE (18) 58

30. John DREYER

31. Aidan DAVISON

MATCH REPORT

After spluttering fitfully for half an hour, Manchester United moved sweetly through their attacking gears, eventually extinguishing the challenge of Premiership strugglers Bradford City with crushing finality.

The Reds' headliners were Yorke, who transformed the game with two strikes inside three minutes, and Beckham, who laid on two goals before adding the fourth himself. Yet it had been the relegation-haunted Bantams who had carried the early menace. After only two minutes, Bosnich spilled a 30-yard drive from Beagrie and needed Phil Neville to rescue him, then he muffed a clearance which rebounded to safety off Cadete. After that Beagrie set up Windass but the striker dallied and Phil Neville made another decisive intervention.

Gradually United shrugged off their lethargy and Giggs might have done better than lobbing wide after being freed by a long-distance pass from Beckham.

Now the visitors' pressure increased and they broke through when Beckham's outswinging corner was met with Yorke's bullet header from eight yards. Soon afterwards the Tobagan exchanged passes with Giggs before netting with a

Dwight Yorke's two goals changed the match

4 MANCHESTER UNITED

38, 40 YORKE
71 SCHOLES
79 BECKHAM

| 1. Mark BOSNICH |
| 2. Gary NEVILLE |
| 12. Phil NEVILLE |
| 16. Roy KEANE |
| 21. Henning BERG |
| 27. Mikael SILVESTRE |
| 7. David BECKHAM |
| 18. Paul SCHOLES |
| 9. Andy COLE |
| 19. Dwight YORKE |
| 11. Ryan GIGGS |
| **SUBSTITUTES** |
| 8. Nicky BUTT |
| 10. Teddy SHERINGHAM |
| 17. Raimond VAN DER GOUW |
| 20. Ole Gunnar SOLSKJAER (11) 80 |
| 30. Ronnie WALLWORK (16) 75 |

Roy Keane was majestic as usual in the United midfield

tantalising scoop from 15 yards, and he would have notched the fastest hat-trick in Premiership history had Clarke not pushed his shot against a post only moments after his first goal.

United assumed total control and only the margin of victory was in doubt. The third goal was a classic, Scholes meeting a Beckham corner with a venomous volley from 20 yards. All that remained was for Beckham to round off a majestic display by scoring with a perfectly placed sidefoot from 18 yards.

MARCH IN REVIEW

WEDNESDAY 1	v FC GIRONDINS BORDEAUX	H	2-0
SATURDAY 4	v LIVERPOOL	H	1-1
TUESDAY 7	v FC GIRONDINS BORDEAUX	A	2-1
SATURDAY 11	v DERBY COUNTY	H	3-1
WEDNESDAY 15	v AC FIORENTINA	H	3-1
SATURDAY 18	v LEICESTER CITY	A	2-0
TUESDAY 21	v VALENCIA CF	A	0-0
SATURDAY 25	v BRADFORD CITY	A	4-0

PLAYER IN THE FRAME

Paul Scholes

Having fully recovered from a mid-season hernia operation, Paul Scholes positively scintillated throughout March. His passing was a delight, while his goal at Bradford will remain vivid in the memory of all those who saw it. Paul goes on improving and, at the moment, his horizons appear limitless.

FA CARLING PREMIERSHIP

		P	W	D	L	F	A	Pts
UP TO AND INCLUDING	MANCHESTER UNITED	30	20	7	3	69	35	67
SUNDAY 26 MARCH 2000	Leeds United	30	19	3	8	49	33	60
	Liverpool	30	16	8	6	44	24	56
	Arsenal	30	16	6	8	53	31	54
	Chelsea	30	14	10	6	40	26	52
	Aston Villa	31	12	10	9	35	27	46
	Sunderland	30	12	9	9	48	45	45
	West Ham United	30	12	9	9	41	40	45
	Tottenham Hotspur	30	12	7	11	45	35	43
	Everton	31	10	11	10	49	42	41
	Leicester City	29	12	5	12	43	43	41
	Newcastle United	30	11	7	12	50	44	40
	Middlesbrough	30	11	7	12	32	40	40
	Coventry City	31	10	8	13	40	39	38
	Southampton	30	9	7	14	36	52	34
	Wimbledon	30	7	11	12	41	56	32
	Derby County	30	7	7	16	33	46	28
	Bradford City	30	6	8	16	28	53	26
	Sheffield Wednesday	30	5	6	19	27	57	21
	Watford	30	5	4	21	26	61	19

APRIL

SATURDAY 1	v WEST HAM	H
TUESDAY 4	v REAL MADRID CF	A
MONDAY 10	v MIDDLESBOROUGH	A
SATURDAY 15	v SUNDERLAND	H
WEDNESDAY 19	v REAL MADRID CF	H
SATURDAY 22	v SOUTHAMPTON	A
MONDAY 24	v CHELSEA	H
SATURDAY 29	v WATFORD	A

MANCHESTER UNITED 7

1. Mark BOSNICH
2. Gary NEVILLE
3. Denis IRWIN
16. Roy KEANE
27. Mikael SILVESTRE
6. Jaap STAM
7. David BECKHAM
18. Paul SCHOLES
9. Andy COLE
19. Dwight YORKE
25. Quinton FORTUNE

SUBSTITUTES

8. Nicky BUTT (16) 57
10. Teddy SHERINGHAM (9) 68
12. Phil NEVILLE
17. Raimond VAN DER GOUW
20. Ole Gunnar SOLSKJAER (18) 68

SCHOLES 24, 51, 63 (penalty)
IRWIN 27
COLE 45
BECKHAM 66
SOLSKJAER 73

MATCH REPORT

The sheer majesty of it all! After West Ham had the temerity to snatch an early lead, Manchester United replied with awesome authority, plundering seven goals, then easing up long before the final whistle ended the procession.

For the Red Devils, all ten outfielders were outstanding, with Keane and Beckham in particularly rapturous form. Yet the Londoners had begun with impressive resolve, their long-ball service to their two big front-men ruffling the home rearguard. Accordingly, it was through a headed flick from the menacing

Roy Keane's presence was felt all over the pitch

1 WEST HAM UNITED

11 WANCHOPE

22. Craig FORREST
13. Marc-Vivien FOE
20. Scott MINTO
4. Steve POTTS
15. Rio FERDINAND
16. John MONCUR
18. Frank LAMPARD
8. Trevor SINCLAIR
12. Paulo WANCHOPE
14. Frederic KANOUTE
11. Steve LOMAS

SUBSTITUTES

2. Gary CHARLES
7. Marc KELLER
26. Joe COLE
29. Ian FEUER
45. Grant McCANN

Kanoute that Wanchope raced ahead of Silvestre, then beat the floundering Bosnich with a soft shot from a narrow angle. The admirably vocal Hammers fans celebrated thunderously, but all that awaited them was torment as the hosts began to exert pressure which paid off twice inside three minutes.

First Scholes seized on to a headed clearance before beating the unsighted Forrest with a skidding 20-yarder, then Keane exchanged passes with Yorke before surging into the box, where he was tripped by Potts. Irwin's penalty was parried by Forrest, but the Irishman tapped home the rebound.

West Ham might have equalised when Bosnich failed to reach Minto's cross and Foe nodded wide, but United's devastating riposte was a magnificent goal just before the break, Cole converting Beckham's beautiful cross.

The rout gathered pace as a Beckham dispatch was back-flicked past Forrest by Scholes, who completed his first Reds hat-trick from the spot after Butt fell over his own feet and the referee thought he had been fouled. Still to come were a free-kick – intoxicatingly delicious even by Beckham standards – and a clinical finish from Solskjaer. Ferguson's men had delivered their most imperious display of the season.

Paul Scholes converted a penalty for his hat-trick

REAL MADRID CF 0

27. Iker CASILLAS

2. Michel SALGADO

3. Roberto CARLOS

12. Ivan CAMPO

15. Ivan HELGUERA

6. Fernando REDONDO

7. RAUL

8. Steve McMANAMAN

9. Fernando MORIENTES

18. Aitor KARANKA

11. SAVIO

SUBSTITUTES

1. Bodo ILLGNER

17. DORADO

20. Elvir BALIC (11) 76

21. GEREMI

22. Christian KAREMBEU

25. Perica OGNJENOVIC (9) 86

34. David AGANZO

MATCH REPORT

To the uncommitted, it was a sumptuous feast of free-flowing entertainment marred only by a mysterious lack of goals; to Real Madrid it was an encouraging encounter which offered genuine hope for the return leg; but to Manchester United, the Bernabeu experience was more than a tad frustrating.

On a night when they owed plenty to a splendid display of goalkeeping by Bosnich, United surrendered possession with alarming frequency and allowed their hosts too much room for manoeuvre in midfield, where McManaman was outstanding. Twice the former Liverpool favourite came desperately close to breaking the deadlock only to be denied by United's keeper, who pulled off an adroit tip-over from a diving header early in the game and an instinctive block with his knee when McManaman was through near the end.

In between both sides created numerous scoring opportunities, with the comfortable majority falling to Real, particularly before the break when scorching drives from Raul and Morientes were repelled expertly by Bosnich.

United's best chances also occurred in the first half, the pick of them being missed by Cole, a two-yard header

Ryan Giggs goes over following a harsh tackle

0 MANCHESTER UNITED

1. Mark BOSNICH
2. Gary NEVILLE
3. Denis IRWIN
16. Roy KEANE
21. Henning BERG
6. Jaap STAM
7. David BECKHAM
18. Paul SCHOLES
9. Andy COLE
19. Dwight YORKE
11. Ryan GIGGS
SUBSTITUTES
8. Nicky BUTT (18) 81
10. Teddy SHERINGHAM (19) 76
12. Phil NEVILLE
14. Jordi CRUYFF
17. Raimond VAN DER GOUW
20. Ole Gunnar SOLSKJAER
27. Mikael SILVESTRE (3) 87

Paul Scholes dodged defenders all night, but to no avail

following Stam's flick from a Beckham corner. When they did manage to find the net – Yorke prodding home after a Scholes shot rebounded – the Tobagan was ruled narrowly offside.

In the second period, the visitors were slightly less profligate with their passing and Giggs embarked on one thrilling run, only to be halted, illegally and violently, by Karanka.

But it was Real who continued to surge forward most convincingly, with Roberto Carlos particularly menacing, and Bosnich came under further heavy fire. He coped magnificently, allowing United to go home with a hard-earned draw but rueing the absence of an away goal.

MIDDLESBROUGH 3

1. Mark SCHWARZER

2. Curtis FLEMING

17. Christian ZIEGE

4. Steve VICKERS

28. Colin COOPER

22. Mark SUMMERBELL

7. Robbie MUSTOE

19. Hamilton RICARD

9. Paul INCE

10. Brian DEANE

18. Andy CAMPBELL

SUBSTITUTES

5. Gianluca FESTA (28) 12

13. Marlon BERESFORD

15. Neil MADDISON

23. JUNINHO (7) 71

27. Robbie STOCKDALE

CAMPBELL 19
INCE 87
JUNINHO 90

MATCH REPORT

Ryan Giggs scores United's first goal early in the second half

Exuberant going forward but often horribly uncertain at the back, United treated their fans to a royally entertaining rollercoaster ride to forge 11 points clear at the Premiership summit.

For half an hour 'Boro were the better side, with the power of Ricard and Deane and the pace of Campbell causing problems to Stam and company, yet only a smart block from Schwarzer prevented Yorke from putting the visitors ahead. Thirty seconds later, though, they were trailing after Ricard dinked over a static defence for Campbell to volley home between Bosnich's legs.

Bryan Robson's men sought to press home their advantage

4 MANCHESTER UNITED

46 GIGGS
60 COLE
74 SCHOLES
88 FORTUNE

1. Mark BOSNICH
2. Gary NEVILLE
3. Denis IRWIN
16. Roy KEANE
21. Henning BERG
6. Jaap STAM
7. David BECKHAM
18. Paul SCHOLES
9. Andy COLE
19. Dwight YORKE
11. Ryan GIGGS

SUBSTITUTES

8. Nicky BUTT (16) 81
10. Teddy SHERINGHAM
17. Raimond VAN DER GOUW
25. Quinton FORTUNE (11) 81
27. Mikael SILVESTRE (3) 32

and it took a splendid reflex save from the Australian to halt Deane's header, then Ricard netted from a Ziege corner only for his effort to be disallowed for Deane's foul on Stam.

Soon Silvestre replaced Irwin to address the aerial threat and the tide began to turn. Giggs, Cole and Yorke all missed good chances, but it was not until the second period that United struck prime form. When they did, however, they did so with a vengeance. First Giggs beat the unsighted Schwarzer with a 20-yard right-footer following a misheaded Ince clearance, then man-of-the-match Beckham took centre stage. After waltzing past two tackles, he shredded the Middlesbrough defence with a sublime through-ball to Cole, who slotted in at his near post. After Scholes had hit the target with a rising 25-yarder that was savage even by his exalted standards, the contest seemed to be over. Far from it.

Bosnich badly misjudged a 'Boro corner allowing Ince to bundle a goal, but United responded instantly with Yorke touching Butt's cross to Fortune, who flicked home coolly. Still there was time for Juninho to register with a 20-yard curler following a clever run, thus completing an evening of pulsating drama.

Paul Scholes scores on the hour

MANCHESTER UNITED 4

1. Mark BOSNICH
2. Gary NEVILLE
12. Phil NEVILLE
16. Roy KEANE
27. Mikael SILVESTRE
6. Jaap STAM
18. Paul SCHOLES
8. Nicky BUTT
20. Ole Gunnar SOLSKJAER
10. Teddy SHERINGHAM
25. Quinton FORTUNE

SUBSTITUTES

7. David BECKHAM (18) 65
11. Ryan GIGGS
17. Raimond VAN DER GOUW (1) h-t
19. Dwight YORKE
21. Henning BERG (6) 56

SOLSKJAER 3, 51
BUTT 65
BERG 70

MATCH REPORT

Treating Old Trafford to yet another joyous goal spree, Manchester United broke the Premiership record for goals scored, and still had five matches to play. After thumping Sunderland, albeit not quite as comprehensively as the scoreline suggests, the Reds had racked up 84 strikes, outstripping the benchmark of 82 set by Newcastle in 1994. With half the side rested for the forthcoming clash with Real Madrid, the achievement was particularly impressive.

The carnage began after only three minutes when Williams underhit a back pass, thus letting in Solskjaer, who danced past Sorensen before netting gleefully. However, the Wearsiders held their own for the remainder of the half, with Quinn twice going close and Stam a trifle fortunate to escape with a booking after appearing to clip Phillips' heels as the England marksman raced goalwards.

Come the second period, though, United dominated and doubled their lead with the goal of the match. After exchanging a slick one-two with Solskjaer in midfield, Sheringham dispatched a long arcing pass towards the right of Sunderland's box. The

A rare goal from Henning Berg capped the emphatic win for the Champions

0 SUNDERLAND

1. Thomas SORENSEN
2. Chris MAKIN
3. Michael GRAY
4. Kevin KILBANE
18. Darren WILLIAMS
17. Jody CRADDOCK
14. Darren HOLLOWAY
29. Eric ROY
9. Niall QUINN
10. Kevin PHILLIPS
16. Alex RAE

SUBSTITUTES

6. Paul BUTLER (18) 75
7. Nicky SUMMERBEE (3) 54
12. Danny DICHIO
13. Andrew MARRIOTT
19. Paul THIRLWELL

predatory Norwegian, who had scampered forward at high speed, flipped the ball delicately over Williams' head before slotting immaculately past Sorensen from ten yards.

The rest of the game was played at a canter. With his first touch after rising from the bench, Beckham crossed to Solskjaer, the ball was touched back to Butt and the workaholic Mancunian sidestepped a tackle before rocketing a shot into the roof of the net. Then another whipped delivery from Beckham caused mayhem in the visitors' defence, allowing substitute Berg to ram in his first goal of the campaign from close range.

All that remained was a sublime effort from Solskjaer, who flicked the ball past a defender before unleashing an explosive left-foot volley from 25 yards, only to be denied by Sorensen's flying save. It was a big step closer to another Premier League Championship.

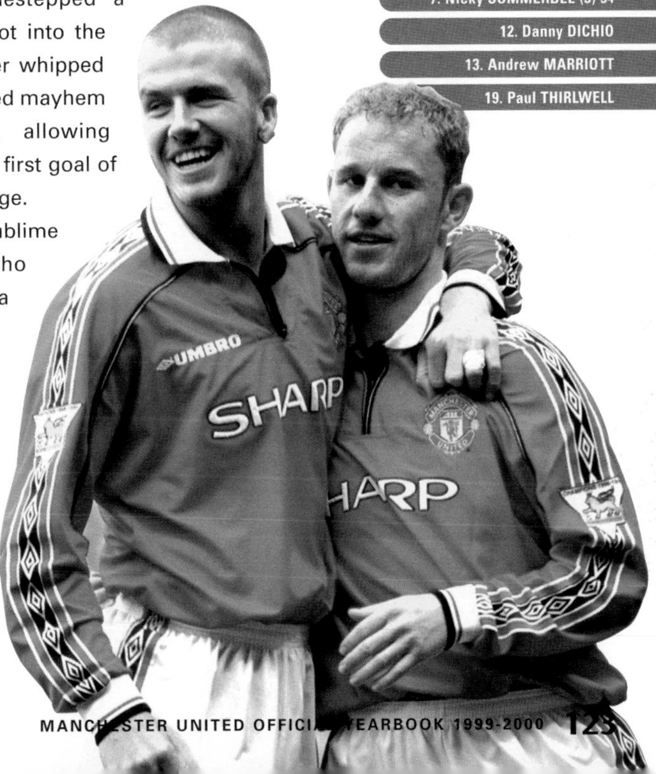

David Beckham and Nicky Butt: united for United

MANCHESTER UNITED   2

17. Raimond VAN DER GOUW
2. Gary NEVILLE
3. Denis IRWIN
16. Roy KEANE
21. Henning BERG
6. Jaap STAM
7. David BECKHAM
18. Paul SCHOLES
9. Andy COLE
19. Dwight YORKE
11. Ryan GIGGS

SUBSTITUTES

8. Nicky BUTT
10. Teddy SHERINGHAM (21) 63
12. Phil NEVILLE
14. Jordi CRUYFF
20. Ole Gunnar SOLSKJAER (9) 63
27. Mikael SILVESTRE (3) h-t
31. Nick CULKIN

BECKHAM 64
SCHOLES (penalty) 88

MATCH REPORT

Dwight Yorke came close to equalising towards the end of the first half

3 REAL MADRID CF

20 KEANE (o.g.)
50, 53 RAUL

| 27. IKER CASILLAS |
| 2. Michel SALGADO |
| 3. Roberto CARLOS |
| 12. Ivan CAMPO |
| 15. HELGUERA |
| 6. Fernando REDONDO |
| 7. RAUL |
| 8. Steve McMANAMAN |
| 9. Fernando MORIENTES |
| 18. Aitor KARANKA |
| 11. SAVIO |

SUBSTITUTES

| 1. Bodo ILLGNER |
| 17. DORADO |
| 19. Nicolas ANELKA (9) |
| 20. Elvir BALIC |
| 21. GEREMI (11) |
| 22. Christian KAREMBEU |
| 23. Julio CESAR (8) |

United surrendered their European crown on a night of crackling excitement, but they went down gloriously, playing some of the best attacking football seen in England this season. In particular, Giggs and Scholes were exceptional, but lack of defensive concentration was to prove calamitous.

Immense credit is due to Real Madrid, who carried the game to their hosts from the outset, and two early mistakes by Gary Neville might have led to a Spanish breakthrough but for sharp saves by van der Gouw from Morientes and Roberto Carlos. Real went ahead fortuitously after 20 minutes when Salgado's low cross was turned into his own net by Keane.

Then Giggs began to run riot and some of United's rapid-fire passing was heavenly, but young keeper Casillas was in inspired form, saving from Yorke, Beckham and Keane before the break. However, two goals in three minutes shortly after the interval settled the game. First McManaman broke through to find Raul, who netted with a curler; then Redondo tricked Berg on the left before setting up a tap-in for the Spanish spearhead.

United stormed back and Beckham gave them hope when he scored a fabulous goal to set up a period of frenzied and extended pressure. But by the time McManaman tripped Keane and Scholes hammered home from the spot, the issue was effectively settled. Sir Alex Ferguson's men had played their part in yet another magnificent contest, but this time they had lost.

David Beckham celebrates his goal – clearly knowing that it wasn't enough

SOUTHAMPTON 1

| 13. Neil MOSS |
| 2. Jason DODD |
| 15. Francis BENALI |
| 4. Chris MARSDEN |
| 5. Claus LUNDEKVAM |
| 6. Dean RICHARDS |
| 21. Jo TESSEM |
| 27. Tahar EL KHALEJ |
| 17. Marian PAHARS |
| 10. Kevin DAVIES |
| 18. Wayne BRIDGE |

SUBSTITUTES

| 7. Matthew LE TISSIER (10) 73 |
| 8. Matthew OAKLEY (27) 83 |
| 20. Scott BEVAN |
| 30. Hassan KACHLOUL (15) h-t |
| 32. Trond SOLTVEDT |

PAHARS 84

MATCH REPORT

Winning the Championship is always special, no matter how often it happens, and Manchester United celebrated at The Dell with all the fervour that greeted the first of their modern titles in 1993. That it was their sixth crown in eight years, and attained with four matches to spare, underlined emphatically the degree of their supremacy in the English game.

Shrugging off their midweek European disappointment, the Reds brushed aside Glenn Hoddle's Southampton with ease, scoring three goals in the first half-hour to render the remainder of the proceedings largely academic.

The quickfire demolition began with Phil Neville surging down the left and crossing to Cole, who was fouled some 25 yards from goal. It was the perfect distance for Beckham, who stepped forward to dispatch a characteristically curvaceous delivery past Moss.

The constant movement of Solskjaer and Cole was causing serial confusion in the home rearguard and Phil Neville took further advantage with another left-flank foray which ended with the full-back's drilled cross being deflected between his own posts by Benali.

Next Moss tipped a Solskjaer drive against an upright, then Cole miskicked from close range with his unfavoured left foot as the pressure continued relentlessly, and any likelihood of the

Roy Keane and Mikael Silvestre stayed in the thick of the action for the entire game

3   MANCHESTER UNITED

8   BECKHAM
15   BENALI (o.g.)
30   SOLSKJAER

17. Raimond VAN DER GOUW
2. Gary NEVILLE
12. Phil NEVILLE
16. Roy KEANE
27. Mikael SILVESTRE
6. Jaap STAM
7. David BECKHAM
8. Nicky BUTT
9. Andy COLE
20. Ole Gunnar SOLSKJAER
11. Ryan GIGGS
SUBSTITUTES
5. Ronny JOHNSEN (11) 59
10. Teddy SHERINGHAM (20) 73
18. Paul SCHOLES
19. Dwight YORKE (9) 73
31. Nick CULKIN

The glorious Reds celebrate their sixth Premier League win

Saints turning the tide disappeared with a third devastating strike.

This time the architect was Beckham, whose raking pass was controlled on the chest of Solskjaer, then rifled unerringly into the far corner of the net from eight yards by the lethal Norwegian's left foot.

Thereafter the visitors were always in control of an increasingly ill-tempered encounter, though Tessem brought two fine saves from van der Gouw and the splendid Pahars reduced the arrears with a sharp finish after cutting in from the right. By then, though, the destination of the Premiership trophy was not in doubt.

MANCHESTER UNITED 3

YORKE 11, 69
SOLSKJAER 40

17. Raimond VAN DER GOUW
2. Gary NEVILLE
3. Phil NEVILLE
16. Roy KEANE
5. Ronny JOHNSEN
27. Mikael SILVESTRE
7. David BECKHAM
8. Nicky BUTT
20. Ole Gunnar SOLSKJAER
19. Dwight YORKE
11. Ryan GIGGS

SUBSTITUTES

10. Teddy SHERINGHAM
14. Jordi CRUYFF (20) 63
18. Paul SCHOLES (16) 50
21. Henning BERG (2) 32
25. Quinton FORTUNE

MATCH REPORT

It was showtime as the Champions celebrated in style

This was a strange contest in which the priorities of the two sides were in stark contrast. There was an unmistakable end-of-term air about the champions and, at times, they might have been playing in an exhibition match. Chelsea, on the other hand, were desperate for points in their quest for a Champions League slot, yet they failed to impose their will and subsided ever more passively as the game wore on.

The Londoners started in sprightly manner, a Flo header

2 CHELSEA

22 PETRESCU
36 ZOLA

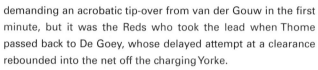

1. Ed DE GOEY
2. Dan PETRESCU
21. Bernard LAMBOURDE
30. Emerson THOME
5. Frank LEBOEUF
18. Gabriele AMBROSETTI
7. Didier DESCHAMPS
15. Mario MELCHIOT
19. Tore Andre FLO
25. Gianfranco ZOLA
11. Dennis WISE

SUBSTITUTES

4. Jes HOGH
9. Chris SUTTON (2) 74
20. Jody MORRIS (7) h-t
23. Carlo CUDICINI
34. Jon HARLEY (18) h-t

demanding an acrobatic tip-over from van der Gouw in the first minute, but it was the Reds who took the lead when Thome passed back to De Goey, whose delayed attempt at a clearance rebounded into the net off the charging Yorke.

Chelsea buzzed back enterprisingly and when Phil Neville failed to clear a cross from Flo, Petrescu pounced to hammer an equaliser from close range. Now the Blues began to dominate and United – for whom Johnsen was making his first start since the European Cup Final – elected for a defensive reshuffle, with Berg coming on for Gary Neville, Silvestre shifting to left-back and Phil Neville moving to the right. With the new formation settling, Zola volleyed the visitors in front from Petrescu's cross, but soon the hosts regained parity when Giggs set up Solskjaer for a 16-yard drive.

Thereafter it was a story of Chelsea possession with United creating the better chances until Yorke bagged what proved to be the winner. Cruyff freed Beckham on the right and the England midfielder's shot was parried by De Goey, leaving the Tobagan to tap home.

The belief seemed to drain from Chelsea, and though Berg diverted a Flo shot against his own bar, the Reds finished in cruise control, turning the tempo up and down seemingly at will.

Dwight Yorke gave Frank Leboeuf nightmares in defence

WATFORD 2

1 Alec CHAMBERLAIN
23 Darren WARD
26 David PERPETUINI
4 Robert PAGE
5 Steve PALMER
6 Paul ROBINSON
36 Neil COX
8 Micah HYDE
37 Heidar HELGUSON
17 Tommy SMITH
33 DominicFOLEY
SUBSTITUTES
9 Tommy MOONEY (33) h-t
10 Richard JOHNSON (37) 88
13 Chris DAY
14 Nordin WOOTER
16 Nigel GIBBS (36) 84

HELGUSON 34
SMITH 78

MATCH REPORT

After a listless first half during which Watford had taken a deserved lead, the Reds roused themselves to record a ninth successive Premiership victory. Sadly, the occasion was tainted by a mindless scuffle between Butt and Hyde, which resulted in the pair being sent off in the 64th minute. Until then, the Hornets had held sway thanks to Helguson's header from Hyde's free-kick, and van der Gouw had been by far the busiest goalkeeper.

However, the champions had no intention of falling to their relegated hosts, and the tables were turned by two goals in five

Some of United's less regular players earned a runout to torment Watford

3 MANCHESTER UNITED

69 YORKE
71 GIGGS
87 CRUYFF

17 Raimond VAN DER GOUW
12 Phil NEVILLE
27 Mikael SILVESTRE
33 Mark WILSON
5 Ronny JOHNSEN
21 Henning BERG
34 Jonathan GREENING
8 Nicky BUTT
20 Ole Gunnar SOLSKJAER
10 Teddy SHERINGHAM
11 Ryan GIGGS

SUBSTITUTES

14 Jordi CRUYFF (34) 71
19 Dwight YORKE (33) h-t
25 Quinton FORTUNE
28 Danny HIGGINBOTHAM (27) 63
31 Nick CULKIN

Jordi Cruyff had a good day, scoring the winner three minutes from time

minutes. The first came as a result of a poor kick by Chamberlain, which allowed Sheringham to find Yorke, who netted via an upright. The Tobagan thus became the first Red Devil to net 20 times in a League campaign since Brian McClair in 1988.

Next it was the turn of Giggs, who ran on to a subtle dink from Solskjaer before lifting the ball delicately over the keeper. That seemed to be that, but plucky Watford refused to capitulate and equalised through the effervescent Smith. To finish the matter, Cruyff ran through onto a Solskjaer pass which he had intercepted as the keeper tried to clear his lines. Game over. Though there had been nothing tangible at stake, the below-strength champions had rolled on regardless.

APRIL IN REVIEW

SATURDAY 1	v WEST HAM	H	7-1
TUESDAY 4	v REAL MADRID CF	A	0-0
MONDAY 10	v MIDDLESBOROUGH	A	4-3
SATURDAY 15	v SUNDERLAND	H	4-0
WEDNESDAY 19	v REAL MADRID CF	H	2-3
SATURDAY 22	v SOUTHAMPTON	A	3-1
MONDAY 24	v CHELSEA	H	3-2
SATURDAY 29	v WATFORD	A	3-2

PLAYER IN THE FRAME

Dwight Yorke
The Tobagan sparkled brightly during April and became the first United man for 12 years to net 20 League goals in a single campaign. His landmark strike came at Vicarage Road as United defeated lowly Watford 3-2.

FA CARLING PREMIERSHIP

UP TO AND INCLUDING
MONDAY 24TH APRIL 2000

	P	W	D	L	F	A	Pts
MANCHESTER UNITED	35	25	7	3	90	42	82
Liverpool	34	19	9	6	51	25	66
Arsenal	33	19	6	8	63	34	63
Leeds United	34	19	4	11	51	41	61
Chelsea	35	16	11	8	46	32	59
Aston Villa	35	15	11	9	43	31	56
Sunderland	35	15	9	11	54	52	54
West Ham United	34	15	9	10	51	49	54
Everton	35	12	13	10	58	45	49
Tottenham Hotspur	35	14	7	14	52	44	49
Leicester City	34	13	7	14	48	50	46
Newcastle United	34	12	8	14	55	50	44
Middlesbrough	34	12	8	14	40	49	44
Coventry City	35	11	8	16	43	50	41
Southampton	35	11	7	17	42	60	40
Derby County	35	9	9	17	43	52	36
Wimbledon	35	7	11	17	44	67	32
Bradford City	35	7	9	19	34	65	30
Sheffield Wednesday	34	7	6	21	30	60	27
Watford	34	5	5	24	30	70	20

MAY

MANCHESTER UNITED 3

17. Raimond VAN DER GOUW

12. Phil NEVILLE

3. Denis IRWIN

18. Paul SCHOLES

27. Mikael SILVESTRE

6. Jaap STAM

7. David BECKHAM

8. Nicky BUTT

20. Ole Gunnar SOLSKJAER

10. Teddy SHERINGHAM

11. Ryan GIGGS

SUBSTITUTES

14. Jordi CRUYFF (20) 79

21. Henning BERG (6) 26

25. Quinton FORTUNE

30. Ronnie WALLWORK

34. Jonathan GREENING (8) 63

SOLSKJAER 5
BECKHAM 34
SHERINGHAM 36

MATCH REPORT

Ryan Giggs holds off Steffen Freund in midfield

On a day when the football match took second place to the celebration, Manchester United brushed aside Tottenham Hotspur with the minimum of fuss and then simply got on with the prizegiving party.

The Reds stroked the ball around with majestic command and there was an air of inevitability about proceedings from the moment they seized an early lead. Phil Neville embarked on the first of many surging sprints down the right flank and was halted

1 TOTTENHAM HOTSPUR

20 ARMSTRONG

1. Ian WALKER
2. Stephen CARR
25. Stephen CLEMENCE
4. Steffen FREUND
5. Sol CAMPBELL
6. Chris PERRY
7. Darren ANDERSON
29. Simon DAVIES
16. Chris ARMSTRONG
10. Steffen IVERSEN
28. Matthew ETHERINGTON

SUBSTITUTES

11. Williams KORSTEN (10) 71
12. Gary DOHERTY (16) 71
19. John SCALES
26. Ledley KING (28) 84
40. Hans SEGERS

only at the expense of a corner. Beckham's arcing delivery was met by Stam, whose header was nodded netwards by Solskjaer and a desperate lunge by Carr failed to keep the ball out.

The visitors toiled manfully to regain a foothold in the game and, against the run of play, they did so when Iversen set up Anderton's cross and Armstrong flung himself horizontal to beat van der Gouw with a fabulous near-post header.

Thus stung, United responded with wave after wave of attacks, and as Giggs and Solskjaer ferried the ball to Beckham, who controlled it imperiously before half-swivelling and passing Walker with a glorious curler from 20 yards.

Two minutes later the Welshman and the Norwegian were the providers again, a penetrating dispatch from Ryan enabling Ole to set up Sheringham. The Londoner, who had thought quicker than Campbell and then outpaced the England centre-half, completed the move with a scorching left-footer from 12 yards.

Thereafter a shirtsleeved crowd was treated to exhibition stuff – with Greening coming closest to another goal. All that remained was the joyous distribution of silverware in the spring sunshine.

Ole Gunnar Solskjaer celebrates his fifth-minute strike

ASTON VILLA 0

39. Peter ENCKELMAN

24. Mark DELANEY

3. Alan WRIGHT

4. Gareth SOUTHGATE

5. Ugo EHIOGU

6. George BOATENG

17. Lee HENDRIE

15. Gareth BARRY

9. Dion DUBLIN

10. Paul MERSON

18. Benito CARBONE

SUBSTITUTES

7. Ian TAYLOR (17) 65

11. Alan THOMPSON (6) 81

12. Julian JOACHIM (18) 59

13. Neil CUTLER

31. Jlloyd SAMUEL

MATCH REPORT

'Four more, we only need four more' chanted United's travelling contingent at the outset of a long, hot afternoon, but in the end the Reds fell three short of a century of League goals. Still, the one supplied by Teddy Sheringham ensured yet another victory – their 28th of the Premiership campaign – and stretched the final margin of their title triumph to a remarkable 18 points, so there were scant grounds for disappointment.

With the Championship long since safe and with Villa's minds on the FA Cup Final, the game was predicatably low-key in nature, enlivened only by isolated pockets of excitement. The first of these materialised in the 24th minute when the perky Merson attempted an audacious chip, but was foiled by van der Gouw's spring-heeled parry.

The visitors responded with a spell of coherent attacks, during which Scholes twice volleyed straight at Enckelman, though the best chance of the first half fell to Villa's Carbone, who swept narrowly wide following a centre from Merson.

After the interval United began to pass with more purpose and might have scored when Cruyff freed Sheringham, only for the Londoner to pull his shot tamely wide.

Ryan Giggs shoots for goal

1 MANCHESTER UNITED

SHERINGHAM 65

17. Raimond VAN DER GOUW

28. Danny HIGGINBOTHAM

3. Denis IRWIN

12. Phil NEVILLE

27. Mikael SILVESTRE

21. Henning BERG

19. Dwight YORKE

18. Paul SCHOLES

20. Ole Gunnar SOLSKJAER

10. Teddy SHERINGHAM

11. Ryan GIGGS

SUBSTITUTES

14. Jordi CRUYFF (20) 33

25. Quinton FORTUNE

30. Ronnie WALLWORK (28) h-t

34. Jonathan GREENING

43. Michael STEWART

Teddy Sheringham beats Enckelman to secure the points for United

He was not long in making amends, however, and again Jordi was the provider. This time the Dutchman crossed from the right, Ehiogu failed to clear and Sheringham netted with a low show from 12 yards.

Thereafter Villa mounted a late aerial bombardment in search of a point. Berg, Silvestre and company stood up well to this examination, although Dublin was unlucky with a header which clipped the bar. Thus United finished the season with 11 straight League wins, one of their many Premeirship records.

MAY IN REVIEW

SATURDAY 6	v TOTTENHAM HOTSPUR	H	3-1
SUNDAY 14	v ASTON VILLA	A	1-0

PLAYER IN THE FRAME

Roy Keane

Injury prevented Roy Keane from leading his troops into their final Premiership fixtures, but he had been a guiding light when it had mattered throughout the campaign, as his crowning as Footballer of the Year by both players and writers confirmed. How appropriate, therefore, that as the Championship trophy was presented, it was the chant of 'Keano' which echoed the loudest around a sun-bathed Old Trafford. Once again, the Irishman had been United's inspiration.

FA CARLING PREMIERSHIP

FINAL TABLE	P	W	D	L	F	A	Pts
MANCHESTER UNITED	38	28	7	3	97	45	91
Arsenal	38	22	7	9	73	43	73
Leeds United	38	21	6	11	58	43	69
Liverpool	38	19	10	9	51	30	67
Chelsea	38	18	11	9	53	34	65
Aston Villa	38	15	13	10	46	35	58
Sunderland	38	16	10	12	57	56	58
Leicester City	38	16	7	15	55	55	55
West Ham United	38	15	10	13	52	53	55
Tottenham Hotspur	38	15	8	15	57	49	53
Newcastle United	38	14	10	14	63	54	52
Middlesbrough	38	14	10	14	46	52	52
Everton	38	12	14	12	59	49	50
Coventry City	38	12	8	18	47	54	44
Southampton	38	12	8	18	45	62	44
Derby County	38	9	11	18	44	57	38
Bradford City	38	9	9	20	38	68	36
Wimbledon	38	7	12	19	46	74	33
Sheffield Wednesday	38	8	7	23	38	70	31
Watford	38	6	6	26	35	77	24

1999–2000 Season in Review

How do you follow the unbeatable? How could Manchester United avoid demoralising anti-climax in the wake of the barely credible treble triumph of 1998/99? In fact, the Red Devils made a good fist of their Millennium campaign. True, the European Cup slipped away, but not until United became the only club to reach the quarter-finals in each of the last four terms. As for the FA Cup, it was not defended because of fixture congestion caused by the Club World Championship, a cause for sadness among all those who hold dear the traditions of the English game.

But to many fans the domestic League crown represents the principal prize and that was retained with a flourish. Sir Alex Ferguson's men served up some of the most sumptuous football of modern times, in the process setting Premiership records for the most points and wins in a 38-game season, scoring more goals than any top-flight title-winners for nearly 40 years and finishing 18 points ahead of their nearest rivals.

To what is all this success due? Many say that it is due to the quality of the midfield. But for all the formidable quality of such world-class performers as David Beckham, Roy Keane, Paul Scholes and Ryan Giggs, it is none of them who holds the outright key to the phenomenal continued success of Manchester United. The lion's share of gratitude for the Red Devils' pre-eminence can be laid at the door of the manager. Both his overwhelming desire to go on winning, and his unshakeable belief that he can and will, are unique. Crucially, so are his knack of communicating these feelings to his players and his ability to recognise which of them share that relentless hunger.

On that unforgettable May day when Old Trafford partied joyously following the presentation of the Premiership trophy, he stressed, with typical eloquence, that such occasions were special, that the title was not come by easily, that nothing should be taken for granted. By the same token, it would be monstrous if anyone involved with Manchester United should ever become the slightest bit blase about the contribution of Sir Alex Ferguson. It is beyond price.

APPEARANCES

substitute appearances shown in parenthesis

Legend:
- FA CARLING PREMIERSHIP
- WORTHINGTON CUP
- UEFA CHAMPIONS LEAGUE
- FIFA CWC
- TOTAL

Player	FA Carling Premiership	Worthington Cup	UEFA Champions League	FIFA CWC	Total
STAM • Jaap	33	0	13	2	48
BECKHAM • David	30 (1)	0	12	1 (1)	43 (2)
GIGGS • Ryan	30	0	11	2	43
KEANE • Roy	28 (1)	0	12	2	42 (1)
YORKE • Dwight	29 (3)	0	9 (2)	2	40 (5)
IRWIN • Denis	25	0	13	2	40
COLE • Andy	23 (5)	0	13	2	38 (5)
SCHOLES • Paul	27 (4)	0	11	0	38 (4)
SILVESTRE • Mikael	30 (1)	0	2 (2)	2	34 (3)
NEVILLE • Phil	25 (4)	0	6 (3)	2 (1)	33 (8)
BOSNICH • Mark	23	1	7	2	33
NEVILLE • Gary	22	0	9	2	33
BERG • Henning	16 (6)	0	11 (1)	1	28 (7)
BUTT • Nicky	21 (11)	0	4 (2)	2	27 (13)
SOLSKJAER • Ole Gunnar	15 (13)	1	4 (7)	2 (1)	22 (21)
VAN DER GOUW • Raimond	11 (3)	0	7	1	19 (3)
SHERINGHAM • Teddy	15 (12)	0	3 (6)	0 (2)	18 (20)
FORTUNE • Quinton	4 (2)	0	1 (3)	1 (1)	6 (6)
CRUYFF • Jordi	1 (7)	1	1 (3)	1 (1)	4 (11)
GREENING • Jonathan	1 (3)	1	1 (1)	1	4 (4)
WILSON • Mark	1 (2)	0	2 (1)	1	4 (3)
HIGGINBOTHAM • Danny	2 (1)	1	0 (1)	1	4 (2)
TAIBI • Massimo	4	0	0	0	4
WALLWORK • Ronnie	0 (5)	1	0	1	2 (5)
CLEGG • Michael	0 (2)	1	1 (1)	0	2 (3)
JOHNSEN • Ronny	2 (1)	0	0	0	2 (1)
CURTIS • John	0 (1)	1	0	0	1 (1)
MAY • David	0 (1)	0	1	0	1 (1)
CHADWICK • Luke	0	1	0	0	1
O'SHEA • John	0	1	0	0	1
TWISS • Michael	0	1	0	0	1
CULKIN • Nick	0 (1)	0	0	0	0 (1)
HEALY • David	0	0 (1)	0	0	0 (1)
RACHUBKA • Paul	0	0	0	0 (1)	0 (1)
WELLENS • Richard	0	0 (1)	0	0	0 (1)

GOALSCORERS

Player	FA Carling Premiership	Worthington Cup	UEFA Champions League	FIFA CWC	Total
YORKE • Dwight	20	0	2	1	23
COLE • Andy	19	0	3	0	22
SOLSKJAER • Ole Gunnar	12	0	3	0	15
SCHOLES • Paul	9	0	3	0	12
KEANE • Roy	5	0	6	0	11
BECKHAM • David	6	0	2	0	8
GIGGS • Ryan	6	0	1	0	7
SHERINGHAM • Teddy	5	0	1	0	6
BUTT • Nicky	3	0	0	1	4
FORTUNE • Quinton	2	0	0	2	4
CRUYFF • Jordi	3	0	0	0	3
IRWIN • Denis	3	0	0	0	3
BERG • Henning	1	0	0	0	1
BENALI Francis (Southampton)	1 o.g.	0	0	0	1 o.g.
CARRAGHER Jamie (Liverpool)	2 o.g.	0	0	0	2 o.g.
Total	**97**	**0**	**21**	**4**	**122**

LEAGUE ATTENDANCES 1999-2000

Home		Away	
61,629	v Tottenham Hotspur	44,929	v Liverpool
61,619	v Derby County	42,026	v Sunderland
61,612	v Sunderland	40,160	v Leeds United
61,611	v West Ham United	39,640	v Sheffield Wednesday
61,593	v Chelsea	39,217	v Aston Villa
61,592	v Liverpool	39,141	v Everton
61,380	v Coventry City	38,147	v Arsenal
61,267	v Middlesbrough	36,470	v Newcastle United
58,293	v Arsenal	36,072	v Tottenham Hotspur
55,249	v Southampton	34,909	v Chelsea
55,211	v Aston Villa	34,775	v Middlesbrough
55,193	v Everton	33,370	v Derby County
55,191	v Leicester City	26,037	v West Ham United
55,190	v Newcastle United	26,129	v Wimbledon
55,189	v Wimbledon	22,170	v Leicester City
55,188	v Bradford City	22,024	v Coventry City
55,188	v Watford	20,250	v Watford
55,187	v Leeds United	18,276	v Bradford City
54,941	v Sheffield Wednesday	15,245	v Southampton

Home		Away	
Highest	v 61,629 (Tottenham Hotspur)	Highest	v 44,929 (Liverpool)
Lowest	v 54,941 (Sheffield Wednesday)	Lowest	v 15,245 (Southampton)
Total	1,102,323	Total	608,987
Average	58,017	Average	32,052

OLD TRAFFORD ATTENDANCES

League & Cup

Total 1,496,807

Average 57,569

Includes: 19 FA Carling Premiership games

7 UEFA Champions League games

Sunday 1 August, 1999 • Wembley • 3.00pm • Attendance 70,185
Referee Graham Barber, Tring

MANCHESTER UNITED 1
37 YORKE

ARSENAL 2
67 KANU (penalty)
77 PARLOUR

MATCH REPORT

Though this was only the phoney war, Manchester United clearly had no intention of kicking off a new season with defeat at the hands of their closest rivals, and for the better part of a brisk workout in the Wembley sunshine they seemed unlikely to suffer their first reverse of the 1999-2000 season.

Though the Gunners looked more spritely during the early exchanges, the treble winners were not unduly stretched and gradually attained the ascendancy. The pressure paid off after Cruyff was fouled by Dixon 30 yards from goal. Beckham delivered an arcing free-kick which cannoned off the underside of the bar and clearly crossed the line. However, the referee did not signal a goal until Yorke had beaten Keown to nod home the bouncing rebound.

In the 65th minute, the lively Parlour went past Irwin and beat Bosnich with a low angled drive that bounced off the far post. During the ensuing confusion Irwin tugged Vieira's shirt, the Frenchman went to ground and Kanu equalised from the spot. The Nigerian began to trouble the United rearguard and ten minutes later he freed Parlour on the right who drove the ball goalwards. Again it struck an upright before entering the net for the winner.

Thus the Red Devils' 17th Wembley outing of the decade ended in defeat, but the result's significance was not being exaggerated in either camp.

MANCHESTER UNITED   1 Mark BOSNICH, 12 Phil NEVILLE, 3 Denis IRWIN, 21 Henning BERG, 18 Paul SCHOLES, 6 Jaap STAM, 7 David BECKHAM, 8 Nicky BUTT, 9 Andy COLE, 19 Dwight YORKE, 14 Jordi CRUYFF **Substitutes:** 4 David MAY (6) h-t, 10 Teddy SHERINGHAM (8) 81, 13 John CURTIS, 20 Ole Gunnar SOLSKJAER (14) 62, 31 Nick CULKIN, 33 Mark WILSON, 34 Jonathan GREENING

ARSENAL   13 Alex MANNINGER, 2 Lee DIXON, 3 Nigel WINTERBURN, 4 Patrick VIEIRA, 5 Martin KEOWN, 18 Gilles GRIMANDI, 15 Ray PARLOUR, 8 Fredrik LJUNGBERG, 25 KANU, 17 Emmanuel PETIT **Substitutes:** 16 SILVINHO, 1 Stuart TAYLOR, 12 Christopher WREH, 19 Stefan MALZ, 21 Luis BOA MORTE (16) 65, 22 Oleg LUZHNY (15) 89, 24 John LUKIC, 30 Paolo VERNAZZA

Friday 27 August 1999 • Stade Louis II, Monaco • 8.45pm • Attendance 14,461
Referee Ryszard Wojcik, Poland

MANCHESTER UNITED 0

SS LAZIO 1
35 SALAS

MATCH REPORT

It is known as the Super Cup, but in view of Manchester United's low-key approach to the match, it merits a less rarified description. But in fairness to Lazio, their desire to win burned brightly and their margin of victory in no way reflected their superiority on the night.

For all that, United were the first to threaten, with Sheringham heading just wide from a fourth minute Phil Neville cross. At the other end van der Gouw had a fortunate escape when his clearance struck Mancini before rebounding onto the top of the net. Then a Mihajlovic free-kick brought a smart save from the Reds' keeper before Lazio took the lead. The scorer was the former United transfer target, Salas, who had entered the fray as a substitute for the injured Inzaghi. The Chilean controlled the ball on his chest, then volleyed past van der Gouw, who got a hand to the ball and will be disappointed that he did not repel it.

Thereafter Lazio grew in confidence, with Veron, Almeyda and Nedved outstanding. That they didn't score more goals owed something to a lenient referee, who waved away penalty appeals when van der Gouw floored Salas, and to the United custodian himself, who saved superbly from Nedved and Mancini. United created chances, too, with Sheringham, Scholes and Solskjaer all going close, but the trophy went to the team which wanted it the most.

MANCHESTER UNITED 17 Raimond VAN DER GOUW, 2 Gary NEVILLE, 12 Phil NEVILLE, 16 Roy KEANE, 21 Henning BERG, 6 Jaap STAM, 7 David BECKHAM, 18 Paul SCHOLES, 9 Andy COLE, 10 Teddy SHERINGHAM, 20 Ole Gunnar SOLSKJAER **Substitutes:** 11 Ryan GIGGS, 13 John CURTIS (6) 57, 14 Jordi CRUYFF (7) 58, 19 Dwight YORKE , 31 Nick CULKIN, 33 Mark WILSON, 34 Jonathan GREENING (9) 78

SS LAZIO 1 Luca MARCHEGIANI, 2 Paolo NEGRO, 15 Giuseppe PANCARO, 20 Dejan STANKOVIC, 13 Alessandro NESTA, 18 Pavel NEDVED, 25 Matias ALMEYDA, 23 Sebastian VERON, 21 Simone INZAGHI, 10 Roberto MANCINI, 11 Sinisa MIHAJLOVIC **Substitutes:** 5 Giuseppe FAVALLI, 7 Sergio CONCEICAO, 9 Marcelo SALAS (21) 23, 14 Diego SIMEONE (18) 66, 16 Attilio LOMBARDO (10) 84, 19 Kennet ANDERSSON, 22 Marco BALLOTTA

Tuesday 30 November, 1999 • Olympic Stadium, Tokyo • 7.10pm
Attendance 53,372 • Referee Hellmut Krug, Germany

MANCHESTER UNITED 1
35 KEANE

SE PALMEIRAS 0

MATCH REPORT

Predictions of a bloodbath failed to materialise as United became the first British winners of the World Club Championship in the 40-year history of a much maligned competition. Though hardly a classic, the game produced genuine excitement and a star performance from Bosnich, whose string of splendid saves was the decisive factor in United's triumph.

The Brazilians dominated the first half, putting the European Champions under some intense pressure. Particularly Asprilla, the former Newcastle marksman, who opened the United defence in the 22nd minute, only for Bosnich to deny Alex with a Schmeichel-type block. The goal came against the run of play when Irwin found Giggs on the left and the Welshman surged past Baiano and dispatched a high cross which brushed the fingertips of Marcos before falling to Keane at the far post, who volleyed into the net from four yards.

The second period was far more open and Giggs might have doubled the lead on 58 minutes when he screwed a shot wide of the gaping goal as Marcos charged from his line. Twice in the time that remained, Bosnich was United's saviour. First he frustrated Oseas from point-blank range, then he tipped over a blazing drive from Alex.

The man-of-the-match award of a new car went to Giggs, but the difference between the two sides was the Australian keeper, who was finally approaching top form after an uncertain start to his second Old Trafford sojourn.

MANCHESTER UNITED   1 Mark BOSNICH, 2 Gary NEVILLE, 3 Denis IRWIN, 16 Roy KEANE, 27 Mikael SILVESTRE, 6 Jaap STAM, 7 David BECKHAM, 8 Nicky BUTT, 20 Ole Gunnar SOLSKJAER, 18 Paul SCHOLES, 11 Ryan GIGGS **Substitutes:** 10 Teddy SHERINGHAM (18) 75, 12 Phil NEVILLE , 19 Dwight YORKE (20) h-t, 25 Quinton FORTUNE, 26 Massimo TAIBI, 28 Danny HIGGINBOTHAM, 30 Ronnie WALLWORK

SE PALMEIRAS   1 MARCOS, 2 ARCE, 3 JUNIOR BAIANO, 4 ROQUE JUNIOR, 5 SAMPAIO, 6 JUNIOR, 7 PAULO NUNES, 15 GALEANO, 20 Faustino ASPRILLA, 10 ALEX, 11 ZINHO **Substitutes:** : 8 ROGERIO, 9 OSEAS (20) 56, 13 TIAGO, 17 EVAIR (15) 54, 18 CLEBER, 19 EULLER (7) 77, 21 SERGIO

v AUSTRALIA (MCG, Melbourne) • Attendance: 70,000 • Won: 2-0

Bosnich • Neville P. • Irwin • May • Berg • Wilson • Greening • **Butt** • Yorke • Sheringham • **Blomqvist**

Substitutes: Stam (for May) • van der Gouw • Cruyff (for Blomqvist) • Cole • Giggs (for Greening) • Brown (for Berg) • Curtis (for Irwin) • Clegg (for Wilson) • Solskjaer

v AUSTRALIA (Stadium Australia, Sydney) • Attendance: 78,032 • Won: 1-0

Bosnich • Neville P. • Irwin • Wilson • Berg • Stam • Cruyff • Butt • Cole • **Yorke** • Giggs

Substitutes: Solskjaer (for Wilson) • van der Gouw (for Bosnich) • Greening (for Cruyff) • Sheringham (for Cole) • May Clegg (for Neville P.) • Blomqvist • Curtis • Brown

v SHENHUA (Shanghai, China) • Attendance: 80,000 • Won: 2-0

van der Gouw • Curtis • Irwin • Wilson • Brown • Stam • Greening • Butt • Cole • **Solskjaer** • Blomqvist

*Substitutes: Neville P. (for Butt) • Bosnich (for van der Gouw) • Yorke (for Wilson) • **Sheringham** (for Cole) • Berg May (for Stam) • Cruyff (for Greening) • Clegg (for Irwin)*

v SOUTH CHINA (Hong Kong, China) • Attendance: 40,000 • Won: 2-0

Bosnich • Brown • Irwin • Neville P. • Berg • Stam • Cruyff • Yorke • **Cole** • **Sheringham** • Blomqvist

Substitutes: May (for Stam) • Wilson • Greening (for Blomqvist) • Curtis (for Irwin) • Clegg (for Berg)

OMAGH MEMORIAL FUND

v OMAGH TOWN (away) • Attendance: 7,000 • Won: 9-0

Culkin • **Clegg 2** • Irwin • May • Neville G. • Keane • Greening • Wilson • **Cole 2** • **Sheringham 4** • Chadwick • **Nixon (o.g.)**

Substitutes: Curtis • Notman (for Wilson) • Healy (for Cole) • Stewart (for Chadwick) • Wellens (for Greening) • Ford (for Neville G.) • O'Shea (for May)

OFFICIAL OPENING OF JJB STADIUM

v WIGAN ATHLETIC (away) • Attendance: 15,000 • Won: 2-0

van der Gouw • Neville P. • Curtis • May • Berg • **Scholes** • Beckham • Butt • **Solskjaer** • Yorke • Cruyff

Substitutes: Clegg (for Neville P.) • Bosnich • Healy (for Butt) • Ford • Wellens • O'Shea (for May) • Stewart • Chadwick • Notman

ALEX FERGUSON TESTIMONIAL

v REST OF THE WORLD XI (home) • Attendance: 54,842 • Lost: 2-4

van der Gouw • Neville P. • Silvestre • Solskjaer • Berg • Stam • Yorke • Butt • Cole • Sheringham • Giggs

Substitutes: Scholes (for Solskjaer) • Bosnich • Cruyff (for Giggs) • Greening (for Cruyff) • Irwin (for Berg) • Curtis (for Stam) • Clegg (for Neville P.)

FABIEN BARTHEZ

Position: goalkeeper
Born: Lavelanet, France, 28 June 1971
Height: 180 cms
Weight: 80 kgs
Transferred: from AS Monaco, 21 May 2000
Other clubs: Toulouse, Olympique Marseille, AS Monaco
Full International: France

Several goalkeepers have tried and failed to fill the mammoth void left by the departure of Peter Schmeichel, but Sir Alex Ferguson believes that he has found the right man at last. Fabien, who helped Marseille to lift the European Cup in 1993 and was a World Cup winner with France in 1998, is agile, courageous and strong. Crucially, too, the £7.8 million recruit from Monaco is a bubbly, forceful character who inspires confidence among fellow defenders.

DAVID BECKHAM

Position: midfielder
Born: Leytonstone, 2 May 1975
Height: 183 cms
Weight: 76 kgs
Signed trainee: 8 July 1991
Signed professional: 23 January 1993
Other club: Preston North End (loan)

Senior United debut: 23 September 1992 v Brighton at the Goldstone Ground (League Cup, substitute for Andrei Kanchelskis)

United record: League: 158 (17) games, 36 goals; FA Cup: 16 (2) games, 5 goals; League Cup: 5 (2) games, 0 goals; Europe: 45 (1) games, 7 goals; Club World Championship: 1 (1) games, 0 goals

Total: 225 (22) games, 48 goals

Full international: England

In 1999/2000: David's crosses from the right flank marked him out as the side's chief provider of goals, while the variety of his distribution became better as the season wore on.

HENNING BERG

Position: defender
Born: Eidsvoll, Norway, 1 September 1969
Height: 183 cms
Weight: 78 kgs
Transferred: from Blackburn Rovers, 11 August 1997
Other clubs: Valerengen IF, Lillestrom, Blackburn Rovers
Senior United debut: 13 August 1997 v Southampton at Old
Trafford (League, substitute for Ronny Johnsen)
United record: League: 49 (16) games, 2 goals; FA Cup: 7 games, 0 goals; League Cup: 3
games, 0 goals; Europe: 19 (4) games, 1 goal; Club World Championship: 1 game, 0 goals
Total: 79 (20) games, 3 goals
Full international: Norway
In 1999/2000: with Ronny Johnsen injured, Henning started the campaign in accomplished
fashion as Jaap Stam's central defensive partner, but lost his place following an uneasy
display against Fiorentina. For a while thereafter he languished in the shadow of newcomer
Mikael Silvestre, but underlined his worth by re-emerging impressively in the spring.

JESPER BLOMQVIST

Position: forward
Born: Tavelsjo, Sweden, 5 February 1974
Height: 175 cms
Weight: 71 kgs
Transferred: from Parma, 21 July 1998
Other clubs: Tavelsjo IK, Umea, IFK Gothenburg, AC Milan,
Parma
Senior United debut: 9 September 1998 v Charlton Athletic at Old Trafford (League)
United record: League: 20 (5) games, 1 goal; FA Cup: 3 (2) games, 0 goals; League Cup: 0
(1) games, 0 goals; Europe: 6 (1) games, 0 goals
Total: 29 (9) games, 1 goal
Full International: Sweden
In 1999/2000: endured a season of overwhelming frustration. After recovering from the foot
problem which hampered his effectiveness in the European Cup Final, Jesper showed lively
form on the summer tour, only to suffer a knee injury which sidelined him for the whole of
campaign. When recovered, the Swede will face a stiff challenge for left-flank opportunities.

MARK BOSNICH

Position: goalkeeper
Born: Sydney, Australia, 13 January 1972
Height: 188 cms
Weight: 92 kgs
Transferred: from Aston Villa, 2 June 1999
Other clubs: Croatia Sydney, Manchester United, Aston Villa
Senior United debut: 30 April 1990 v Wimbledon at Old Trafford
(League)/8 August 1999 v Everton at Goodison Park (League)
United record: League: 26 games, 0 goals; FA Cup: 0 games, 0 goals; League Cup: 1 game, 0 goals; Europe: 7 games, 0 goals; Club World Championship: 2 games, 0 goals
Total: 36 games, 0 goals
Full international: Australia
In 1999/2000: exuded confidence as he faced the task of replacing Peter Schmeichel, but experienced mixed fortunes. Mark confirmed his reputation as a magnificent shot-stopper, notably in Madrid, but rarely commanded his area in the manner of his predecessor. Determined to overcome inevitable competition for his jersey in the 2000/01 season.

WES BROWN

Position: defender
Born: Manchester, 13 October 1979
Height: 185 cms
Weight: 87 kgs
Signed trainee: 8 July 1996
Signed professional: 4 November 1996
Senior United debut: 4 May 1998 v Leeds United at Old Trafford
(League, substitute for David May)
United record: League: 12 (4) games, 0 goals; FA Cup: 2 games, 0 goals; League Cup: 0 (1) games, 0 goals; Europe: 3 (1) games, 0 goals
Total: 17 (6) games, 0 goals
Full international: England
In 1999/2000: his campaign ended before it had begun when he severely damaged a knee in pre-season training. This was particularly vexing as the cool, skilful young defender had made such prodigious progress during 1998/99, winning a full England cap in the process. However, hopes were high that he would make a full recovery in time for 2000/01.

NICKY BUTT

Position: midfielder
Born: Manchester, 21 January 1975
Height: 178 cms
Weight: 75 kgs
Signed trainee: 8 July 1991
Signed professional: 23 January 1993
Senior United debut: 21 November 1992 v Oldham Athletic at Old Trafford (League, substitute for Paul Ince)
United record: League: 140 (38) games, 16 goals; FA Cup: 16 (2) games, 1 goal; League Cup: 5 games, 0 goals; Europe: 30 (8) games, 1 goals; Club World Championship: 2 games, 1 goal
Total: 193 (48 games), 19 goals
Full international: England
In 1999/2000: an absolute nugget, particularly if Roy Keane is unavailable. Buzzing tirelessly to all corners of the pitch and invariably doing the simple things well, the flinty Mancunian offers priceless near-metronomic consistency. As a bonus, sometimes he surprises opponents and fans alike with a sudden shaft of delicacy. Every squad needs a Nicky Butt.

LUKE CHADWICK

Position: forward
Born: Cambridge, 18 November 1980
Height: 180 cms
Weight: 73 kgs
Signed trainee: 30 June 1997
Signed professional: 5 February 1999
Other club: Royal Antwerp (loan)
Senior United debut: 13 October 1999 v Aston Villa at Villa Park (League Cup)
United record: League: 0 games, 0 goals; FA Cup: 0 games, 0 goals; League Cup: 1 game, 0 goals; Europe: 0 games, 0 goals
Total: 1 game, 0 goals
In 1999/2000: didn't qualify for a championship medal with United, but pocketed a title gong of his own, having helped Royal Antwerp to lift the Belgian Second Division crown during a fruitful springtime loan spell. The effervescent right-sided attacker, who was on Arsenal's books as a schoolboy, has also excelled at England under-21 level and is regarded as an exciting prospect.

MICHAEL CLEGG

Position: defender
Born: Ashton-under-Lyne, 3 July 1977
Height: 173 cms
Weight: 74 kgs
Signed trainee: 5 July 1993
Signed professional: 1 July 1995
Other clubs: Ipswich Town (loan), Wigan Athletic (loan) Senior

United debut: 23 November 1996 v Middlesbrough at Riverside Stadium (League)
United record: League: 4 (5) games, 0 goals; FA Cup: 3 (1) games, 0 goals; League Cup: 5 games, 0 goals; Europe: 1 (2) games, 14 goals
Total: 13 (8) games, 0 goals
In 1999/2000: let no one down on his limited senior opportunities with the Reds, but has been unable to mount a concerted challenge for a regular berth. Three years on from his debut, that must be disappointing for the cool, competent full-back, who spent loan stints with Ipswich Town and Wigan Athletic during the second half of the season.

ANDY COLE

Position: forward
Born: Nottingham, 15 October 1971
Height: 180 cms
Weight: 77 kgs
Transferred: from Newcastle United, 12 January 1995
Other clubs: Arsenal, Fulham (loan), Bristol City, Newcastle United

Senior United debut: 22 January 1995 v Blackburn Rovers at Old Trafford (League)
United record: League: 139 (26) games, 80 goals; FA Cup: 18 (2) games, 9 goals; League Cup: 2 games, 0 goals; Europe: 32 (4) games, 14 goals; Club World Championship: 2 games, 0 goals
Total: 193 (32) games, 103 goals
Full international: England
In 1999/2000: since arriving at Old Trafford his all-round game has improved out of all recognition, and he has triumphed over earlier vilification. Indeed, some of his recent strikes have provoked comparison with those of Eric Cantona. Enough said.

NICK CULKIN

Position: goalkeeper
Born: York, 6 July 1978
Height: 188 cms
Weight: 87 kgs
Transferred: from York City, 25 September 1995
Other club: York City, Hull City (loan)
Senior United debut: 22 August 1999 v Arsenal at Highbury
(League, substitute for Raimond van der Gouw)
United record: League: 0 (1) games, 0 goals; FA Cup: 0 games, 0 goals; League Cup: 0 games, 0 goals; Europe: 0 games, 0 goals
Total: 0 (1) games, 0 goals
In 1999/2000: saw a mere ten seconds of senior service and touched the ball once, a free-kick to clear his lines after coming on for the injured Raimond van der Gouw at Highbury. Did well during a mid-term interlude on loan with Hull City, though that stint cost him the chance of a trip to Rio de Janeiro for the Club World Championship.

QUINTON FORTUNE

Position: forward or midfielder
Born: Cape Town, South Africa, 21 May 1977
Height: 175 cms
Weight: 74 kgs
Transferred: from Atletico Madrid, 21 August 1999
Other club: Atletico Madrid
Senior United debut: 30 August 1999 v Newcastle United at Old Trafford (League, substitute for Paul Scholes)
United record: League: 4 (2) games, 2 goals; FA Cup: 0 games, 0 goals; League Cup: 0 games, 0 goals; Europe: 1 (3) games, 0 goals; Club World Championship: 1 (1) games, 2 goals
Total: 6 (6) games, 4 goals
Full international: South Africa
In 1999/2000: can be proud of his progress in his first Premiership campaign. Though a central midfielder for South Africa and versatile enough to double as a striker or even full-back, it has been as left-flank cover for Ryan Giggs that Quinton has excelled as a Red Devil. Quick and skilful, a good crosser and a confident finisher, he is a promising prospect.

RYAN GIGGS

Position: forward
Born: Cardiff, 29 November 1973
Height: 180 cms
Weight: 70 kgs
Signed trainee: 9 July 1990
Signed professional: 29 November 1990
Senior United debut: 2 March 1991 v Everton at Old Trafford
(League, substitute for Denis Irwin)
United record: League: 267 (23) games, 59 goals; FA Cup: 34 (3) games, 7 goals; League Cup: 17 (4) games, 6 goals; Europe: 42 (1) games, 11 goals; Club World Championship: 2 games, 0 goals
Total: 362 (31) games, 83 goals
Full international: Wales
In 1999/2000: Ryan was virtually unplayable at times, shredding defences with his direct running and his mesmeric ability to nip past opponents while retaining perfect control of the ball. Now poised on the threshold of his prime, he could get even better!

JONATHAN GREENING

Position: forward or midfielder
Born: Scarborough, 2 January 1979
Height: 183 cms
Weight: 76 kgs
Transferred: from York City, 24 March 1998
Other club: York City
Senior United debut: 28 October 1998 v Bury at Old Trafford
(League Cup)
United record: League: 1 (6) games, 0 goals; FA Cup: 0 (1) games, 0 goals; League Cup: 4 games, 0 goals; Europe: 1 (1) games, 0 goals; Club World Championship: 1 game, 0 goals
Total: 7 (8) games, 0 goals
In 1999/2000: continued to hint at a hugely productive future, but was never afforded the settled first-team sequence needed to prove himself. An exciting, long-striding, attacking midfielder, Jonathan revels in wrong-footing defenders with a beguiling body-swerve. The former York City starlet also packs a savage shot and on several occasions he was unlucky not to break his senior goal duck.

DAVID HEALY

Position: forward
Born: Downpatrick, Northern Ireland, 5 August 1979
Height: 173 cms
Weight: 70 kgs
Signed trainee: 8 July 1996
Signed professional: 24 November 1997
Other club: Port Vale (loan)

Senior United debut: 13 October 1999 v Aston Villa at Villa Park (substitute for Danny Higginbotham)
United record: League 0 games, 0 goals; FA Cup: 0 games, 0 goals; League Cup: 0 (1) games, 0 goals; Europe: 0 games, 0 goals
Total: 0 (1) games, 0 goals
Full international: Northern Ireland
In 1999/2000: enjoyed international prominence with Northern Ireland, scoring three goals in his first two outings. David also made his senior entrance for United before impressing on loan with Port Vale. Fast, skilful and with a predatory eye for goal, he is one to watch.

DANNY HIGGINBOTHAM

Position: defender
Born: Manchester, 29 December 1978
Height: 185 cms
Weight: 79 kgs
Signed trainee: 10 July 1995
Signed professional: 1 July 1997
Other club: Royal Antwerp (loan)

Senior United debut: 10 May 1998 v Barnsley at Oakwell (League, substitute for Michael Clegg)
United record: League: 2 (2) games, 0 goals; FA Cup: 0 games, 0 goals; League Cup:1 game, 0 goals; Europe: 0 (1) games, 0 goals; Club World Championship: 1 game, 0 goals
Total: 4 (3) games, 0 goals
In 1999/2000: continued his development as one of the most self-possessed young defenders at the club. Tall and strong, Danny is blessed with assured ball control, he passes both imaginatively and accurately, and he is a smooth contributor to attacking moves. Profited immensely from his successful loan period with Royal Antwerp in 1998/99.

DENIS IRWIN

Position: defender
Born: Cork, 31 October 1965
Height: 173 cms
Weight: 68 kgs
Transferred: from Oldham Athletic, 8 June 1990
Other clubs: Leeds United, Oldham Athletic
Senior United debut: 25 August 1990 v Coventry City at Old Trafford (League)
United record: League: 326 (9) games, 22 goals; FA Cup: 41 (1) games, 7 goals; League Cup: 28 (3) games, 0 goals; Europe: 58 games, 2 goals; Club World Championship: 2 games, 0 goals
Total: 455 (13) games, 31 goals
Full international: Republic of Ireland
In 1999/2000: though he retired from the international scene, Denis remained the Red Devils' most reliable full-back and signed a new contract for 2000/01. That's good news for United's defence which would sorely miss his vast experience.

RONNY JOHNSEN

Position: defender or midfielder
Born: Sandefjord, Norway, 10 June 1969
Height: 190 cms
Weight: 85 kgs
Transferred: from Besiktas, 10 July 1996
Other clubs: Stokke, EIK-Tonsberg, Lyn Oslo, Lillestrom, Besiktas
Senior United debut: 17 August 1996 v Wimbledon at Selhurst Park (League, substitute for Nicky Butt)
United record: League: 65 (13) games, 5 goals; FA Cup: 8 (2) games, 1 goal; League Cup: 2 games, 0 goals; Europe: 20 (2) games, 0 goals
Total: 95 (17) games, 6 goals
Full international: Norway
In 1999/2000: after playing through pain towards the climax of the treble-winning campaign, the versatile Norwegian was forced to undergo operations on both his knees. The upshot was that he didn't kick a ball for the first team until the April afternoon at Southampton when the title was clinched. His speed and decisiveness at the back will be welcome as the Reds set out to defend their crown.

ROY KEANE

Position: midfielder
Born: Cork, 10 August 1971
Height: 180 cms
Weight: 74 kgs
Transferred: from Nottingham Forest, 19 July 1993
Other clubs: Cobh Ramblers, Nottingham Forest
Senior United debut: 15 August 1993 v Norwich City at Carrow Road (League)
United record: League: 177 (8) games, 24 goals; FA Cup: 29 (1) games, 1 goal; League Cup: 9 (2) games, 0 goals; Europe: 40 games, 12 goals; Club World Championship: 2 games, 0 goals
Total: 257 (11) games, 37 goals
Full international: Republic of Ireland
In 1999/2000: the skipper attained new heights of excellence, being rewarded with both major Player of the Year awards. The mid-season announcement that he had signed a new contract was greeted with the euphoria usually reserved for star signings. Massively influential in every area of play, Roy is one of United's all-time greats.

DAVID MAY

Position: defender
Born: Oldham, 24 June 1970
Height: 183 cms
Weight: 85 kgs
Transferred: from Blackburn Rovers, 1 July 1994
Other club: Blackburn Rovers, Huddersfield Town (loan)
Senior United debut: 20 August 1994 v Queen's Park Rangers at Old Trafford (League)
United record: League: 65 (15) games, 6 goals; FA Cup: 6 games, 0 goals; League Cup: 7 games, 1 goal; Europe: 12 (1) games, 1 goal
Total: 90 (16) games, 8 goals
In 1999/2000: endured his most infuriating Old Trafford campaign. His hopes were high after an outstanding performance in the 1999 FA Cup Final, but injury ruled David out until the autumn. Further fitness problems disrupted a loan stint at Huddersfield and no sooner had he recovered again than a ruptured achilles tendon jeopardised his prospects for 2000/01.

GARY NEVILLE

Position: defender
Born: Bury, 18 February 1975
Height: 180 cms
Weight: 78 kgs
Signed trainee: 8 July 1991
Signed professional: 23 January 1993
Senior United debut: 16 September 1992 v Torpedo Moscow at Old Trafford (UEFA Cup, substitute for Lee Martin)
United record: League: 167 (4) games, 2 goals; FA Cup: 21 (3) games, 0 goals; League Cup: 4 (1) games, 0 goals; Europe: 41 (3) games, 0 goals; Club World Championship: 2 games, 0 goals
Total: 235 (10) games, 2 goals
Full international: England
In 1999/2000: missed the start of the season through injury, then took time to find his form. Two uncharacteristic mistakes against Vasco da Gama in Rio dented his confidence, but soon one of the most reliable right-backs in the British game was back in the groove. A canny defensive organiser, Gary gets forward, too, meshing with David Beckham on the right flank.

PHIL NEVILLE

Position: defender
Born: Bury, 21 January 1977
Height: 180 cms
Weight: 76 kgs
Signed trainee: 5 July 1993
Signed professional: 1 June 1994
Senior United debut: 28 January 1995 v Wrexham at Old Trafford (FA Cup)
United record: League: 105 (26) games, 1 goal; FA Cup: 14 (4) games, 0 goals; League Cup: 5 (1) games, 0 goals; Europe: 18 (9) games, 1 goal; Club World Championship: 2 (1) games, 0 goals
Total: 144 (41) games, 2 goals
Full international: England
In 1999/2000: started fewer games than he would have liked, particularly during the second half of the campaign, but he remains an immensely valuable squad member. Phil is naturally right-footed but usually he featured at left-back. When Denis Irwin eventually retires, Neville Jnr seems a likely candidate to replace the evergreen Irishman.

ALEX NOTMAN

Position: forward
Born: Edinburgh, 10 December 1979
Height: 170 cms
Weight: 68 kgs
Signed trainee: 10 December 1995
Signed professional: 17 December 1996
Other clubs: Aberdeen (loan), Sheffield United (loan)

Senior United debut: 2 December 1998 v Tottenham Hotspur at White Hart Lane (League Cup, substitute for Nicky Butt)
United record: League: 0 games, 0 goals; FA Cup: 0 games, 0 goals; League Cup: 0 (1) games, 0 goals; Europe: 0 games, 0 goals
Total: 0 (1) games, 0 goals
In 1999/2000: Alex's most notable contribution to the United cause was a four-goal spree for the reserves at Sheffield Wednesday, but he received no senior opportunities as a Red Devil. Away from Old Trafford, the diminutive Scottish marksman netted three times in a dozen First Division outings on loan with Sheffield United.

JOHN O'SHEA

Position: defender
Born: Waterford, Republic of Ireland, 30 April 1981
Height: 190 cms
Weight: 81 kgs
Signed professional: 3 August 1998
Other club: Bournemouth (loan)
Senior United debut: 13 October 1999 v Aston Villa at Villa Park (League Cup)
United record: League: 0 games, 0 goals; FA Cup: 0 games, 0 goals; League Cup: 1 game, 0 goals; Europe: 0 games 0 goals
Total: 1 game, 0 goals
In 1999/2000: distinguished himself during ten League outings on loan at Bournemouth, now faces a battle royal if he is to make a lasting mark at Old Trafford. However, if his composed performance in an inexperienced side at Villa Park is anything to go by, the tall, young centre-half from across the Irish Sea has a realistic chance of making the grade.

PAUL RACHUBKA

Position: goalkeeper
Born: San Luis Obispo, California, 21 May 1981
Height: 185 cms
Weight: 83 kgs
Signed trainee: 30 June 1997
Signed professional: 1 July 1999
Senior United debut: 11 January 2000 v South Melbourne at the
Maracana Stadium (Club World Championship, substitute for Raimond van der Gouw)
United record: League: 0 games, 0 goals; FA Cup: 0 games, 0 goals; League Cup: 0 games, 0
goals, Europe: 0 games, 0 goals; Club World Championship: 0 (1) games, 0 goals
Total: 0 (1) games, 0 goals
In 1999/2000: the agile, supple young six-footer tasted senior action for the first time in no
less daunting a venue than the Maracana. True, it was only for seven minutes and against
moderate opposition, but the cool Californian was not overawed by the occasion, which
augurs well for his long-term Old Trafford ambitions.

PAUL SCHOLES

Position: midfielder or forward
Born: Salford, 16 November 1974
Height: 170 cms
Weight: 70 kgs
Signed trainee: 8 July 1991
Signed professional: 23 January 1993
Senior United debut: 21 September 1994 v Port Vale at Vale Park
(League Cup)
United record: League: 117 (43) games, 41 goals; FA Cup: 8 (7) games, 4 goals; League Cup:
6 (2) games, 5 goals; Europe: 28 (10) games, 10 goals
Total: 159 (62) games, 60 goals
Full international: England
In 1999/2000: further enhanced his reputation as one of the most complete footballers in
the country. There is no more precise or visionary passer at the club, his commitment is
total and he specialises in memorable goals, his range of strikes running the whole gamut
from subtle flick to savage volley. A modest fellow who prefers the quiet life to the media
glare, Paul is a star whether he likes it or not.

TEDDY SHERINGHAM

Position: forward
Born: Highams Park, London, 2 April 1966
Height: 183 cms
Weight: 80 kgs
Transferred: from Tottenham Hotspur, 27 June 1997
Other clubs: Millwall, Aldershot (loan), Djurgaarden (loan), Nottingham Forest, Tottenham Hotspur
Senior United debut: 10 August 1997 v Tottenham Hotspur at White Hart Lane (League)
United record: League: 50 (25) games, 16 goals; FA Cup: 3 (4) games, 4 goals; League Cup: 1 game, 1 goal; Europe: 12 (8) games, 4 goals; Club World Championship: 0 (2) games, 0 goals
Total: 66 (39) games, 25 goals
Full international: England
In 1999/2000: spent too much time on the bench for his liking, but remains an effective striking option. A perceptive footballer, he often brings the best out of colleagues with his intelligent instant lay-offs and he represents a more potent aerial menace than any of his fellow front-runners. Teddy signed a new United contract just after the end of the season.

MIKAEL SILVESTRE

Position: defender
Born: Chambray-Les-Tours, France, 9 August 1977
Height: 183 cms
Weight: 83 kgs
Transferred: from Internazionale, 10 September 1999
Other clubs: Rennes, Internazionale
United record: League: 30 (1) games, 0 goals; FA Cup: 0 games, 0 goals; League Cup: 0 games, 0 goals; Europe: 2 (2) games, 0 goals; Club World Championship: 2 games, 0 goals
Total: 34 (3) games, 0 goals
In 1999/2000: made a foot-perfect start at left-back, then underlined his credentials as a pacy, skilful and intelligent utility defender as the season wore on. However, when switched to his preferred central role, Mikael looked uneasy at times, but he is young and gifted, and his undoubted quality can be expected to prevail in the long term.

OLE GUNNAR SOLSKJAER

Position: forward
Born: Kristiansund, Norway, 26 February 1973
Height: 178 cms
Weight: 75 kgs
Transferred: from Molde, 29 July 1996
Other clubs: Clausenengen FK, Molde
Senior United debut: 25 August 1996 v Blackburn Rovers at Old Trafford (League, substitute for David May)
United record: League: 64 (38) games, 48 goals; FA Cup: 5 (8) games, 3 goals; League Cup: 4 games, 3 goals; Europe: 16 (17) games, 7 goals; Club World Championship: 2 (1) games, 0 goals
Total: 91 (64) games, 61 goals
Full international: Norway
In 1999/2000: Ole's form was matched only by his patience as he contributed massively to United's continued success, but without cementing the regular starting place. Some of his goals – notably those at home to Liverpool and away to Bordeaux – offered supreme examples of predatory marksmanship. The Norwegian is a gem to be cherished.

JAAP STAM

Position: defender
Born: Kampen, Holland, 17 July 1972
Height: 190 cms
Weight: 95 kgs
Transferred: from PSV Eindhoven, 1 July 1998
Other clubs: Dos Kampen, FC Zwolle, Cambuur Leeuwarden, Willem II, PSV Eindhoven
Senior United debut: 12 August 1998 v LKS Lodz at old Trafford (Champions League)
United record: League: 63 games, 1 goal; FA Cup: 6 (1) games, 0 goals; League Cup: 0 games, 0 goals; Europe: 26 games, 0 goals; Club World Championship: 2 games, 0 goals
Total: 97 (1) games, 1 goal
Full international: Holland
In 1999/2000: cut a Herculean figure at the heart of United's rearguard, oozing authority and reinforcing his status as one of the world's top stoppers. However, there were moments – mercifully few – when even the mighty Dutchman seemed vulnerable, an understandable consequence of the unsettled goalkeeping situation. Proved ideal to deputise as skipper when Roy Keane was absent.

MASSIMO TAIBI

Position: goalkeeper
Born: Palermo, Italy, 18 February 1970
Height: 190 cms
Weight: 92 kgs
Transferred: from Venezia, 31 August 1999
Other clubs: Licata, Trento, AC Milan (twice), Como, Piacenza, Venezia, Reggina (loan)
Senior United debut: 11 September 1999 v Liverpool at Anfield (League)
United record: League: 4 games, 0 goals; FA Cup: 0 games, 0 goals; League Cup: 0 games, 0 goals; Europe: 0 games, 0 goals
Total: 4 games, 0 goals
In 1999/2000: after being hailed as man of the match for his brave and acrobatic debut display at Anfield, Massimo suffered a torrid Premiership interlude which terminated in a loan transfer to Reggina. The big, self-assured Italian was not accustomed to the high incidence of crosses in the English game, but he promised to return and fight for his place in 2000/01.

RAIMOND VAN DER GOUW

Position: goalkeeper
Born: Oldenzaal, Holland, 24 March 1963
Height: 190 cms
Weight: 87 kgs
Transferred: from Vitesse Arnhem, 1 July 1996
Other clubs: Go Ahead Eagles, Vitesse Arnhem
Senior United debut: 21 September 1996 v Aston Villa at Villa Park (League)
United record: League: 21 (5) games, 0 goals; FA Cup: 0 games, 0 goals; League Cup: 6 games, 0 goals; Europe: 9 games, 0 goals; Club World Championship: 1 game, 0 goals **Total:** 37 (5) games, 0 goals
In 1999/2000: apart from one high-profile error in Bordeaux, Raimond was a model of competence and consistency, leaving the fans to rue the fact that he was not a decade younger. An admirably reliable gatherer of crosses and an assured kicker, he was acrobatic at need and unfailingly courageous, exuding an aura of solidity and composure which was often lacking in his absence.

RONNIE WALLWORK

Position: defender or midfielder
Born: Manchester, 10 September 1977
Height: 178 cms
Weight: 83 kgs
Signed trainee: 11 July 1994
Signed professional: 17 March 1995
Other clubs: Carlisle United (loan), Stockport County (loan), Royal Antwerp (loan)
Senior United debut: 25 October 1997 v Barnsley at Old Trafford (League, substitute for Gary Pallister)
United record: League: 0 (6) games, 0 goals; FA Cup: 0 games, 0 goals; League Cup: 1 (1) games, 0 goals; Europe: 0 games, 0 goals; Club World Championship: 1 game, 0 goals
Total: 2 (7) games, 0 goals
In 1999/2000: spent the early part of the season under threat of a life ban, following an incident while on loan at Royal Antwerp in 1999/2000. Happily that cloud lifted and Ronnie confirmed himself a hugely promising central defender. In addition, when called on as a substitute for Nicky Butt at Anfield, he shone as an industrious and skilful midfielder.

MARK WILSON

Position: midfielder
Born: Scunthorpe, 9 February 1979
Height: 183 cms
Weight: 79 kgs
Signed trainee: 10 July 1995
Signed professional: 9 February 1996
Other club: Wrexham (loan)
Senior United debut: 21 October 1998 v Brondby at the Parken Stadium (Champions League, substitute for Dwight Yorke)
United record: League: 1 (2) games, 0 goals; FA Cup: 0 games, 0 goals; League Cup: 2 games, 0 goals; Europe: 2 (2) games, 0 goals; Club World Championship: 1 game, 0 goals
Total: 6 (4) games, 0 goals
In 1999/2000: ended on a high as the reserves' Player of the Season, but didn't quite justify forecasts that he would break through at senior level. Other clubs expressed interest in signing Mark before the transfer deadline, but no deal was done and there is still time for the tall, Scunthorpe-born midfielder to achieve an impact at Old Trafford.

DWIGHT YORKE

Position: forward
Born: Canaan, Tobago, 3 November 1971
Height: 178 cms
Weight: 77 kgs
Transferred: from Aston Villa, 28 August 1998
Other club: Aston Villa
Senior United debut: 22 August 1998 v West Ham United at Upton Park (League)

United record: League: 61 (3) games, 38 goals; FA Cup: 5 (3) games, 3 goals; League Cup: 0 games, 0 goals; Europe: 20 (2) games, 10 goals; Club World Championship: 2 games, 1 goal
Total: 88 (8) games, 52 goals
Full international: Trinidad and Tobago
In 1999/2000: became the first man since Brian McClair in 1988 to score 20 League goals in a season for United. However, there were periods when his form and confidence seemed to desert him, perhaps an inevitable consequence of his phenomenally successful first term as a Red Devil. An endlessly inventive front runner, Dwight can double as a midfield playmaker, as he showed to telling effect at Watford for example.

YOUNG PROFESSIONALS

GEORGE CLEGG
Position: forward
Birthdate: 16 November 1980
Birthplace: Manchester
Height: 178 cms
Weight: 75 kgs
Signed trainee: 30 June 1997
Signed professional: 1 July 1999

CRAIG COATES
Position: forward
Birthdate: 26 October 1982
Birthplace: Dryburn
Height: 170 cms
Weight: 68 kgs
Signed trainee: 5 July 1999
Signed professional: 26 October 1999

STEPHEN COSGROVE
Position: midfield
Birthdate: 29 December 1980
Birthplace: Glasgow
Height: 175 cms
Weight: 66 kgs
Signed trainee: 30 June 1997
Signed professional: 1 July 1998

JIMMY DAVIS
Position: forward
Birthdate: 6 February 1982
Birthplace: Bromsgrove
Height: 173 cms
Weight: 72 kgs
Signed trainee: 6 July 1999
Signed professional: 31 August 1999

ASHLEY DODD
Position: midfield
Birthdate: 7 January 1982
Birthplace: Stafford
Height: 178 cms
Weight: 64 kgs
Signed trainee: 6 July 1998
Signed professional: 31 August 1999

BOJAN DJORDJIC
Position: midfield
Birthdate: 6 February 1982
Birthplace: Belgrade, Yugoslavia
Height: 178 cms
Weight: 70 kgs
Signed professional: 17 February 1999
Previous Club: Brommapojkarna IF (Sweden)

WAYNE EVANS
Position: midfield
Birthdate: 23 October 1980
Birthplace: Carmarthen
Height: 176 cms
Weight: 61 kgs
Signed trainee: 30 June 1997
Signed professional: 21 November 1997

KIRK HILTON
Position: defender
Birthdate: 2 April 1981
Birthplace: Flixton
Height: 170 cms
Weight: 64 kgs
Signed trainee: 30 June 1997
Signed professional: 1 July 1999

RHODRI JONES
Position: defender
Birthdate: 19 January 1982
Birthplace: Cardiff
Height: 183 cms
Weight: 78 kgs
Signed trainee: 6 July 1998
Signed professional: 31 August 1999

MARK LYNCH
Position: defender
Birthdate: 2 September 1981
Birthplace: Manchester
Height: 180 cms
Weight: 71 kgs
Signed trainee: 6 July 1998
Signed professional: 31 August 1999

ALAN McDERMOTT
Position: defender
Birthdate: 22 January 1982
Birthplace: Dublin
Height: 185 cms
Weight: 73 kgs
Signed trainee: 6 July 1998
Signed professional: 22 January 1999

BEN MUIRHEAD
Position: forward
Birthdate: 5 January 1983
Birthplace: Doncaster
Height: 175 cms
Weight: 66 kgs
Signed trainee: 5 July 1999
Signed professional: 5 January 2000

DANIEL NARDIELLO
Position: forward
Birthdate: 22 October 1982
Birthplace: Coventry
Height: 180 cms
Weight: 72 kgs
Signed trainee: 5 July 1999
Signed professional: 22 October 1999

LEE ROCHE
Position: defender
Birthdate: 28 October 1980
Birhtplace: Bolton
Height: 178 cms
Weight: 68 kgs
Signed trainee: 30 June 1997
Signed professional: 5 February 1999

MICHAEL ROSE
Position: defender
Birthdate: 28 July 1982
Birthplace: Salford
Height: 180 cms
Weight: 70 kgs
Signed trainee: 6 July 1998
Signed professional: 31 August 1999

MICHAEL STEWART
Position: midfield
Birthdate: 26 February 1981
Birthplace: Edinburgh
Height: 180 cms
Weight: 75 kgs
Signed trainee: 30 June 1997
Signed professional: 13 March 1998

GARETH STRANGE
Position: midfield
Birthdate: 3 October 1981
Birthplace: Bolton
Height: 175 cms
Weight: 66 kgs
Signed trainee: 6 July 1998
Signed professional: 3 October 1998

MARK STUDLEY
Position: defender
Birthdate: 27 December 1881
Birthplace: Manchester
Height: 168 cms
Weight: 64 kgs
Signed trainee: 6 July 1998
Signed professional: 31 August 1999

MAREK SZMID
Position: defender
Birthdate: 2 March 1982
Birthplace: Nuneaton
Height: 173 cms
Weight: 73 kgs
Signed trainee: 6 July 1998
Signed professional: 21 September 1999

PAUL TEATHER
Position: defender
Birthdate: 26 December 1977
Birthplace: Rotherham
Height: 183 cms
Weight: 76 kgs
Signed trainee: 11 July 1994
Signed professional: 29 December 1994

JOSHUA WALKER
Position: midfield
Birthdate: 20 December 1981
Birthplace: Birmingham
Height: 185 cms
Weight: 70 kgs
Signed trainee: 6 July 1998
Signed professional: 31 August 1999

DANNY WEBBER
Position: forward
Birthdate: 28 December 1981
Birthplace: Manchester
Height: 175 cms
Weight: 67 kgs
Signed trainee: 6 July 1998
Signed professional: 28 December 1998

MATTHEW WILLIAMS
Position: forward
Birthdate: 5 November 1982
Birthplace: St Asaph
Height: 173 cms
Weight: 62 kgs
Signed trainee: 5 July 1999
Signed professional: 26 January 2000

NEIL WOOD
Position: forward
Birthdate: 4 January 1983
Birthplace: Manchester
Height: 178 cms
Weight: 83 kgs
Signed trainee: 5 July 1999
Signed professional: 4 January 2000

PLAYER PROFILES

TRAINEE PROFESSIONALS 2000-2001

THIRD YEAR

Name	Position	Birthdate	Birthplace	Date Signed
Kevin GROGAN	midfield	15 November 1981	Dublin	6 July 1998

SECOND YEAR

Name	Position	Birthdate	Birthplace	Date Signed
Nick BAXTER	goalkeeper	25 March 1983	Bridlington	18 October 1999
Steven CLEGG	defender	16 April 1982	Ashton-under-Lyne	5 July 1999
David MORAN	goalkeeper	21 January 1983	Ballinasloe	5 July 1999
Danny PUGH	midfield	19 October 1982	Manchester	5 July 1999
John RANKIN	midfield	27 June 1983	Bellshill	5 July 1999
Gary SAMPSON	midfield	13 September 1982	Manchester	5 July 1999
Alan TATE	defender	2 September 1982	Easington	5 July 1999
Andrew TAYLOR	midfield	17 September 1982	Exeter	5 July 1999
Paul TIERNEY	midfield	15 September 1982	Salford	5 July 1999
Marc WHITEMAN	forward	1 October 1982	St Hellier	5 July 1999

FIRST YEAR

Name	Position	Birthdate	Birthplace	Date Signed
John COGGER	defender	12 September 1983	Waltham Forest	3 July 2000
Darren FLETCHER	midfield	1 February 1984	Edinburgh	3 July 2000
David FOX	midfield	13 December 1983	Stoke-on-Trent	3 July 2000
Colin HEATH	forward	31 December 1983	Chesterfield	3 July 2000
Chris HUMPHREYS	forward	22 September 1983	Manchester	3 July 2000
James JOWSEY	goalkeeper	24 November 1983	Scarborough	3 July 2000
Kalam MOONIARUCK	forward	22 November 1983	Yeovil	3 July 2000
Kris TAYLOR	midfield	12 January 1984	Stafford	3 July 2000

DEPARTURES 1999-2000

Name	Details	Date
Ben CLARK	declined trainee contract	July 1999
Jordi CRUYFF	free transfer	30 June 2000
John CURTIS	to Blackburn Rovers	31 May 2000
Ian FITZPATRICK	to Halifax Town	2 March 2000
Joshua HOWARD	free transfer	30 June 2000
Ryan FORD	to Notts County	31 January 2000
Allan MARSH	free transfer	30 June 2000
Erik MOLLOY	free transfer	30 June 2000
Erik NEVLAND	to Viking Stavanger	20 December 1999
Stephen ROSE	free transfer	30 June 2000
Dominic STUDLEY	free transfer	30 June 2000
*John THORRINGTON-SMITH	free transfer	30 June 1999
Michael TWISS	free transfer	30 June 2000
Richard WELLENS	to Blackpool	23 March 2000
Paul WHEATCROFT	free transfer	30 June 2000
*Jamie WOOD	free transfer	30 June 1999

* Carried over from 1998-1999

Jordi Cruyff

FA PREMIER RESERVE LEAGUE – NORTH

Mike Phelan's first season in charge of United's 2nd XI may not have ended with the FA Premier Reserve League trophy on the OldTrafford sideboard, but he would be the first to admit that his new job didn't suffer from a dearth of incident and variety.

Though he had to be content with sixth place finish to United's inaugural campaign in a new competition, he could nevertheless look back on a season which ultimately fell short of his own expectations, but on the credit side provided some excellent entertainment for the regulars at Gigg Lane.

For it was at their adopted home in the outer reaches of Greater Manchester that they produced the majority of their best performances in the 24-match league programme. They won seven of the fixtures played at Bury and embroidered several of them with a quality of football which was enough to keep the die-hards happy on bitterly cold and damp nights. And that was never more evident in defeating Newcastle United (3-0) and Bradford City (5-1) in the month of February.

Away from home there wasn't such a good picture to paint. There was the spectacular 5-2 win against Sheffield Wednesday at Hillsborough when Alex Notman helped himself to four goals and encouraging wins at Bolton, Bradford and Villa, but overall the reserves weren't at their best on the road.

Disappointment in the league was offset in good measure by success once again in the newly formatted Manchester Senior Cup. The long established competition, which was first contested by clubs from the Manchester region in the late 19th century, was staged as a mini-league again with United and Oldham Athletic finishing in the top two spots. That provided a repeat of the previous season's final, held again at Boundary Park, Latics' home ground, where a small but enthusiastic crowd – a far cry from the days when the Manchester Cup final could attract upwards of 25,000 – saw United retain the trophy for a second successive year.

names in bold indicate goalscorers

v SHEFFIELD WEDNESDAY (home, at Gigg Lane, Bury) • Won: 3-1 — Wednesday 18 August 1999

Culkin • Clegg • Curtis • Roche • O'Shea • Stewart • Wellens • **Twiss** • Greening **2 (1 pen)** • Notman • Chadwick.
Substitutes: Howard • Rose S. • Hilton (for O'Shea) • Davis (for Twiss)

v LEEDS UNITED (away) • Lost: 1-2 — Tuesday 7 September 1999

Culkin • Clegg • Hilton • Wallwork • Roche • Ford • Wellens • Wilson • Fortune • **Notman** • Twiss
Substitutes: Fitzpatrick (for Ford) • Rachubka • Howard • O'Shea • Stewart

v LIVERPOOL (away) • Drawn: 0-0 — Wednesday 15 September 1999

Bosnich • Roche • Curtis • Wallwork • O'Shea • Healy • Wellens • Cruyff • Greening • Notman • Chadwick
Substitutes: Nevland (for Notman) • Culkin • Twiss • Ford (for Wellens) • Hilton (for Curtis)

v ASTON VILLA (home, at Gigg Lane, Bury) • Lost: 2-3 — Thursday 23 September 1999

Culkin • Clegg • Curtis • Wallwork • O'Shea • Twiss • Wellens • **Healy** • **Greening (pen)** • Fortune • Chadwick
Substitutes: Notman (for Greening) • Rachubka • Roche • Ford • Nevland (for Fortune)

v SUNDERLAND (home, at Gigg Lane, Bury) • Drawn: 1-1 — Thursday 30 September 1999

Rachubka • Clegg • Higginbotham • Wallwork • Curtis • Healy • **Wilson** • Cruyff • Greening • Fortune • Chadwick
Substitutes: Notman (for Greening) • Roche • Ford • Nevland (for Fortune) • Twiss (for Healy)

v BOLTON WANDERERS (away) • Won: 2-0 — Thursday 21st October 1999

Culkin • Clegg • Higginbotham • May • Neville G. • Fortune • Wellens • Wilson • Greening • **Notman** • **Chadwick**
Substitutes: Curtis • Rachubka • Healy (for Fortune) • Twiss • O'Shea

v NEWCASTLE UNITED (away, at Kingston Park, Newcastle RUFC) • Lost: 0-2 — Tuesday 9 November 1999

Taibi • Clegg • Higginbotham • O'Shea • Roche • Cruyff • Wellens • Wilson • Greening • Healy • Twiss
Substitutes: Notman (for Healy) • Culkin • Rose S • Webber • Stewart

v EVERTON (home, at Gigg Lane, Bury) • Won: 4-2 — Saturday 13 November 1999

Culkin • Clegg • Higginbotham • Curtis • O'Shea • Fortune • Wellens • Wilson • **Healy 3** • Notman • **Greening**
Substitutes: Twiss (for Notman) • Marsh • Roche • Ford • Cosgrove

RESERVES

Tuesday 16 November 1999

v BLACKBURN ROVERS (home, at Gigg Lane, Bury) • Drawn: 1-1

van der Gouw • Clegg • Higginbotham • Curtis • Wallwork • Cruyff • Wilson • Butt • **Greening** • Sheringham • Fortune
Substitutes: Twiss • Culkin • Healy (for Fortune) • Roche • Wellens

Thursday 25 November 1999

v BRADFORD CITY (away) • Won: 3-1

Taibi • Clegg • Higginbotham • Roche • Wallwork • Stewart • Chadwick • Wilson • **Healy** • **Notman** • **Fortune**
Substitutes: Twiss • Culkin • Webber (for Chadwick) • Ford (for Stewart) • Rose S.

Wednesday 1 December 1999

v BARNSLEY (home, at Gigg Lane, Bury) • Won: 3-1

van der Gouw • Clegg • Rose S. • Roche • O'Shea • Stewart • **Chadwick** • Wilson • **Healy** • **Notman** • Twiss
Substitutes: Nevland (for Healy) • Culkin • Howard • Cosgrove

Monday 17 January 2000

v MIDDLESBROUGH (home, at Gigg Lane, Bury) • Lost: 1-2

van der Gouw • Clegg • Higginbotham • Roche • Wallwork • Ford • Wellens • Wilson • Healy • Notman • Twiss **(Cooper o.g.)**
Substitutes: Wheatcroft • Rachubka • Stewart (for Wellens) • Rose S. • Studley D. (for Notman)

Tuesday 25 January 2000

v EVERTON (away, at Autoquest Stadium, Widnes RLFC) • Lost: 1-2

Rachibka • Neville P. • Higginbotham • Berg • Wallwork • Cruyff, Fletcher • Wilson • Healy • **Solskjaer** • Scholes
Substitutes: Djordjic • Twiss (for Healy) • Stewart (for Wilson) • Wellens • Roche

Thursday 3 February 2000

v NEWCASTLE UNITED (home, at Gigg Lane, Bury) • Won: 3-0

van der Gouw • Clegg • Higginbotham • Roche • Wallwork • Fletcher • Wellens • Wilson • **Healy 2** • Greening • **Twiss**
Substitutes: Stewart (for Fletcher) • Rachubka • Rose S. • Webber (for Stewart) • Cosgrove

Wednesday 16 February 2000

v BLACKBURN ROVERS (away) • Lost: 1-2

Culkin • Roche • **Higginbotham** • Berg • Wallwork • Neville P. • Stewart • Wilson • Healy • Cruyff • Greening
Substitutes: Djordjic • Rachubka • Howard • Davis (for Healy) • Cosgrove

Wednesday 23 February 2000

v BRADFORD CITY (home, at Gigg Lane, Bury) • Won: 5-1

van der Gouw • Lynch • Higginbotham • Roche • Wallwork • Stewart • **Davis** • **Wilson** • **Fortune 2** • **Greening** • Djordjic
Substitutes: Teather (for Wilson) • Culkin • Howard • Fitzpatrick (for Djordjic) • Wheatcroft (for Davis)

names in bold indicate goalscorers

v BARNSLEY (away) • Lost: 1-2 — Thursday 2 March 2000

Culkin • Lynch • Higginbotham • Berg • Teather • Stewart • Evans • Wilson • Davis • **Greening** • Djordjic
Substitutes: Cosgrove • Rachubka • Studley M. (for Berg)

v SUNDERLAND (away) • Lost: 1-2 — Monday 27 March 2000

Culkin • Roche • Higginbotham • O'Shea • Wallwork • Stewart • Evans • **Wilson** • Greening • Davis • Twiss
Substitutes: Teather (for Evans) • Rachubka • Cosgrove • Rose S. • Studley D.

v SHEFFIELD WEDNESDAY (away) • Won: 5-2 — Thursday 30 March 2000

Culkin • Roche • Higginbotham • Teather • Wallwork • Stewart • Evans • Wilson • **Greening (pen)** • **Notman 4** • Twiss
Substitutes: Studley D. (for Stewart) • Cosgrove • Rose S. (for Roche) • Davis

v ASTON VILLA (away) • Won: 2-1 — Monday 3 April 2000

Culkin • Lynch • Higginbotham • Wallwork • Johnsen • Stewart • Evans • Twiss • Greening • **Notman** • Djordjic
(Bewers o.g.)
Substitutes: Studley D. • Rachubka • Cosgrove • Howard • Sampson (for Djordjic)

v BOLTON WANDERERS (home, at Gigg Lane, Bury) • Won: 4-0 — Wednesday 12 April 2000

van der Gouw • Roche • Higginbotham • Wallwork • Johnsen • Stewart • Evans • **Wilson** • **Greening 3 (1 pen)** • Notman • Twiss
Substitutes: Studley D. • Culkin • Cosgrove • Howard • O'Shea

v LIVERPOOL (home, at Gigg Lane, Bury) • Lost: 0-2 — Monday 17 April 2000

Culkin • Roche • Higginbotham • Wallwork • Johnsen • Fletcher • Evans • Wilson • Greening • Notman • Twiss
Substitutes: Wheatcroft • Rachubka • Rose S. • Cosgrove (for Twiss) • Howard (for Evans)

v MIDDLESBROUGH (away) • Lost: 0-2 — Wednesday 26 April 2000

Culkin • Roche • Higginbotham • Rose S. • O'Shea • Stewart • Evans • Wilson • Greening • Fortune • Twiss
Substitutes: Cosgrove (for Greening) • Howard • Tierney (for Evans) • Coates (for Fortune)

v LEEDS UNITED (home, at Gigg Lane, Bury) • Won: 2-0 — Thursday 4 May 2000

Culkin • Roche • Higginbotham • Wallwork • O'Shea • Stewart • **Davis** • Wilson • **Greening** • Notman • Djordjic
Substitutes: Fletcher (for Greening) • Rachubka • Evans • Cosgrove (for Wilson)

RESERVES

APPEARANCES

GOALSCORERS

Name	Appearances (as sub)	Name	Appearances (as sub)	Name	Goals (penalties)
WILSON • Mark	20	FORD • Ryan	2 (2)	GREENING • Jonathan	12
GREENING • Jonathan	19	TEATHER • Paul	2 (2)	NOTMAN • Alex	9
HIGGINBOTHAM • Danny	19	ROSE • Stephen	2 (1)	HEALY • David	8
WALLWORK • Ronnie	17	NEVILLE • Phil	2	WILSON • Mark	4
ROCHE • Lee	16	RACHUBKA • Paul	2	FORTUNE • Quinton	3
NOTMAN • Alex	13 (3)	TAIBI • Massimo	2	CHADWICK • Luke	2
TWISS • Michael	13 (3)	HILTON • Kirk	1 (2)	DAVIS • Jimmy	2
CULKIN • Nick	13	BOSNICH • Mark	1	TWISS • Michael	2
STEWART • Michael	12 (3)	BUTT • Nicky	1	HIGGINBOTHAM • Danny	1
CLEGG • Michael	12	MAY • David	1	SOLSKJAER • Ole Gunnar	1
HEALY • David	11 (2)	NEVILLE • Gary	1		
FORTUNE • Quinton	9	SCHOLES • Paul	1	**Own Goals**	
O'SHEA • John	9	SHERINGHAM • Teddy	1	BEWERS • Jonathan (Aston Villa)	1
WELLENS • Richard	9	SOLSKJAER • Ole Gunnar	1	COOPER • Colin (Middlesbrough)	1
CHADWICK • Luke	7	NEVLAND • Erik	0 (4)		
EVANS • Wayne	7	COSGROVE • Stephen	0 (3)		
CRUYFF • Jordi	6	FITZPATRICK • Ian	0 (2)		
CURTIS • John	6	STUDLEY • Dominic	0 (2)		
VAN DER GOUW • Raimond	6	WEBBER • Danny	0 (2)		
DAVIS • Jimmy	4 (2)	COATES • Craig	0 (1)		
DJORDJIC • Bojan	4	HOWARD • Joshua	0 (1)		
FLETCHER • Darren	3 (1)	SAMPSON • Gary	0 (1)		
BERG • Henning	3	STUDLEY • Mark	0 (1)		
JOHNSEN • Ronny	3	TIERNEY • Paul	0 (1)		
LYNCH • Mark	3	WHEATCROFT • Paul	0 (1)		

FA PREMIER RESERVE LEAGUE – NORTH

		P	W	D	L	F	A	Pts
FINAL TABLE 1999-2000	Liverpool	24	16	7	1	55	18	55
	Sunderland	24	12	5	7	35	27	41
	Blackburn Rovers	24	11	6	7	37	27	39
	Bradford City	24	12	3	9	44	45	39
	Newcastle United	24	11	4	9	37	35	37
	MANCHESTER UNITED	24	11	3	10	46	32	36
	Leeds United	24	10	6	8	48	38	36
	Middlesbrough	24	10	6	8	34	33	36
	Everton	24	7	10	7	44	40	31
	Aston Villa	24	8	5	11	37	42	29
	Bolton Wanderers	24	6	4	14	22	59	22
	Sheffield Wednesday	24	5	4	15	35	52	19
	Barnsley	24	3	5	16	22	48	14

names in bold indicate goalscorers   # MANCHESTER SENIOR CUP

v BURY (away) • Won: 5-0   Wednesday 25 August 1999

Rachubka • Neville G. • Hilton • Roche • O'Shea • **Twiss 2** • Healy • Wilson • **Greening** • **Notman 2** • Chadwick
Substitutes: Rose S. (for Neville G.) • Marsh • Wellens • Fitzpatrick (for Greening) • Howard (for Twiss)

v MANCHESTER CITY (home, at Gigg Lane, Bury) • Drawn: 1-1*   Thursday 28 October 1999

Taibi • Neville G. • Higginbotham • May • Curtis • Cruyff • Wellens • **Wilson** • Greening • Notman • Chadwick
Substitutes: Clegg • Culkin • Healy • Twiss (for Chadwick) • O'Shea
*Won 5-4 on penalties *Penalty-scorers: Neville G. • Cruyff • Greening • Wilson • May*

v MANCHESTER CITY (away, at Ewen Fields, Hyde) • Won: 3-1   Tuesday 8 February 2000

van der Gouw • Clegg M. • Higginbotham • Roche • Wallwork • Webber • **Wellens** • Wilson • Healy • **Greening** • Twiss
*Substitutes: Cosgrove (for Wellens) • Rachubka • Howard (for Fletcher) • Rose S. • **Fletcher** (for Webber)*

v BURY (home, at Gigg Lane, Bury) • Won: 4-0   Monday 28 February 2000

Culkin • Lynch • Higginbotham • Teather • Wallwork • Stewart • Davis • Wilson • **Fitzpatrick** • **Greening 2** • **Djordjic**
Substitutes: Howard (for Wallwork) • Rachubka • Evans • Wheatcroft (for Davis) • Studley M. (for Higginbotham)

v OLDHAM ATHLETIC (away) • Won: 2-1   Thursday 23 March 2000

Culkin • Roche • Higginbotham • **Wallwork** • Johnsen • Teather • Evans • Wilson • Greening • Solskjaer • Stewart
*Substitutes: O'Shea (for Johnsen) • Rachubka • **Notman** (for Solskjaer) • Cosgrove (for Evans)*

v OLDHAM ATHLETIC (home, at The Cliff) • Lost: 0-2   Wednesday 5 April 2000

Rachubka • Roche • Tierney • Tate • McDermott • Howard • Walker • Studley D. • Muirhead • Molloy • Rose M.
Substitutes: Davis (for Walker) • Pugh (for Studley D.) • Clegg S. • Sampson (for Rose M.)

	P	W	D	L	F	A	Pts
MANCHESTER UNITED	6	5	0	1	15	5	15
Oldham Athletic	6	5	0	1	12	7	15
Bury	6	2	0	4	6	15	6
Manchester City	6	0	0	6	6	12	0

v OLDHAM ATHLETIC – FINAL (away, at Boundary Park) • Won: 2-0   Tuesday 2 May 2000

Culkin • Roche • Higginbotham • Wallwork • O'Shea • Stewart • Fletcher • **Wilson** • Greening • Notman •
Djordjic **(Smith o.g.)**
Substitutes: Twiss • Rachubka • Evans • Cosgrove • Davis (for Fletcher)

FRIENDLIES

Tuesday 20 July 1999   v ALTRINCHAM (away) • Won: 1-0

Culkin • Rose S. • Hilton • Roche • O'Shea • Ford • Wellens • Nevland • Notman • **Scholes** • Chadwick
Substitutes: Healy (for Nevland) • Stewart (for Wellens) • Fitzpatrick • Cosgrove • Clegg G. (for Notman)

Saturday 24 July 1999   v SELBY TOWN (away) • Won: 6-1

Culkin • Rose S. • Hilton • Roche • O'Shea • Ford • Beckham • Nevland • Healy • **Scholes** • Chadwick
*Substitutes: **Notman 3 (1 pen)** (for Nevland) • Stewart (for Beckham) • Wellens (for Scholes) • **Wheatcroft 2** (for Healy)*

Tuesday 27 July 1999   v ALFRETON TOWN (away) • Lost: 0-1

Culkin • Rose S. • Hilton • Roche • O'Shea • Ford • Wellens • Stewart • Healy • Notman • Chadwick
Substitutes: Fitzpatrick (for Healy) • Howard (for Ford) • Clegg G. (for Stewart)

Friday 30 July 1999   v BRISTOL ROVERS (away) (Lee Martin Testimonial) • Drawn: 2-2

Culkin • Clegg M. • Curtis • May • O'Shea • Greening • Beckham • Scholes • **Solskjaer** • Ford • Chadwick
*Substitutes: Notman (for Solskjaer) • **Healy** (for Ford) • Stewart (for Beckham) • Wellens (for Scholes) • Hilton (for O'Shea)*

Thursday 5 August 1999   v CHORLEY (away) • Won: 3-0

Culkin • Clegg S. • Twiss • Tate • O'Shea • Ford • Wellens • Stewart • **Healy** • Notman • Chadwick
*Substitutes: Sampson (for Wellens) • **Nardiello** (for Healy) • **Molloy** (for Chadwick) • Dodd (for Twiss)*

Monday 8 August 1999   v SHELBOURNE (away) (The Amstel Challenge Cup) • Lost: 0-1

Culkin • Clegg M. • Hilton • Curtis • O'Shea • Ford • Greening • Wilson • Healy • Notman • Twiss
Substitutes: Stewart (for Twiss) • Clegg G. • Howard • Wellens (for Ford) • Rose S. • McDermott

Tuesday 31st August 1999   v ROYAL ANTWERP (Belgium) (away) • Drawn: 2-2

Rachubka • Clegg M. • Hilton • Roche • O'Shea • Srewart • **Wilson** • Fortune • **Greening** • Notman • Twiss
Substitutes: Ford (for Twiss) • Wellens (for Stewart) • Howard (for Fortune) • Rose S. (for O'Shea)

Thursday 18 November 1999   v ROYAL AIR FORCE FA (home, at The Cliff) • Won: 4-2

Culkin • Howard • Studley D. • Roche • Rose S. • Cosgrove • **Wellens** • Stewart • **Healy** • **Notman 2** • Twiss
Substitute: Rachubka

names in bold indicate goalscorers

v SCARBOROUGH (away) • Won: 2-1   Thursday 9 December 1999

Culkin • Clegg M. • Higginbotham • May • Wallwork • Stewart • Chadwick • **Wilson** • Healy • Notman • Fortune
*Substitutes: **Nevland** (for Chadwick) • Rachubka (for Culkin) • Twiss (for Notman) • Wellens (for Stewart) •
Roche (for Clegg M.) • O'Shea (for May)*

v HALIFAX TOWN (home, at The Cliff) • Lost: 0-1   Wednesday 2 February 2000

Rachubka • Lynch • Studley M. • Rose S. • Jones • Howard • Evans • Cosgrove • Wheatcroft • Fitzpatrick • Studley D.
Substitutes: Szmid • Rose M.

v NEWPORT (home, at Trafford Training Centre) • Won: 2-0   Wednesday 8 March 2000

Baxter • Rankin • Pugh • Tate • Jones • Walker • Muirhead • Castillo (trialist) • **Trialist 2** • Nardiello • Molloy
Substitutes: Tierney (for Tate) • Rose M. (for Nardiello)

v STALYBRIDGE CELTIC (away) • Won: 5-2   Thursday 16 March 2000

Culkin • Roche • Higginbotham • Wallwork • Johnsen • Teather • Evans • **Wilson 2** • Davis • **Stewart** • **Greening**
*Substitutes: Wheatcroft (for Davis) • Rachubka • Studley D. (for Evans) • Studley M. • **Cosgrove** (for Teather) •
Lynch (for Johnsen)*

v OXFORD UNITED (away) (Mike Ford Testimonial) • Lost: 2-3   Monday 8 May 2000

Culkin • Clegg M. • Higginbotham • Wallwork • O'Shea • Stewart • **Fletcher** • Twiss • **Greening** • Notman • Djordjic
Substitutes: Roche (for Higginbotham) • Rachubka (for Culkin) • Evans (for Fletcher) • Cosgrove (for Djordjic)

v ROYAL ANTWERP (away) • Lost: 0-1   Friday 12 May 2000

Culkin • Clegg M. • Higginbotham • Roche • O'Shea • Fletcher • Davis • Wilson • Healy • Notman • Djordjic
Substitutes: Evans • Rachubka • Cosgrove (for Fletcher) • Clegg G. (for Notman) • Twiss

ARP

FA PREMIER RESERVE LEAGUE – UNDER 19s

David Williams must have the whitest knuckles in football after the roller-coaster ride the Under 19s took him on during the 1999-2000 season. David was forced to endure numerous highs and lows during a campaign which saw his team capable of beating the best one day and then change course to slip to defeat in the most inexplicable of circumstances.

That said, it is also true that the Under 19s enjoyed an extended purple patch during the second half of the season which saw them complete an unbeaten run of 10 games from December through March. But, sadly it wasn't enough to help them challenge for the top spot in the table following an erratic opening few months to the term.

They began the season with a couple of defeats against north-east opposition in Middlesbrough and Sunderland, but then luck changed for the better and hat-trick of wins, including a 7-2 home success over Sheffield Wednesday and 5-0 triumph against Stoke City at the Britannia Stadium.

But then, just when the future began to look brighter, they ran into a sequence of eight games, which scuppered their chances of the title. Just two wins – 5-0 away at Bolton and 4-0 against Newcastle United at The Cliff – and two draws were mixed in with four defeats to leave them playing catch-up with the teams at the head of the table.

Never more was the nature of the season emphasised than in the closing couple of games – both in the play-offs – when they demolished Leeds United 6-1 at The Cliff only to go out of the competition the following week after losing 5-0 against West Ham United at the Boleyn Ground.

names in bold indicate goalscorers

v MIDDLESBROUGH (away) • Lost: 0-2 — Saturday 28 August 1999

Marsh • Szmid • Studley D. • Rose S. • O'Shea • Cosgrove • Evans • Howard • Davis • Wheatcroft • Djordjic

Substitutes: Fitzpatrick (for Evans) • Williams B. • Rose M. • Jones • Walker (for Davis)

v SUNDERLAND (home) • Lost: 0-2 — Saturday 4 September 1999

Marsh • Szmid • Studley M. • McDermott • Jones • Rose M. • Walker • Howard • Davis • Fitzpatrick • Djordjic

Substitutes: Rose S. • Williams B. • Wheatcroft • Dodd (for Walker) • Molloy (for Djordjic)

v SHEFFIELD WEDNESDAY (home) • Won: 7-2 — Saturday 11 September 1999

Rachubka • Rose S. • Studley M. • Rose M. • Jones • Clegg. • **Evans** • **Cosgrove** • **Wheatcroft 3** • **Fitzpatrick 2** • Studley D.

Substitutes: Dodd (for Evans) • Davis • Szmid • Djordjic

v BARNSLEY (away) • Won: 2-0 — Saturday 18 September 1999

Marsh • Strange • Hilton • Rose S. • McDermott • Szmid • Evans • Howard • **Webber 2** • Clegg • Studley D.

Substitutes: Dodd • Walker • Studley M. (for Rose S.) • Rose M. (for Studley D.)

v STOKE CITY (away) • Won: 5-0 — Saturday 25 September 1999

Rachubka • Szmid • Studley M. • Cosgrove • Rose S. • Hilton • Strange • **Davis 3** • **Webber** • **Rose M.** • Djordjic

Substitutes: Evans (for Djordjic) • Dodd • Walker

v CREWE ALEXANDRA (home) • Lost: 0-1 — Saturday 2 October 1999

Marsh • Szmid • Studley M. • Strange • Roche • Rose M. • Davis • Howard • Webber • Clegg • Studley D.

Substitutes: Rose S. • Dodd (for Studley D.) • Djordjic (for Szmid)

v EVERTON (away) • Drawn: 1-1 — Saturday 16 October 1999

Rachubka • Cosgrove • Studley M. • Szmid • Rose S. • Stewart • Evans • Wood • **Webber** • Rose M. • Djordjic

Substitutes: Studley D (for Evans) • Dodd • Molloy (for Studley M.)

v BOLTON WANDERERS (away) • Won: 5-0 — Saturday 23 October 1999

Marsh • Studley M. • Studley D. • Szmid • Rose S. • Cosgrove • **Dodd** • **Howard** • **Webber** • **Davis 2** • Djordjic

Substitutes: Rose M. (Webber) • Molloy (Djordjic) • Walker (Cosgrove)

JUNIORS

v BLACKBURN ROVERS (away) • Lost: 1-2

Rachubka • Studley M. • Studley D. • Rose S. • Roche • Stewart • Evans • Howard • **Webber** • Davis • Rose M.
Substitutes: Dodd (for Howard) • Djordjic (for Rose M.) • Molloy • Walker

v LIVERPOOL (home) • Drawn: 1-1

Marsh • Szmid • Studley M. • Rose S. • Roche • Cosgrove • Walker • Davis • Webber • Rose M. • Djordjic
*Substitutes: Studley D. (for Rose M.) • Rachubka • **Dodd** (for Cosgrove) • Molloy*

v MANCHESTER CITY (away) • Lost: 1-2

Rachubka • Studley M. • Studley D. • Szmid • Rose S. • Stewart • Walker • Howard • **Webber** • Davis • Rose M.
Substitutes: Dodd • Molloy

v NEWCASTLE UNITED (home) • Won: 4-0

Marsh • Lynch • Studley M. • Szmid • Roche • Rose M. • Muirhead • Walker • **Webber** • **Nardiello 2** • **Molloy**
Substitutes: Dodd (for Walker) • Studley D. (for Webber) • Cosgrove (for Rose M.)

v CREWE ALEXANDRA (away) • Lost: 0-2

Rachubka • Lynch • Studley D. • Strange • Rose S. • Cosgrove • Walker • Howard • Nardiello • Dodd • Molloy
Substitutes: Davis (for Dodd) • Webber • Rose M. • Szmid • Studley M.

v EVERTON (home) • Won: 2-0

Marsh • Lynch • Studley D. • Strange • Szmid • Cosgrove • Dodd • Howard • **Nardiello** • **Davis** • Molloy
Substitutes: Webber (for Dodd) • Rachubka (for Nardiello) • Wood • Studley M. • Rose M. (for Molloy)

v BOLTON WANDERERS (home, at Littleton Road) • Won: 4-0

Rachubka • Lynch • Studley M. • Strange • Szmid • Dodd • Muirhead • Wood • **Webber** • **Nardiello 3** • Rose M.
Substitutes: Walker (for Dodd) • Davis (for Muirhead) • Molloy (for Rose M.)

v LIVERPOOL (away) • Drawn: 1-1

Rachubka • Lynch • Studley M. • Strange • Rose S. • Szmid • **Muirhead** • Wheatcroft • Nardiello • Djordjic • Rose M.
Substitutes: Jones • Dodd (for Wheatcroft) • Walker

names in bold indicate goalscorers

v BLACKBURN ROVERS (home) • Drawn: 0-0 — Saturday 29 January 2000

Rachubka • Lynch • Studley M. • Strange • Rose S. • Szmid • Dodd • Wheatcroft • Webber • Djordjic • Rose M.
Substitutes: Walker (for Rose M.) • Molloy (for Wheatcroft) • Jones

v MANCHESTER CITY (away, at The Cliff) • Won: 2-1 — Saturday 5 February 2000

Rachubka • Lynch • Studley M. • Rose S. • Jones • Szmid • Davis • **Nardiello** • **Webber** • Dodd • Rose M.
Substitutes: Walker (for Dodd) • Molloy

v HUDDERSFIELD TOWN (away) • Won: 5-2 — Saturday 12 February 2000

Rachubka • Lynch • Studley M. • Strange • Jones • **Dodd 2** • **Davis** • Fitzpatrick • **Nardiello 2** • Djordjic • Molloy
Substitutes: Szmid • Rose M. • Walker (for Molloy)

v LEEDS UNITED (away) • Won: 2-1 — Saturday 19 February 2000

Rachubka • Lynch • Studley M. • Strange • Jones • Szmid • **Evans (pen)** • Molloy • **Davis** • Djordjic • Rose M.
Substitutes: Dodd • Forde • Cogger • Humphreys

v ASTON VILLA (home) • Drawn: 1-1 — Saturday 26 February 2000

Rachubka • Lynch • Studley M. • Strange • Jones • Szmid • **Evans** • Molloy • Davis • Walker • Rose M.
Substitutes: Djordjic (for Rose M.) • Muirhead • Cogger

v BIRMINGHAM CITY (home) • Won: 3-1 — Saturday 4 March 2000

Rachubka • Studley M. • Pugh • Szmid • Jones • Cosgrove • **Muirhead** • Evans • Molloy • Walker • **Rose M. 2**
Substitutes: Studley D. (for Muirhead) • Djordjic • Davis (for Molloy) • Nardiello

v LEEDS UNITED (home) Play-Off, Second Round • Won: 6-1 — Saturday 25 March 2000

Rachubka • Lynch • Studley M. • **McDermott** • Jones • Szmid • **Evans** • **Davis 2** • **Nardiello 2** • Djordjic • Studley D.
Substitutes: Rose M. (for Evans) • Walker (for Studley D.) • Molloy (for Djordjic)

v WEST HAM UNITED (away) Play-Off, Third Round • Lost: 0-5 — Wednesday 12 April 2000

Rachubka • Lynch • Studley M. • McDermott • Jones • Szmid • Davis • Cosgrove • Nardiello • Djordjic • Studley D.
Substitutes: Walker (for Studley D.) • Molloy • Tate (for Cosgrove) • Sampson

UNDER 19s APPEARANCES

GOALSCORERS

Name	Appearances (as sub)	Name	Appearances (as sub)	Name	Goals (penalties)
STUDLEY • Mark	20 (1)	MARSH • Allan	8	NARDIELLO • Daniel	11
SZMID • Marek	20	WALKER • Joshua	7 (8)	DAVIS • Jimmy	10
ROSE • Michael	16 (4)	DODD • Ashley	7 (7)	WEBBER • Danny	10
RACHUBKA • Paul	16 (1)	MOLLOY • Eric	7 (6)	DODD • Ashley	4
DAVIS • Jimmy	15 (3)	McDERMOTT • Alan	4	EVANS • Wayne	4
ROSE • Stephen	13	MUIRHEAD • Ben	4	WHEATCROFT • Paul	3
DJORDJIC • Bojan	12 (3)	ROCHE • Lee	4	FITZPATRICK • Ian	2
WEBBER • Danny	12 (1)	WHEATCROFT • Paul	4	MUIRHEAD • Ben	2
LYNCH • Mark	12	FITZPATRICK • Ian	3 (1)	ROSE • Michael	2
STUDLEY • Dominic	11 (4)	CLEGG • George	3	COSGROVE • Stephen	1
STRANGE • Gareth	11	STEWART • Michael	3	HOWARD • Joshua	1
COSGROVE • Stephen	10 (1)	HILTON • Kirk	2	McDERMOTT • Alan	1
EVANS • Wayne	9 (1)	WOOD • Neil	2	MOLLOY • Eric	1
HOWARD • Joshua	9	O'SHEA • John	1	ROSE • Stephen	1
JONES • Rhodri	9	PUGH • Danny	1		
NARDIELLO • Daniel	9	TATE • Alan	0 (1)		

FA PREMIER ACADEMY LEAGUE UNDER–19S

		P	W	D	L	F	A	Pts
GROUP B FINAL TABLE 1999-2000	Blackburn Rovers	22	15	5	2	55	18	50
	Everton	22	14	3	5	38	22	45
	MANCHESTER UNITED	22	11	5	6	47	22	38
	Manchester City	22	12	2	8	45	32	38
	Liverpool	22	11	3	8	45	37	36
	Crewe Alexandra	22	7	8	7	29	34	29
	Bolton Wanderers	22	3	3	16	18	55	12

names in bold indicate goalscorers

16TH INTERNATIONAL
YOUTH TOURNAMENT
– REAL SOCIEDAD, SPAIN

v SEVILLA Group B • Lost: 0-2   Friday 21 April 2000

Rachubka • Lynch • Studley • Rose • Jones • McDermott • Szmid • Molloy • Davis • Nardiello • Djordjic

v OSASUNA Group B • Drawn: 1-1   Saturday 22 April 2000

Rachubka • Tate • Studley • Sampson • Jones • **Rose** • Szmid • Walker • Davis • Molloy • Djordjic

Substitute: Pugh (for Walker)

v REAL SOCIEDAD • Won: 4-1   Sunday 23 April 2000

Rachubka • **Tate** • Djordjic • **Sampson** • Jones • **McDermott** • Szmid • Walker • Davis • **Nardiello** • Pugh

Substitutes: Molloy (for Nardiello) • Williams (for Rachubka) • Rose (for Djordjic)

United did not qualify for the final

TOURNAMENT SQUAD

1. Paul RACHUBKA	9. Jimmy DAVIS
2. Mark LYNCH	10. Daniel NARDIELLO
3. Mark STUDLEY	11. Daniel PUGH
4. Gary SAMPSON	12. Eric MOLLOY
5. Rhodri JONES	13. Ben WILLIAMS
6. Alan McDERMOTT	14. Michael ROSE
7. Marek SZMID	15. Bojan DJORDJIC
8. Joshua WALKER	16. Alan TATE

FRIENDLIES

Saturday 17 July 1999 v SALFORD CITY (away) • Won: 5-1

Rachubka • Lynch • Studley M. • Cosgrove • **McDermott** • Clegg • **Studley D.** • Howard • Wheatcroft • **Webber 2** • Djordjic
Substitutes: **Davis** *(for Wheatcroft)* • *Walker (for Howard)* • *Rose M. (for Djordjic)* • *Molloy (for Studley D.)* • *Djordjic (for Webber)* • *Studley D. (for Cosgrove)*

Saturday 24 July 1999 v WORKSOP TOWN (away) • Won: 5-1

Rachubka • Lynch • Studley D. • **Howard** • McDermott • Clegg G. • Walker • Rose M. • **Davis** • **Fitzpatrick 3** • Djordjic
Substitutes: Cosgrove (for Rose M.) • *Evans (for Walker)* • *Studley M. (for McDermott)* • *Webber (for Davis)* • *Molloy (for Djordjic)* • *Walker (for Evans)*

Thursday 29 July 1999 v BOCA JUNIORS (Argentina) (home) • Lost: 1-3

Marsh • Lynch • Studley M. • Rose M. • McDermott • Sammutt (trialist) • Farrugia (trialist) • Davies (trialist) • Wheatcroft • Mifsud (trialist) • Etherington (trialist)
Substitutes: Studley D. (for Studley M.) • *Clegg G. (for McDermott)* • *Szmid (for Lynch)* • **Webber** *(for Wheatcroft)* • *Howard*

Monday 2 August 1999 v. BRISTOL CITY (away) • Drawn: 1-1

Rachubka • Szmid • Studley M. • Rose S. • Hilton • Rose M. • Evans • Clegg G. • Wheatcroft • Fitzpatrick • **Studley D.**
Substitutes: Lynch (Szmid) • *Howard (Rose M.)* • *Cosgrove (Clegg G.)* • *Webber (Fitzpatrick)* • *Davis (Wheatcroft)* • *Djordjic (Studley D.)*

Wednesday 4 August 1999 v YEOVIL TOWN (away) • Lost: 3-5

Rachubka • Lynch • Hilton • Cosgrove • McDermott • Clegg G. • Szmid • Howard • **Webber 2 (1 pen)** • **Davis (pen)** • Djordjic
Substitutes: Rose S. (for Djordjic) • *Marsh* • *Studley M.* • *Rose M.* • *Evans* • *Wheatcroft* • *Fitzpatrick* • *Studley D.*

Saturday 6 August 1999 v FOREST GREEN ROVERS (away) • Lost: 2-5

Marsh • Lynch • Studley M. • Howard • McDermott • Rose S. • Evans • Rose M. • Wheatcroft • **Fitzpatrick 2** • Studley D
Substitutes: Cosgrove (for Howard) • *Rachubka* • *Hilton* • *Clegg G.* • *Szmid* • *Webber* • *Davis* • *Djordjic*

Tuesday 10 August 1999 v UPTON A.A. (away) • Won: 5-0

Marsh • Szmid • Studley M. • Lynch • Roche • **Dodd** • Davis • Cosgrove • **Webber** • **Wheatcroft 2** • **Molloy**
Substitutes: Studley D. (for Studley M.) • *Rose M. (for Wheatcroft)* • *Evans (for Cosgrove)* • *Strange (for Lynch)* • *Wheatcroft (for Davis)*

Saturday 14 August 1999 v RANGERS (Scotland) JERSEY TOURNAMENT • Won: 2-1

Rachubka • Rose S. • Hilton • Roche • McDermott • Cosgrove • Davis • Howard • **Webber** • **Wheatcroft** • Studley D.
Substitutes: Lynch (for McDermott) • *Evans (for Webber)* • *Szmid* • *Rose M.* • *Molloy* • *Dodd* • *Clegg G*

names in bold indicate goalscorers

v SL BENFICA (Portugal) JERSEY TOURNAMENT • Lost: 0-2   Sunday 15 August 1999

Rachubka • Lynch • Hilton • Roche • Rose S. • Cosgrove • Evans • Howard • Davis • Wheatcroft • Studley D.
Substitutes: Szmid (for Lynch) • Clegg G. (for Cosgrove) • McDermott • Webber • Rose M. • Molloy • Dodd

v HUDDERSFIELD TOWN (away) • Won: 7-1   Saturday 21 August 1999

Marsh • Neville G. • Studley M. • Strange • **McDermott 2** • **Szmid** • Walker • Rose M. • **Davis** •
Fitzpatrick (2 pens) • Djordjic
Substitutes: Evans (for Walker) • Rachubka • Dodd (for Studley M.) • Molloy (for Djordjic)

v WREXHAM (away) • Lost: 0-2   Wednesday 22 September 1999

Marsh • Ford • Studley M. • Stewart • Rose S. • Cosgrove • Walker • Nevland • Clegg G. • Dodd • Rose M.
Substitutes: Evans (for Clegg G.) • Studley D. (for Rose S.) • Davis

v NEWTOWN (away) • Won: 1-0   Wednesday 19 January 2000

Rachubka • Lynch • Studley D. • Rose S. • Tate • Wood • Evans • Wheatcroft • **Nardiello** • Djordjic • Rose M.
Substitutes: Jones (for Tate) • Dodd (for Wood) • Walker (for Djordjic)

v DERBY COUNTY (away, at Baseball Ground) • Won: 4-3   Saturday 18 March 2000

Rachubka • Lynch • Studley M. • Walker • Jones • Szmid • **Evans** • Cosgrove • **Davis 2** • **Wheatcroft** • Studley D.
Substitutes: Rose M. (for Evans) • Molloy (for Wheatcroft)

v BROMMAPOJKARNA IF (Sweden) (home, at The Cliff) • Won: 2-1   Friday 14 April 2000

Rachubka • Lynch • Studley M. • McDermott • Jones • Szmid • **Muirhead** • **Rose M.** • Nardiello • Davis • Djordjic
Substitutes: Walker (for McDermott) • Molloy (for Nardiello)

v IFK GOTHENBURG (Sweden) (home, at The Cliff) • Won: 6-0   Tuesday 18 April 2000

Williams B. • Szmid • Studley M. • Walker • Jones • **Cosgrove** • Muirhead • **Howard** • **Wheatcroft** • **Coates 2** • Djordjic
Substitutes: Davis (for Muirhead) • Lynch (for Szmid) • Rose M. (for Studley M.)

MUFC Juniors in action

CITY OF GLASGOW INTERNATIONAL FOOTBALL FIVES (UNDER 18s)

v ST MIRREN Section 1 • Won: 6-0　　Saturday 8 January 2000

Goalscorers: **Wood 2 • Studley • Djordjic • Strange • Nardiello**

v RANGERS Section 1 • Lost: 1-6　　Saturday 8 January 2000

Goalscorer: **Wood**

v QUEEN'S PARK • Won: 3-2　　Sunday 9 January 2000

Goalscorers: **Lynch • Djordjic • Wood**

SECTION 1 – FINAL TABLE

	P	W	D	L	F	A	Pts
Rangers	3	3	0	0	19	3	9
Manchester United	3	2	0	1	10	8	6
St Mirren	3	1	0	2	7	16	3
Queen's Park	3	0	0	3	5	14	0

v NEWCASTLE UNITED • Drawn: 5-5*　　Sunday 9 January 2000

Goalscorers: **Davis 2 • Nardiello • Lynch • Studley**
*Lost 3-5 on penalties
Penalty-scorers: **Djordjic • Studley • Wood**

v CELTIC – Third/Fourth Place Play-Off • Lost: 0-2　　Sunday 9 January 2000

TOURNAMENT SQUAD

1. Jimmy DAVIS
2. Bojan DJORDJIC
3. Mark LYNCH
4. Daniel NARDIELLO
5. Gareth STRANGE
6. Mark STUDLEY
7. Marek SZMID
8. Danny WEBBER
9. Ben WILLIAMS
10. Neil WOOD

FA PREMIER RESERVE LEAGUE – UNDER 17s

While David Williams had a roller coaster ride with the Under 19s there was not much change for Neil Bailey with the Under 17s. They too had ups and downs.

After a helter-skelter opening saw them run up seven straight wins, including a 9-0 rampage against Barnsley which promised much they began to stumble and the remainder of the season was littered with a series of impressive victories and frustrating defeats.

Their hopes of success in the end-of-season play-offs were ended in the last minute of extra-time by Coventry City at Littleton Road.

There was also disappointment in the FA Youth Cup with United falling at first hurdle against Nottingham Forest at Gigg Lane.

names in bold indicate goalscorers

v MIDDLESBROUGH (away) • Won: 4-0   Saturday 28 August 1999

Moran • Clegg • Pugh • Tierney • Tate • Wood • Muirhead • Sampson • **Nardiello** • Williams • **Rankin**

*Substitutes: Taylor A. • **Whiteman 2** (for Williams) • Heath • Humphreys*

v SUNDERLAND (home) • Won: 1-0   Saturday 4 September 1999

Moran • Clegg • Pugh • Tierney • Tate • Taylor A. • Muirhead • Sampson • Nardiello • **Williams** • Wood

Substitutes: Whiteman (for Taylor A.) • Humphreys • Heath • Taylor K

v SHEFFIELD WEDNESDAY (home) • Won: 1-0   Saturday 11 September 1999

Moran • Clegg • Pugh • Tierney • Tate • Wood • Muirhead • Sampson • Nardiello • **Williams** • Rankin

Substitutes: Whiteman • Mooniaruck • Taylor K. • Humphreys • Heath

v BARNSLEY (away) • Won: 4-1   Saturday 18 September 1999

Baxter • Clegg • Pugh • Tierney • Tate • Wood • **Muirhead** • Sampson • **Whiteman** • Williams • Rankin

*Substitutes: Nardiello • **Coates 2** (for Williams) • Taylor A. • Taylor K*

v SUNDERLAND (away) • Won: 6-1   Saturday 25 September 1999

Baxter • Clegg • Pugh • **Tierney** • Tate • **Wood** • Muirhead • Sampson • **Nardiello 2** • Coates • Rankin

*Substitutes: Whiteman • **Taylor A.** (for Humphreys) • Cogger • Humphreys (for Nardiello) • Eckersley (for Sampson)*

v CREWE ALEXANDRA (away) • Won: 5-2   Saturday 2 October 1999

Baxter • Clegg • Pugh • Tierney • **Taylor A.** • **Wood** • Muirhead • Humphreys • **Nardiello 3** • Coates • Rankin

Substitutes: Whiteman (for Coates) • Mooniaruck • Waud • Cogger • Taylor K

v BARNSLEY (home) • Won 9-0   Saturday 16 October 1999

Baxter • Clegg • Pugh • Tierney • Tate • Taylor A. • **Muirhead** • **Sampson** • **Nardiello 3** • **Whiteman 2** • Rankin

(Oldham o.g.)

*Substitutes: Coates (for Muirhead) • **Humphreys** (for Nardiello) • Taylor K. • Mooniaruck (for Rankin)*

v BOLTON WANDERERS (away) • Lost: 1-3   Saturday 23 October 1999

Baxter • Clegg • Pugh • Tierney • Tate • Wood • Muirhead • Sampson • Nardiello • **Whiteman** • Mooniaruck

Substitutes: Coates (for Whiteman) • Cogger (for Nardiello) • Humphreys (for Muirhead)

Saturday 30 October 1999   v BLACKBURN ROVERS (away) • Lost: 1-2

Baxter • Taylor A. • Pugh • Tierney • **Tate** • Wood • Muirhead • Sampson • Nardiello • Coates • Rankin
Substitutes: Whiteman (for Coates) • Williams • Mooniaruck (for Rankin) • Taylor K. • Cogger

Saturday 6 November 1999   v LIVERPOOL (home) • Drawn: 0-0

Baxter • Clegg • Pugh • Tierney • Tate • Wood • Muirhead • Sampson • Nardiello • Coates • Rankin
Substitutes: Williams (for Coates) • Taylor A. • Whiteman • Mooniaruck

Saturday 13 November 1999   v MANCHESTER CITY (away) • Lost: 1-2

Baxter • Clegg • Pugh • Taylor A. • Tate • Wood • Muirhead • Sampson • **Nardiello (pen)** • Williams • Rankin
Substitutes: Coates • Whiteman • Mooniaruck • Taylor K

Saturday 20 November 1999   v NEWCASTLE UNITED (home) • Won: 4-2

Baxter • Taylor A. • Pugh • Tierney • Tate • **Wood (pen)** • Mooniaruck • Sampson • **Whiteman** • **Williams 2** • Rankin
Substitutes: Coates (for Whiteman) • Clegg (for Sampson) • Rea

Saturday 27 November 1999   v CREWE ALEXANDRA (away) • Lost: 1-3

Baxter • Clegg • Pugh • Tierney • Tate • Wood • Mooniaruck • Sampson • **Whiteman** • Williams • Rankin
Substitutes: Coates • Muirhead • Taylor K. • Humphreys

Saturday 4 December 1999   v ASTON VILLA (away) • Lost: 0-2

Forde • Clegg • Pugh • Taylor K. • Tate • Rankin • Mooniaruck • Sampson • Coates • Williams • Tierney
Substitutes: Whiteman (for Williams) • Humphreys (for Sampson) • Thompson

Saturday 11 December 1999   v BOLTON WANDERERS (home) • Won: 5-0

Forde • Clegg • Tierney • Taylor K. • Tate • Rankin • Mooniaruck • Sampson • **Whiteman 2** • **Williams** • Pugh
*Substitutes: **Coates 2** (for Williams) • Humphreys • Thompson*

Saturday 22 January 2000   v LIVERPOOL (away) • Won: 2-1

Forde • Clegg • Rankin • Tierney • Tate • Fletcher • Mooniaruck • Sampson • **Whiteman** • **Coates** • Pugh
Substitutes: Williams • Heath • Taylor K. (for Tate) • Cogger

names in bold indicate goalscorers

v BLACKBURN ROVERS (home) • Won: 1-0   Saturday 29 January 2000

Forde • Clegg • Rankin • Tierney • Taylor K. • **Fletcher** • Mooniaruck • Sampson • Whiteman • Coates • Pugh
Substitutes: Williams (for Coates) • Baxter • Taylor A. • Heath

v MANCHESTER CITY (away, Littleton Road) • Lost: 0-1   Saturday 5 February 2000

Forde • Clegg • Tierney • Taylor K. • Tate • Fletcher • Taylor A. • Sampson • Whiteman • Coates • Pugh
Substitutes: Heath (for Taylor A.) • Baxter • Cogger • Richardson

v COVENTRY CITY (away) • Drawn: 2-2   Saturday 12 February 2000

Baxter • Clegg • Tierney • Taylor K. • **Tate** • Fletcher • Whiteman • Sampson • Heath • Coates • Mooniaruck
Substitutes: Richardson • Forde • **Johnson J.** (for Clegg) • Meredith

v LEEDS UNITED (away) • Won: 5-1   Saturday 19 February 2000

Baxter • Clegg • Tierney • Taylor K. • Tate • Fletcher • **Whiteman** • Sampson • **Heath 3** • **Coates** • Mooniaruck
Substitutes: Johnson J. (for Heath) • Forde • Richardson (for Fletcher) • Byrne (for Whiteman)

v ASTON VILLA (home) • Lost: 0-3   Saturday 26 February 2000

Baxter • Clegg • Rankin • Tierney • Tate • Fletcher • Whiteman • Sampson • Heath • Coates • Mooniaruck
Substitutes: Castillo • Forde • Humphreys • Johnson E.

v BIRMINGHAM CITY (home) • Won: 6-3   Saturday 4 March 2000

Baxter • Clegg • Tierney • Taylor K. • Tate • Rankin • **Mooniaruck** • Sampson • **Heath 2** • **Coates 3** • Castillo
Substitutes: Humphreys (for Coates) • Forde • Cogger (for Clegg) • Johnson J. • Richardson (for Rankin)

v LEEDS UNITED (home) Play-Off, First Round • Won: 3-1   Saturday 18 March 2000

Forde • Clegg • Tierney • Taylor K. • Tate • Fletcher • Muirhead • Sampson • **Nardiello 2** • **Coates** • Pugh
Substitutes: Heath • Mooniaruck • Humphreys • Cogger

v COVENTRY CITY (home) Play-Off, Second Round • Lost: 2-3   Saturday 25 March 2000

Forde • Clegg • Rankin • Tierney • **Tate** • Fletcher • Mooniaruck • Sampson • **Heath** • Coates • Pugh
Substitutes: Humphreys (for Heath) • Baxter (for Forde) • Cogger • Johnson E. (for Mooniaruck)

UNDER 17s APPEARANCES

GOALSCORERS

Name	Appearances (as sub)	Name	Appearances (as sub)	Name	Goals (penalties)
SAMPSON • Gary	23	TAYLOR • Kris	8 (1)	NARDIELLO • Daniel	12
TIERNEY • Paul	23	FLETCHER • Darren	8	WHITEMAN • Marc	12
CLEGG • Steven	22 (1)	TAYLOR • Andrew	7 (1)	COATES • Craig	10
TATE • Alan	22	FORDE • Mark	7	HEATH • Colin	6
PUGH • Danny	20	HEATH • Colin	5 (1)	WILLIAMS • Matthew	5
RANKIN • John	18	MORAN • David	3	MUIRHEAD • Ben	3
COATES • Craig	14 (5)	HUMPHREYS • Chris	1 (6)	TATE • Alan	3
BAXTER • Nick	14 (1)	CASTILLO • Nery	1	WOOD • Neil	3
WHITEMAN • Marc	12 (5)	COGGER • John	0 (2)	TAYLOR • Andrew	2
MOONIARUCK • Kalam	12 (2)	JOHNSON • Jemal	0 (2)	FLETCHER • Darren	1
MUIRHEAD • Ben	12	RICHARDSON • Kieran	0 (2)	HUMPHREYS • Chris	1
WOOD • Neil	12	BYRNE • Danny	0 (1)	JOHNSON • Jemal	1
NARDIELLO • Daniel	11	ECKERSLEY • Michael	0 (1)	MOONIARUCK • Kalam	1
WILLIAMS • Matthew	9 (2)	JOHNSON • Eddie	0 (1)	RANKIN • John	1
				SAMPSON • Gary	1
				TIERNEY • Paul	1

Own Goals

OLDHAM • Adam (Barnsley)   1

FA PREMIER ACADEMY LEAGUE UNDER 17s

	P	W	D	L	F	A	Pts
GROUP B FINAL TABLE 1999-2000 Crewe Alexandra	22	13	3	6	74	35	42
MANCHESTER UNITED	22	13	2	7	59	29	41
Blackburn Rovers	22	11	5	6	43	34	38
Liverpool	22	12	2	8	41	32	38
Manchester City	22	11	2	9	42	25	35
Bolton Wanderers	22	3	1	18	19	61	10

NIVEA 20TH JUNIOR (UNDER 17s) FOOTBALL TOURNAMENT – BLUDENZ, AUSTRIA

names in bold indicate goalscorers

v CROATIA ZAGREB (Croatia) Group A • Drawn: 0-0   Saturday 22 April 2000

Baxter • Clegg • Rankin • Cogger • Moran • Humphreys • Muirhead • Fox • Heath • Johnson E. • Mooniaruck
Substitutes: Johnson J. (for Heath) • Richardson (for Mooniaruck)

v VORARLBERG (Austria) Group A • Won: 2-0   Sunday 23 April 2000

Jowsey • Clegg • Rankin • Cogger • Moran • Humphreys • **Muirhead 2** • Fox • Johnson E. • Richardson • Johnson J.
Substitutes: Heath (for Johnson J.) • Mooniaruck (for Richardson)

v TURKEY Group A • Won: 1-0   Sunday 23 April 2000

Baxter • Clegg • Rankin • Cogger • Moran • Lawrence • **Muirhead** • Johnson J. • Heath • Collett • Mooniaruck
Substitutes: Richardson (for Collett) • Johnson E. (for Johnson J.)

v USA SELECT Semi-Final • Lost: 0-1   Monday 24 April 2000

Jowsey • Lawrence • Rankin • Cogger • Moran • Humphreys • Muirhead • Fox • Johnson E. • Richardson • Johnson J.
Substitutes: Heath (for Johnson E.) • Collett (for Richardson) • Mooniaruck (for Johnson J.)

v CROATIA ZAGREB Third/Fourth Place Play-Off • Drawn: 0-0 *   Monday 24 April 2000

Baxter • Clegg • Rankin • Cogger • Moran • Humphreys • Muirhead • Fox • Heath • Johnson E. • Mooniaruck
Substitutes: Johnson J. (for Heath) • Richardson (for Mooniaruck)
*Lost: 4-5 on penalties Penalty-scorers: *Fox • Rankin • Mooniaruck • Heath*

TOURNAMENT SQUAD

1. Nick BAXTER	9. Colin HEATH
2. Steven CLEGG	10. Kieran RICHARDSON
3. John RANKIN	11. Kalam MOONIARUCK
4. John COGGER	12. Jemal JOHNSON
5. Martin MORAN	13. James JOWSEY
6. Chris HUMPHREYS	14. Lee LAWRENCE
7. Ben MUIRHEAD	15. Eddie JOHNSON
8. David FOX	16. Ben COLLETT

FRIENDLIES

Saturday 31 July 1999   v FULWOOD AMATEURS (away) • Won: 6-0

Williams B. • Clegg S. • Pugh • Tierney • Tate • Sampson • Evans • **Dodd** • **Nardiello 2 (1 pen)** • **Williams M 2**. • Molloy
*Substitutes: Taylor (for Evans) • **Szmid** (for Dodd) • Davis (for Williams M.) • Williams M. (for Sampson)*

Wednesday 11 August 1999   v SAN DIEGO NOMADS (USA) (home) • Won: 6-0

Williams B. • Clegg S. • Pugh • Tierney • Tate • **Taylor A**. • Muirhead • Sampson • **Nardiello 2** • **Williams M**. • **Rankin**
*Substitutes: **Whiteman** (for Muirhead) • Cogger (for Tate) • Ward (for Tierney) • Taylor K. (for Pugh) • Heath (for Sampson)*

Friday 13 August 1999   v FLIXTON (away) • Won: 6-0

Williams B. • Clegg S. • Pugh • Tierney • Tate • **Strange** • **Whiteman 2** • **Walker** • **Nardiello 2** • Williams M. • Rankin
Substitutes: Muirhead • Sampson • Taylor A. • Heath (for Williams M.) • Taylor K. (for Rankin) • Ward (for Tate)

Wednesday 18 August 1999   v HALIFAX TOWN (home) • Won: 3-0

Williams B. • Clegg S. • Pugh • Tierney • Tate • Taylor A. • **Muirhead** • Sampson • Whiteman • **Williams M. 2** • Rankin
*Substitutes: Moran (for Williams B.) • Nardiello (for Tierney) • Walker (for Tierney) • Dodd • Tierney (for Walker) •
Tierney (for Clegg S.)*

Wednesday 8 December 2000   v AUSTRALIA Under-18 XI (home) • Drawn: 3-3

Williams B. • Clegg S. • Tierney • Cogger • Tate • **Rankin** • Muirhead • Sampson • **Whiteman** • **Coates** • Pugh
Substitutes: Nardiello (for Whiteman) • Wood (for Pugh) • Williams M. (for Coates)

Saturday 11 March 2000   v DERBY COUNTY (home, at Trafford Training Centre) • Won: 3-2

Forde • Clegg S. • Rankin • Taylor K. • Cogger • Fletcher • Mooniaruck • Castillo (trialist) • **Trialist 2** •
Humphreys • Pugh
*Substitutes: **Heath** (for Humphreys) • Tierney (for Rankin) • Fletcher (for Sampson).*

Saturday 1 April 2000   v LIVERPOOL (away) • Won: 2-1

Baxter • Clegg S. • Taylor K. • Tierney • Cogger • Humphreys • **Mooniaruck** • Spann (trialist) • Heath • Coates • Pugh
*Substitutes: Lawrence • Sims • Johnson E. • **Poole** (for Spann [trialist]) • Collett*

Saturday 15 April 2000   v BROMMAPOJKARNA IF (Sweden) (home, at The Cliff) • Won: 7-2

Baxter • Clegg S. • Rankin • Tierney • **Tate** • **Fletcher** • Mooniaruck • Sampson • **Heath** • **Coates 3** • **Pugh**
Substitutes: Fox • Jowsey (for Baxter) • Cogger • Humphreys

names in bold indicate goalscorers

v DERBY COUNTY (away, at Baseball Ground) • Lost: 0-1　Saturday 29 April 2000

Moran • Strange • Tierney • Essien (trialist) • Tate • Dodd • Mooniaruck • Sampson • Atiku (trialist) • Coates • Pugh

Substitutes: Baxter • Humphreys • Johnson J. • Cogger

THE TIMES FA YOUTH CUP – THIRD ROUND

v NOTTINGHAM FOREST (Home, at Gigg Lane, Bury) • Lost: 1-2　Thursday 2nd December 1999

Williams B. • Lynch • Studley M. • Strange • Szmid • Walker • Muirhead • Rose M. • **Webber** • Davis, Wood

Substitutes: Dodd • Tate • Pugh • Nardiello (for Walker) • Sampson

OTHER EVENTS AT OLD TRAFFORD

JJB Sports Super League Grand Final　Saturday 9 October 1999

BRADFORD BULLS 6　　**ST HELENS 8**
Try: Paul H.　　　　　Try: Iro
Goal: Paul H.　　　　 Goals: Long 2
Attendance: 50,717

English Schools' Football Association • Under-15 Final Second Leg　Sunday 7 May 2000

SALFORD 2　　　**CARDIFF 1**
Traynor, Moore　　 Cachia
Salford won 3-1 on aggregate
Attendance: 3,021

MANCHESTER UNITED ACADEMY (Under 16s)

Monday 26 July 1999 v BAYER LEVERKUSEN (Germany) (away, at Bitburg) • Lost: 1-2

Woodcock • Thompson • Taylor • Waud • Fitzgerald • Fletcher • **Eckersley** • Humphreys • Heath • Kinsella • Mooniaruck
Substitutes: Ahmed (for Fletcher) • Rea (for Mooniaruck) • Thewlis (for Woodcock) • Ennis (for Fitzgerald) • Poole (for Kinsella)

Wednesday 29 July 1999 v KAISERSLAUTERN (Germany) (away, at Bitburg) • Won: 1-0

Thewlis • Thompson • Taylor • Ennis • **Fitzgerald** • Humphreys • Eckersley • Ahmed • Poole • Kinsella • Rea
Substitutes: Waud • Woodcock (for Thewlis) • Fletcher • Heath • Mooniaruck (for Kinsella) • Bancroft

Sunday 5 September 1999 v STOKE CITY (home) • Won: 7-0

Nelson • Sims • Thompson • Taylor • Cogger • **Humphreys 3** • Ahmed • Johnson E. • **Heath 3** • Poole • **Mooniaruck**
Substitutes: Hough • Forde • Collett • Bancroft • Hutchinson

Sunday 12 September 1999 v HUDDERSFIELD TOWN (home) • Won: 3-1

Forde • Simms • Thompson • Taylor • Cogger • **Fletcher** • Ahmed • Humphreys • **Heath 2** • Hough • Mooniaruck
Substitutes: Hutchinson • Poole • Eckersley • Rea • Bancroft

Sunday 19 September 1999 v EVERTON (home) • Won: 2-1

Forde • Simms • Thompson • Taylor • Cogger • Humphreys • Ahmed • Eckersley • **Heath 2** • Hough • Mooniaruck
Substitutes: Bancroft • Poole • Rea • Waud • Hutchinson

Sunday 26 September 1999 v CREWE ALEXANDRA (away) • Won: 5-2

Forde • Thompson • **Taylor** • Waud • Cogger • **Rea** • Ahmed • Eckersley • Humphreys • Hutchinson • **Mooniaruck**
Substitutes: Hough 2 • Murray • Bancroft • Nelson

Sunday 3 October 1999 v NOTTINGHAM FOREST (away) • Won: 2-1

Forde • Thompson • Taylor • Waud • Cogger • Rea • Ahmed • Eckersley • Hough • **Mooniaruck 2** • Hutchinson
Substitutes: Bancroft • Humphreys

Sunday 17 October 1999 v MANCHESTER CITY (home) • Lost: 0-1

Forde • Thompson • Taylor • Waud • Cogger • Rea • Hutchinson • Eckersley • Humphreys • Hough • Mooniaruck
Substitutes: Bancroft • Ahmed

names in bold indicate goalscorers

v LIVERPOOL (home) • Drawn: 1-1   Sunday 24 October 1999

Nelson • Thompson • Taylor • Waud • Cogger • Humphreys • **Ahmed** • Eckersley • Poole • Hutchinson • Rea

Substitutes: Mooniaruck • Bancroft • Hough

v BLACKBURN ROVERS (away) • Won: 3-2   Sunday 31 October 1999

Nelson • Sims • **Taylor** • Waud • Cogger • Rea • Mooniaruck • Fletcher • **Humphreys 2** • Johnson J. • Richardson

Substitutes: Eckersley • Hutchinson • Ahmed • Thompson

v SHEFFIELD WEDNESDAY (home) • Lost: 2-4   Sunday 7 November 1999

Nelson • Thompson • Taylor • Waud • Cogger • Rea • Bancroft • Eckersley • Humphreys • Hutchinson • **Mooniaruck**

*Substitutes: **Hough** • Forde • Ahmed*

v LEEDS UNITED (home) • Drawn: 1-1   Sunday 14 November 1999

Forde • Thompson • Taylor • Waud • Cogger • Rea • **Ahmed** • Eckersley • Humphreys • Mooniaruck • Hutchinson

Substitutes: Bancroft • Hough

v EVERTON (away) • Drawn: 3-3   Friday 19 November 1999

Forde • Thompson • Lawrence • **Taylor** • **Waud** • Rea • Ahmed • Eckersley • Poole • **Johnson J.** • Richardson

Substitutes: Humphreys • Bailey • Hutchinson • Bancroft • Hough

v MANCHESTER CITY (away) • Won: 3-1   Sunday 28 November 1999

Nelson • Thompson • Lawrence • Taylor • Waud • Eckersley • Mooniaruck • **Fletcher** • **Humphreys** • **Johnson J.** • Richardson

Substitutes: Rea • Forde • Ahmed • Hutchinson • Bancroft

v NEWCASTLE UNITED (away) • Won: 2-0   Sunday 5 December 1999

Nelson • Thompson • Taylor • Waud • Cogger • Fletcher • **Bancroft** • Ahmed • **Humphreys** • Mooniaruck • Hutchinson

Substitute: Collett

v STOKE CITY (away) • Won: 2-0   Sunday 23 January 2000

Forde • Thompson • Taylor • Waud • Cogger • Eckersley • **Ahmed** • **Bancroft** • Heath • Mooniaruck • Richardson

Substitute: Hutchinson

ACADEMY

names in bold indicate goalscorers

v BLACKBURN ROVERS (home) • Won: 2-1

Hickson • Sims • Lawrence • Taylor • Cogger • Johnson E. • **Mooniaruck** • **Humphreys** • Heath • Poole • Richardson
Substitutes: Johnson J. • Byrne • Collett • Conner

NORTHERN IRELAND MILK CUP
INTERNATIONAL YOUTH TOURNAMENT 1999 (Under 16s)

Monday 19 July 1999   v COUNTY ANTRIM (Northern Ireland) Group One • Won: 3-2

Murphy • Clegg • Rankin • Dodd • **Tate** • Jones • **Muirhead** • Sampson • Szmid • Wood • Pugh
*Substitutes: **Nardiello** (for Wood) • Taylor (for Sampson) • Williams (for Dodd)*

Tuesday 20 July 1999   v BRONDBY (Denmark) Group One • Won: 3-0

Murphy • Clegg • Tierney • Dodd • Tate • Jones • Muirhead • Taylor • **Nardiello** • **Wood** • Szmid
*Substitutes: Rankin (for Clegg) • **Sampson** (for Taylor) • Whiteman (for Nardiello) • Williams (for Dodd)*

Wednesday 21 July 1999   v CHERRY ORCHARD Group One • Drawn: 0-0

Murphy • Clegg • Rankin • Dodd • Szmid • Jones • Muirhead • Fletcher • Whiteman • Heath • Pugh.
Substitutes: Sampson (for Muirhead) • Tierney (for Rankin)

Wednesday 21 July 1999   v DUNDALK SCHOOLBOYS' LEAGUE (Northern Ireland) Quarter-Final • Won: 4-0

Murphy • Tierney • Rankin • Szmid • Tate • Jones • **Muirhead** • Sampson • **Nardiello 2** • Wood • Williams
*Substitutes: Pugh (for Rankin) • Whiteman (for Williams) • **Heath** (for Nardiello) • Fletcher (for Muirhead)*

Thursday 22 July 1999   v COUNTY DOWN (Northern Ireland) Semi-Final • Won: 3-1

Murphy • Tierney • Rankin • Szmid • Tate • **Jones** • Muirhead • Fletcher • **Nardiello** • Wood • **Williams**
Substitutes: Pugh (for Rankin) • Whiteman (for Nardiello) • Taylor (for Fletcher) • Heath (for Williams)

Friday 23 July 1999   v CREWE ALEXANDRA Final • Lost: 1-2

Murphy • Tierney • Rankin • Szmid • Tate • Jones • **Muirhead** • Sampson • Nardiello • Wood • Fletcher
Substitutes: Clegg (for Jones) • Heath (for Nardiello)

TOURNAMENT SQUAD

1. Brian MURPHY	5. Alan TATE	9. Daniel NARDIELLO	15. Paul TIERNEY
2. Steven CLEGG	6. Rhodri JONES	10. Neil WOOD	16. Matthew WILLIAMS
3. John RANKIN	7. Ben MUIRHEAD	11. Danny PUGH	17. Colin HEATH
4. Ashley DODD	8. Gary SAMPSON	12. Marc WHITEMAN	18. Darren FLETCHER
		14. Andrew TAYLOR	19. Marek SZMID

HILDEN CUP 1999
(Under 16s) BITBURG, GERMANY

v EINTRACHT FRANKFURT (Germany) Group Stage • Drawn: 0-0 Friday 30 July 1999

Woodcock • Ennis • Taylor • Waud • Fitzgerald • Fletcher • Eckersley • Humphreys • Heath • Kinsella • Mooniaruck
Substitute: Poole (for Mooniaruck)

v VfB 03 EV HILDEN (Germany) Group Stage • Won: 3-0 Friday 30 July 1999

Thewlis • Thompson • **Taylor 2** • Waud • Ennis • Fletcher • Bancroft • Ahmed • **Heath** • Kinsella • Rea
Substitutes: Fitzgerald (for Waud) • Woodcock (for Thewlis) • Eckersley (for Kinsella) • Poole (for Ahmed)

v TOIN GAKUEN JUNIOR HIGH SCHOOL (Japan) Group Stage • Lost: 1-2 Saturday 31 July 1999

Woodcock • Ennis • Taylor • Waud • Fitzgerald • Fletcher • Eckersley • Humphreys • Heath • Kinsella • **Mooniaruck**
Substitute: Poole (for Eckersley)

v 1.FC KAISERSLAUTERN (Germany) Group Stage • Drawn: 1-1 Saturday 31 July 1999

Thewlis • Thompson • Taylor • Waud • Fitzgerald • Fletcher • Eckersley • Humphreys • **Heath** • Poole • Mooniaruck
Substitute: Ennis (for Humphreys)

United did not qualify for final.

TOURNAMENT SQUAD

1. Gary WOODCOCK	6. Darren FLETCHER	12. Matthew REA
2. Jim THOMPSON	7. Michael ECKERSLEY	13. John THEWLIS
3. Kris TAYLOR	8. Adnan AHMED	14. Pierre ENNIS
4. Ben WAUD	9. Colin HEATH	15. Jamie BANCROFT
5. John FITZGERALD	10. Alan KINSELLA	16. Chris HUMPHREYS
	11. Kalam MOONIARUCK	17. David POOLE

MANCHESTER UNITED ACADEMY (Under 15s)

Sunday 5 September 1999   v STOKE CITY (away) • Won: 5-1

Yeomans • Bardsley • Lawrence • Connor • Moran • Jones • McKay • **Byrne** • **Henson 2** • Johnson J. • **Richardson 2**
Substitutes: Bruce • Gray • Baguley • Gregory

Sunday 12 September 1999   v HUDDERSFIELD TOWN (home) • Won: 5-0

Nelson • Bardsley • Lawrence • Connor • Moran • **Jones** • McKay • Johnson E. • **Henson 2** • **Johnson J. 2** • Collett
Substitutes: Bruce • Yeomans • Gregory • Baguley • Byrne • Eames

Sunday 19 September 1999   v EVERTON (away) • Won: 2-1

Yeomans • Bardsley • Lawrence • Connor • Moran • **Jones** • McKay • Bruce • **Henson** • Johnson E. • Collett
Substitutes: Byrne • Gregory • Eames • Baguley

Sunday 26 September 1999   v CREWE ALEXANDRA (home) • Lost: 0-1

Yeomans • Sims • Lawrence • Connor • Moran • Jones • Byrne • Richardson • Poole • Henson • Collett
Substitutes: Bruce • Baguley • Gregory • Eames

Sunday 3 October 1999   v NOTTINGHAM FOREST (away) • Won: 4-2

Yeomans • Sims • Lawrence • **Moran** • Connor • Jones • Byrne • Bruce • **Henson** • Johnson E. • **Collett**
*Substitutes: **Baguley** • Bardsley • Eames • Gregory*

Sunday 17 October 1999   v MANCHESTER CITY (away) • Lost: 0-3

Yeomans • Gregory • Lawrence • Picken • Connor • Richardson • Byrne • Poole • Johnson J. • Henson • Collett
Substitutes: Bruce • Bardsley • Baguley • Eames

Sunday 24 October 1999   v LIVERPOOL (away) • Won: 2-1

Yeomans • Picken • Lawrence • Sims • Connor • Jones • Bruce • Richardson • **Johnson J.** • **Henson** • Collett
Substitutes: Bardsley • Baguley • Eames

Sunday 7 November 1999   v SHEFFIELD WEDNESDAY (away) • Won: 1-0

Yeomans • Sims • Lawrence • Moran • Connor • Jones • Byrne • Bruce • Johnson J. • **Poole** • Richardson
Substitutes: Collett • Baguley • Gregory • Eames

names in bold indicate goalscorers

v LEEDS UNITED (home) • Won: 4-2 — Sunday 14 November 1999

Nelson • Picken • Lawrence • Sims • Connor • **Jones** • Byrne • Bruce • **Johnson J.** • **Poole** • **Richardson**
Substitutes: Baguley • Yeomans • Eames • Gregory • Collett

v BOLTON WANDERERS (home) • Lost: 0-1 — Sunday 21 November 1999

Nelson • Picken • Lawrence • Sims • Moran • Jones • McKay • Bruce • Johnson J. • Poole • Richardson
Substitutes: Collett • Yeomans • Johnson J. • Bardsley • Gregory • Connor • Baguley • Eames

v BARNSLEY (away) • Won: 4-2 — Sunday 28 November 1999

Yeomans • Pickin • Moran • Sims • Connor • Jones • Byrne • Bruce • **Poole 4** • Johnson E. • Collett
Substitutes: Bardsley • Baguley

v NEWCASTLE UNITED (away) • Won: 4-1 — Sunday 5 December 1999

Yeomans • Pickin • Lawrence • Moran • Connor • Jones • Byrne • **Bruce** • **Johnson J. 2** • Johnson E. • **Richardson**
Substitutes: Bardsley • Baguley

v LIVERPOOL (home) • Lost: 0-1 — Wednesday 15 December 1999

Yeomans • Sims • Lawrence • Connor • Moran • Jones • Byrne • Johnson E. • Poole • Johnson J. • Collett
Substitutes: Bruce • Eames • Baguley • Bardsley • Gregory

v STOKE CITY (home) • Won: 6-1 — Sunday 23 January 2000

Yeomans • Picken • Lawrence • Sims • Moran • **Jones** • Byrne • **Bruce** • **Johnson J. 2** • **Johnson E. 2** • Collett
Substitutes: Bardsley • Baguley • Redshaw

v EVERTON (home) • Lost: 1-4 — Sunday 6 February 2000

Yeomans • Picken • Lawrence • Sims • Moran • Jones • Byrne • Bruce • Johnson J. • **Collett** • Richardson
Substitutes: Bardsley • Baguley • Redshaw

v CREWE ALEXANDRA (away) • Won: 3-2 — Sunday 13 February 2000

Murray • Picken • Lawrence • Sims • Moran • **Richardson** • Byrne • Bruce • **Johnson J.** • **Johnson E.** • Collett
Substitutes: Connor • Yeomans • Bardsley • Redshaw

ACADEMY

Wednesday 16 February 2000 **v LIVERPOOL (away) • Won: 1-0**

Yeomans • Sims • Lawrence • Connor • Moran • Richardson • Byrne • Bruce • Johnson J. • **Johnson E.** • Collett
Substitutes: Bardsley • Jones • Redshaw

Sunday 20 February 2000 **v NOTTINGHAM FOREST (home) • Lost: 0-2**

Yeomans • Reed • Lawrence • Connor • Moran • Jones • Byrne • Bardsley • Johnson J. • Shiels • Collett
Substitutes: Poole • Johnson E. • Bruce • Richardson

Tuesday 22nd February 2000 **v NORWICH CITY (away) • Won: 3-0**

Yeomans • Reed • Lawrence • Sims • Moran • Jones • Byrne • **Richardson** • **Johnson E.** • **Poole** • Collett
Substitutes: Connor • Heaton • Johnson J. • Bardsley • Greenwood

Sunday 5 March 2000 **v LIVERPOOL (home) • Won: 2-1**

Yeomans • Reed • Lawrence • Sims • Moran • Richardson • Byrne • Johnson E. • **Johnson J.** • Poole • Collett
Substitutes: Jones • Bruce • Bardsley • Connor • Redshaw • Gray **(one o.g.)**

Thursday 16 March 2000 **v NIRASAKI HIGH SCHOOL (Japan) (at L.F.A. Ground, Leyland) • Won: 2-0**

Yeomans • Sims • Lawrence • **Connor** • Moran • Jones • **Byrne** • Johnson E. • Johnson J. • Poole • Richardson
Substitutes: Bruce • Collett • Bardsley • Gray

Sunday 19 March 2000 **v SHEFFIELD WEDNESDAY (home) • Won: 1-0**

Yeomans • Reed • Lawrence • Sims • Moran • Jones • Byrne • **Bruce** • Johnson J. • Poole • Collett
Substitutes: Bardsley • Gray • Connor

Sunday 26 March 2000 **v LEEDS UNITED (away) • Won: 4-0**

Yeomans • Reed • Lawrence • Sims • Moran • Jones • Byrne • Bruce • **Johnson J. 2** • **Johnson E.** • **Richardson**
Substitutes: Collett • Connor • Bardsley

Sunday 9 April 2000 **v BARNSLEY (home) • Won: 3-1**

Yeomans • Picken • Lawrence • Sims • **Moran** • Collett • **Poole** • Jones • Johnson J. • **Johnson E.** • Richardson
Substitutes: Bruce • Connor • Bardsley • Byrne • Gray

names in bold indicate goalscorers

v NEWCASTLE UNITED (home) • Won: 4-2   Sunday 7 May 2000

Hickson • Sims • Lawrence • Connor • **Moran** • Collett • Bardsley • Bruce • **Johnson J.** • **Johnson E. 2** • Richardson

Substitutes: Picken • Gray

MANCHESTER UNITED ACADEMY (Under 14s)

v HUDDERSFIELD TOWN (away) • Won: 2-0   Tuesday 31 August 1999

Heaton • Greenwood • Kelliher • Jennions • Howard • Corvins • Jones • Picken • Smith • **Redshaw 2** • Coffey

Substitutes: Dyke • Flanagan • Yeomans.

v STOKE CITY (Home) • Won: 9-0   Sunday 5 September 1999

Heaton • Greenwood • Eckersley • Jennions • Howard • Corvins • **Kingsbury** • Pickin • **Flanagan 2** • **Redshaw 5** • Coffey

Substitutes: Jones • Kelliher

v HUDDERSFIELD TOWN (away) • Won: 3-1   Sunday 12 September 1999

Heaton • Greenwood • Kelliher • Jennions • Howard • **Corvins** • Kingsbury • Pickin • Fllanagan • **Redshaw 2** • Coffey

Substitute: Jones

v EVERTON (home) • Won: 3-1   Sunday 19 September 1999

Heaton • Greenwood • Kelliher • Jennions • Howard • **Corvins** • **Kingsbury** • Pickin • Flanagan • Redshaw • **Coffey**

Substitute: Jones

v CREWE ALEXANDRA (away) • Won: 5-1   Sunday 26 September 1999

Heaton • Greenwood • Eckersley • Jennions • Howard • Corvins • **Kingsbury** • Bardsley • Pickin • **Redshaw 4** • Coffey

Substitutes: Jones • Kelliher

v NOTTINGHAM FOREST (home) • Won: 2-1   Sunday 3 October 1999

Heaton • Greenwood • **Eckersley** • Pickin • Howard • Corvins • **Kingsbury** • Jones • Gibb • Redshaw • Coffey

Substitutes: Kelliher • Flanagan

Sunday 17 October 1999   **v MANCHESTER CITY (away) • Lost: 0-1**

Heaton • Greenwood • Eckersley • Jennions • Howard • Corvins • Kingsbury • Jones • Gibb • Redshaw • Coffey
Substitutes: Kelliher • Flanagan

Saturday 23 October 1999   **v WUHAN HIGH SCHOOL (China) (home) • Lost: 0-4**

Heaton • Gregory • Kelliher • Howard • Jennions • Bardsley • Jones • Eames • Flanagan • Redshaw • Baguley
Substitutes: Eckersley • Corvins • Coffey

Sunday 24 October 1999   **v LIVERPOOL (home) • Won: 3-0**

Heaton • Jones • **Eckersley** • Jennions • Howard • Corvins • Kingsbury • Greenwood • **Flanagan** • **Redshaw** • Coffey
Substitute: Kelliher

Sunday 31 October 1999   **v BLACKBURN ROVERS (home) • Lost: 0-2**

Heaton • Greenwood • Eckersley • Jennions • Howard • Corvins • Kingsbury • Pickin • Gibb • Redshaw • Coffey
Substitutes: Kelliher • Jones • Flanagan

Sunday 7 November 1999   **v SHEFFIELD WEDNESDAY (home) • Won: 1-0**

Heaton • Greenwood • Kelliher • Jennions • Howard • Eckersley • Jones • Bardsley • Gibb • Horrocks • Coffey
*Substitutes: **Flanagan** • Corvins*

Sunday 14 November 1999   **v LEEDS UNITED (away) • Lost: 2-3**

Heaton • Greenwood • Kelliher • **Jennions** • Howard • Eckersley • Jones • Bardsley • Horrocks • **Redshaw** • Coffey
Substitutes: Flanagan • Corvins

Tuesday 16 November 1999   **v LIVERPOOL (away) • Drawn: 1-1**

Heaton • Simpson • Eckersley • **Jennions** • Howard • Jones • Kelliher • Pickin • Horrocks • Redshaw • Coffey
Substitutes: Flanagan • Corvins • Jones

Sunday 21 November 1999   **v BOLTON WANDERERS (away) • Won: 7-0**

Heaton • Jones • Eckersley • Jennions • Howard • **Corvins** • **Coffey** • Greenwood • **Horrocks 2** • **Redshaw 2** • Kelliher
*Substitute: **Flanagan***

names in bold indicate goalscorers

v BARNSLEY (home) • Won: 3-1 — Sunday 28 November 1999

Heaton • Jones • Eckersley • Jennions • Howard • Corvins • Coffey • Greenwood • Horrocks • **Redshaw 3** • Kelliher
Substitute: Flanagan

v NEWCASTLE UNITED (home) • Lost: 1-2 — Sunday 5 December 1999

Heaton • Jones • Eckersley • Holt • Howard • Corvins • Coffey • Greenwood • Flanagan • **Redshaw** • Kelliher
Substitute: Horrocks

v STOKE CITY (away) • Won: 3-0 — Sunday 23 January 2000

Lee • Simpson • Kelliher • Eckersley • Howard • Nix • Salmon • Jones • **Flanagan 2 (1 pen)** • Sheridan • **Coffey**
Substitutes: Corvins • Jones

v HUDDERSFIELD TOWN (home) • Won: 2-1 — Sunday 30 January 2000

Heaton • Simpson • Eckersley • Greenwood • Howard • Nix • Salmon • Jones • **Flanagan 2 (1 pen)** • Sheridan • Coffey
Substitutes: Kelliher • Jones

v EVERTON (away) • Won: 6-0 — Sunday 6 February 2000

Heaton • Greenwood • Eckersley • Jennions • Howard • Nix • Salmon • **Jones 2** • **Flanagan** • **Sheridan 3** • Coffey
Substitutes: Kelliher • Jones

v CREWE ALEXANDRA (home) • Won: 1-0 — Sunday 13 February 2000

Heaton • Greenwood • Baguley • Eckersley • Howard • Nix • Salmon • Jones • **Flanagan** • Sheridan • Coffey
Substitutes: Jennions • Jones

v NOTTINGHAM FOREST (away) • Won: 4-1 — Sunday 20 February 2000

Heaton • Greenwood • Jones • Jennions • Howard • **Nix** • **Redshaw** • Jones • **Flanagan 2** • Sheridan • Coffey
Substitute: Salmon

v MANCHESTER CITY (home) • Drawn: 2-2 — Sunday 27 February 2000

Heaton • Greenwood • Eckersley • Picken • Howard • Nix • Shields • Jones • **Flanagan** • **Sheridan** • Coffey
Substitutes: Kelliher • Jones • Jennions

Sunday 5 March 2000   v LIVERPOOL (away) • Drawn: 3-3

Heaton • Greenwood • Eckersley • **Jennions** • Howard • Nix • Shields • Pickin • **Flanagan** • **Fishwick** • Coffey
Substitutes: Kelliher • Jones

Sunday 12 March 2000   v BLACKBURN ROVERS (away) • Won: 2-0

Heaton • Greenwood • Eckersley • Jennions • Howard • Nix • Shields • Pickin • **Flanagan** • **Fishwick** • Coffey
Substitutes: Jones • Kelliher • Corvins

Sunday 19 March 2000   v SHEFFIELD WEDNESDAY (away) • Won: 6-1

Heaton • **Greenwood** • Eckersley • Holt • Howard • Nix • McMahon • Pickin • Shields • **Fishwick 3** • Coffey
*Substitutes: **Flanagan 2** • Jennions*

Sunday 26 March 2000   v LEEDS UNITED (home) • Drawn: 2-2

Heaton • Greenwood • Eckersley • Holt • Howard • Nix • Flanagan • Pickin • **Shields 2** • Fishwick • Coffey.

Sunday 9 April 2000   v BARNSLEY (away) • Lost: 1-3

Heaton • Greenwood • Eckersley • **Jennions** • Howard • Nix • Flanagan • Nevins • Fishwick • Marsh • Coffey
Substitutes: Holt • McMahon

Sunday 7 May 2000   v NEWCASTLE UNITED (away) • Lost: 1-2

Lee • Greenwood • Eckersley • Jennions • Howard • Nix • McMahon • Nevins • Flanagan • **Marsh** • Coffey

MANCHESTER UNITED ACADEMY (Under 13s)

Sunday 5 September 1999   v STOKE CITY (away) • Won: 6-0

Lee • Simpson • Adams • Holt • Knights M. • **Guthrie** • Salmon • Jones • **Wilcox-Crooks 3** • McMahon • **Marsh 2**
Substitute: Bolton

names in bold indicate goalscorers

v HUDDERSFIELD TOWN (away) • Won: 4-0 — Sunday 12 September 1999

Ratchford • Wilcox-Crooks • Adams • Holt • Simpson • **Guthrie** • **Salmon** • Jones • **Marsh 2** • Grimes • McMahon
Substitute: Bolton

v EVERTON (away) • Drawn: 1-1 — Sunday 19 September 1999

Lee • Simpson • Adams • Holt • Evans • Guthrie • Salmon • Jones • Wilcox-Crooks • Grimes • McMahon
*Substitutes: Bolton • Tuffy • Best • Wilson • Howland • **Marsh***

v CREWE ALEXANDRA (home) • Won: 4-0 — Sunday 26 September 1999

Lee • McMahon • Adams • Simpson • Knights M. • Guthrie • Salmon • Jones • Marsh • **Grimes 2** • **Bolton**
*Substitute: **Burns***

v NOTTINGHAM FOREST (home) • Won: 4-0 — Sunday 3 October 1999

Lee • **Simpson** • Adams • Holt • Knights M. • Guthrie • Salmon • Jones • **Marsh 3** • Grimes • McMahon
Substitutes: Bolton • Burns

v MANCHESTER CITY (home) • Drawn: 0-0 — Sunday 17 October 1999

Lee • Simpson • Adams • Holt • Knights M. • Guthrie • Salmon • Jones • Grimes • Marsh • McMahon
Substitutes: Bolton • Burns

v LIVERPOOL (away) • Won: 6-2 — Sunday 24 October 1999

Lee • Simpson • Adams • Holt • Knights M. • Guthrie • McMahon • **Jones** • Burns • Marsh • **Bolton 2**
*Substitutes: **Wilcox-Crooks 2** • Salmon • **Grimes***

v BLACKBURN ROVERS (away) • Won: 4-0 — Sunday 31 October 1999

Lee • Simpson • Adams • Holt • Knights M. • McMahon • Salmon • Jones • **Burns 2** • **Marsh** • Bolton
*Substitutes: **Grimes** • Wilcox-Crooks*

v SHEFFIELD WEDNESDAY (away) • Lost: 2-3 — Sunday 7 November 1999

Lee • Simpson • Adams • Holt • Knights M. • McMahon • **Salmon** • Jones • **Marsh** • Grimes • Bolton
Substitute: Wilcox-Crooks

Sunday 14 November 1999   v LEEDS UNITED (away) • Won: 5-2

Lee • Simpson • Adams • Holt • Knights M. • McMahon • Salmon • Jones • Marsh • **Grimes 4** • **Wilcox-Crooks**
Substitutes: Bolton • Burns

Thursday 18 November 1999   v HUDDERSFIELD TOWN (home) • Won: 2-1

Lee • Adams • McMahon • Holt • Knights M. • Guthrie • Salmon • Wilcox-Crooks • Marsh • **Grimes** • Bolton
*Substitutes: Jones • Ratchford • Burns • **Campbell** • Simpson*

Sunday 21 November 1999   v BOLTON WANDERERS (home) • Won: 2-0

Lee • Simpson • Adams • Holt • Knights M. • **Guthrie** • Salmon • Jones • **Marsh** • Grimes • McMahon
Substitutes: Bolton • Wilcox-Crooks

Sunday 28 November 1999   v BARNSLEY (away) • Won: 4-1

Lee • Simpson • Adams • Holt • Knights M. • Guthrie • Salmon • Jones • **Marsh 2** • **Grimes 2** • Wilcox-Crooks
Substitutes: Bolton • McMahon

Sunday 5 December 1999   v NEWCASTLE UNITED (home) • Drawn: 1-1

Lee • McMahon • Adams • Simpson • Knights M. • Guthrie • Salmon • Jones • **Marsh** • Grimes • Wilcox-Crooks
Substitutes: Bolton • Campbell

Sunday 23 January 2000   v STOKE CITY (home) • Won: 9-1

Ratchford • McMahon • Adams • Wilcox-Crooks • Knights M. • **Guthrie** • **Campbell** • Baker • Evans • **Grimes 3** • Bolton
(one o.g.)
*Substitute: **Burns 3***

Sunday 30 January 2000   v HUDDERSFIELD TOWN (home) • Won: 10-0

Lee • McMahon • Adams • **Wilcox-Crooks** • Knights M. • **Guthrie 2** • **Campbell 2** • Baker • Evans • Grimes • **Bolton**
*Substitute: **Burns***

Sunday 6 February 2000   v EVERTON (home) • Lost: 1-3

Lee • McMahon • Adams • Wilcox-Crooks • Knights M. • Guthrie • Campbell • Baker • Evans • **Grimes** • Bolton
Substitutes: Burns • Marsh

names in bold indicate goalscorers

v CREWE ALEXANDRA (away) • Lost: 5-8
Sunday 13 February 2000

Stephenson • Baker • Adams • Wilcox-Crooks • Knights M. • **Guthrie** • McMahon • **Evans** • Marsh • **Grimes** • **Bolton 2**
Substitute: Holt

v NOTTINGHAM FOREST (away) • Lost: 3-4
Sunday 20 February 2000

Lee • Baker • Adams • Wilcox-Crooks • **Knights M.** • **Guthrie** • McMahon • Evans • **Marsh** • Baguley • Bolton
Substitutes: Burns • Salmon

v MANCHESTER CITY (away) • Lost: 0-1
Sunday 27 February 2000

Lee • McMahon • Adams • Knights J. • Knights M. • Guthrie • Salmon • Baker • Marsh • Evans • Wilcox-Crooks
Substitutes: Bolton • Burns • Campbell • Grimes

v LIVERPOOL (home) • Won: 5-1
Sunday 5 March 2000

Lee • Simpson • Adams • Holt • Knights M. • Guthrie • Wilcox-Crooks • Jones • **Marsh 2** • **Grimes 3** • McMahon
Substitutes: Bolton • Salmon

v BLACKBURN ROVERS (home) • Won: 2-0
Sunday 12 March 2000

Lee • Wilcox-Crooks • Adams • Holt • Simpson • Guthrie • Salmon • Jones • **Marsh 2** • Grimes • McMahon
Substitutes: White • Oxley • Bolton

v SHEFFIELD WEDNESDAY (home) • Won: 2-1
Sunday 19 March 2000

Lee • Wilcox-Crooks • Adams • Simpson • Oxley • Guthrie • Salmon • Jones • Marsh • **White** • **Bolton**
Substitutes: Grimes • Knights

v LEEDS UNITED (home) • Drew: 2-2
Sunday 26 March 2000

Lee • Wilcox-Crooks • Adams • Simpson • Oxley • **Guthrie** • McMahon • Jones • Marsh • White • Bolton
*Substitutes: **Grimes** • Salmon • Knights M.*

v BARNSLEY (away) • Lost: 2-3
Sunday 9 April 2000

Lee • Wilcox-Crooks • Adams • Simpson • Oxley • Guthrie • McMahon • Jones • **White** • **Grimes** • Bolton
Substitute: Knights M.

names in bold indicate goalscorers

Thursday 27 April 2000 | **v BOLTON WANDERERS (home) • Won: 5-1**

Lee • Simpson • Adams • Holt • Oxley • **Guthrie** • McMahon • Jones • **Marsh 2** • **Grimes 2** • Bolton

Substitutes: White • Salmon

Sunday 7 May 2000 | **v NEWCASTLE UNITED (away) • Drawn: 1-1**

Ratchford • Wilcox-Crooks • Adams • Holt • Simpson • **Guthrie** • Salmon • Jones • White • Grimes • Bolton

Substitutes: Hewitt • Salmon.

Under 12s

SQUAD

Chris BAGULEY
Richard BAKER
Lee BARNES
Aaron BURNS
Fraser CAMPBELL
Leigh CRAVEN
Luke DANIELS
Gareth EVANS
Gary HILLMAN
Iain HOWARD

Jonathan HUNT
Michael LEA
Anthony MARSHALL
James MOORE
Daniel PRINCE
James QUINN
Aaron RATCHFORD
Ryan SHAWCROSS

Under 11s

SQUAD

Fabian BRANDY
James CHESTER
Theodore COLEMAN
Christopher COOKE
Rico COULIO
Alex DRINKWATER
Richard ECKERSLEY
Dominic GALLACHER
Lee HANSON
Gianluca HAVERN
Sam HEWSON
Callum HIGGINBOTHAM

Adam INGRAM-HUGHES
Lee JOHNSON
Zac JONES
Matthew KENDRICK
Scott McMANUS
Luke MORGAN
David OWENS
Joshua PARRY
Thomas ROWE
Daniel TOWNSEND
Joseph THOMPSON
Gavin WESTWELL

Under 10s

SQUAD

Nicky BLACKMAN
Jacob BUTTERFIELD
Jon CROMPTON
James DERBYSHIRE
Daniel DRINKWATER
Dominic HUGHES
Daniel McDONALD
Michael McFALONE
Matthew MAINWARING

Jay McGARVEY
Tom MELLOR
Chris OVINGTON
Matthew ROBERTS
Alex SKIDMORE
James WAGGETT
Adam YATES

Under 9s

SQUAD

Thomas CAHILL
Joseph DUDGEON
Jonathan EDGE
Shaun JOHNSON
Matthew JONES
Lee LATHAM
Jacob LAWLOR
Ben MARSHALL
Adam MITCHELL

Oliver NORWOOD
Michael O'BRIEN
Justin PICKERING
Matthew PIOTROWSKI
Daniel WELBECK
Jordan WHITE
David WILLIAMS
Jake WILLIAMS
Matthew WILLIAMS

4TH INTERNATIONAL CHAMPIONSHIP OF FOOTBALL 7
(Under 12s) – BARCELONA, SPAIN

Monday 27 December 1999
v RCD ESPANOL (Spain) Group A • Won: 1-0
Ratchford • Simpson • Baker • Campbell • Guthrie •
McMahon • Burns
Substitutes: *Baguley (for Burns) • Evans (for Campbell)*

Monday 27 December 1999
v FC BARCELONA (Spain) Group A • Lost: 0-2
Ratchford • Simpson • Hunt • Campbell • Guthrie
McMahon • Baguley
Substitutes: *Baker (for Campbell) • Evans (for Guthrie)*

Monday 27 December 1999
v PARIS ST GERMAIN (France) Group A • Lost: 0-1
Ratchford • Simpson • Baker • Evans • Guthrie • McMahon •
Baguley
Substitutes: *Lea (for McMahon) • Campbell (for Baguley)*

Monday 27 December 1999
v ATLETICO MADRID (Spain) Group A • Lost: 1-4
Jones • Simpson • Hunt • Evans • Guthrie • McMahon •
Baguley
Substitutes: *Baker (for Hunt) • Lea (for McMahon) •*
***Burns** (for Baguley)*

United did not qualify for the final.

TOURNAMENT SQUAD

Christopher BAGULEY	Gareth EVANS	Michael LEA
Richard BAKER	Danny GUTHRIE	Christopher McMAHON
Aaron BURNS	Jonathan HUNT	Aaron RATCHFORD
Frazier CAMPBELL	Zachariah JONES	Daniel SIMPSON

MICROTEC CUP 2000 – BINGEN, GERMANY
FIVE-A-SIDE TOURNAMENT (Under 12s)

Saturday 15 January 2000
v BFV HASSIA BINGEN (Germany) Group A • Won: 4-0
Ratchford • **Simpson** • McMahon • **Guthrie** • Wilcox-Crooks
Substitutes: *Campbell • **Baguley** • Hillman • Howard •*
Evans

Saturday 15 January 2000
v ARMINIA BIELEFELD (Germany) Group A • Won: 1-0
Jones • Simpson • Guthrie • Evans • Baguley
Substitutes: *Campbell • **McMahon** • Howard •*
Wilcox-Crooks

Saturday 15 January 2000
v STUTTGARTER KICKERS (Germany) Group A • Won: 3-0
Ratchford • Simpson • McMahon • Guthrie • Wilcox-
Crookes
Substitutes: ***Campbell 2** • Baguley • Howard • Hillman •*
Evans

Saturday 15 January 2000
v SSV ULM (Germany) Second Phase • Lost: 0-2
Ratchford • Simpson • Evans • Guthrie • Baguley
Substitutes: *Campbell • McMahon • Wilcox-Crooks*

Saturday 15 January 2000
v ALEMANNIA AACHEN (Germany) Second Phase •
Won: 3-2
Jones • Simpson • Evans • Campbell • **Baguley**
*Substitutes: Ratchford • Howard • **Hillman** • Campbell •*
McMahon • Wilcox-Crooks • Guthrie

Saturday 15 January 2000
v SV WALDHOF MANNHEIM (Germany) Semi-Final •
Lost: 1-3
Jones • Simpson • **Evans** • Campbell • Baguley
Substitutes: Campbell • McMahon • Wilcox-Crooks

TOURNAMENT SQUAD

Christopher BAGULEY
Frazier CAMPBELL
Gareth EVANS
Danny GUTHRIE
Gary HILLMAN
Iain HOWARD

Zachariah JONES
Christopher McMAHON
Aaron RATCHFORD
Daniel SIMPSON
Christopher WILCOX-CROOKS

Saturday 15 January 2000
v MAINZ 05 (Germany) Third/Fourth Place Play-Off •
Won: 4-1
Ratchford • **Simpson** • Evans • **Campbell 2** • Baguley
(one o.g.)
Substitutes: Jones • Hillman • Howard • McMahon •
Guthrie • Wilcox-Crooks

DANONE CUP (UNDER 12s) – PARC DES PRINCES, PARIS

Sunday 28 May 2000
v RC LENS (France) Group C • Drawn: 0-0
Ratchford • Morgan • Chester • Drinkwater • Hewson •
Thompson • Evans • Brandy • Hanson
Substitutes: Jones • Coleman • Owens

Sunday 28 May 2000
v RSC ANDERLECHT (Belgium) Group C • Lost: 0-1
Jones • Morgan • Chester • Drinkwater • Hewson •
Thompson • Evans • Brandy • Hanson
Substitutes: Ratchford • Owens • Coleman

Sunday 28 May 2000
v NAGOYA GRAMPUS EIGHT (Japan) Group C •
Drawn: 0-0
Jones • Chester • Drinkwater • Thompson • Brandy • Owens
• Evans • Hanson • Coleman
Substitutes: Ratchford • Hewson • Morgan

Sunday 28 May 2000
v PARIS ST GERMAIN (France) Second Phase • Lost: 0-1
Ratchford • Chester • Drinkwater • Thompson • Brandy •
Owens • Hewson • Evans • Hanson
Substitutes: Jones • Morgan • Brandy

Sunday 28 May 2000
v FC GIRONDINS BORDEAUX (France) Eleventh/Twelfth
Place Play-Off • Lost: 0-2
Jones • Chester • Drinkwater • Hewson • Morgan •
Thompson • Evans • Owens • Hanson
Substitutes: Ratchford • Brandy • Coleman

TOURNAMENT SQUAD

Fabian BRANDY
James CHESTER
Theodore COLEMAN
Alex DRINKWATER
Gare EVANS
Lee HANSON

Sam HEWSON
Zachariah JONES
Luke MORGAN
David OWENS
Aaron RATCHFORD
Joe THOMPSON

INTERNATIONAL 'ASCENSION' TOURNAMENT (UNDER 11s)
BRUSSELS, BELGIUM

Saturday 3 June 2000
v RSC VISE (Belgium) Group B • Drawn: 0-0
Waggett • Eckersley • Chester • Crompton • Roberts •
Brandy • Thompson • Butterfield • Mellor • Hanson •
McGarvey
Substitutes: Ingram-Hughes • Drinkwater • Coleman

Saturday 3 June 2000
v LILLE OSC (France) Group B • Lost: 0-2
Ingram-Hughes • Eckersley • Chester • Crompton • Roberts •
Coleman • Thompson • Butterfield • Mellor • Brandy •
Hanson
Substitutes: Waggett • Drinkwater • McGarvey

Saturday 3 June 2000
v RSC CHARLEROI (Belgium) Group B • Won: 1-0
Waggett • Eckersley • Roberts • Crompton • Drinkwater •
Brandy • Thompson • Chester • McGarvey • **Coleman** •
Hanson
Substitutes: Ingram-Hughes • Mellor • Butterfield

Saturday 3 June 2000
v KAA GEENT (Belgium) Group B • Won: 5-0
Waggett • Eckersley • Roberts • Crompton • Drinkwater •
Brandy • Thompson • Chester • McGarvey • **Coleman 3** •
Hanson 2
Substitutes: Ingram-Hughes • Mellor • Butterfield

Sunday 4 June 2000
v STANDARD LIEGE (Belgium) Group B • Lost: 0-3
Waggett • Eckersley • Roberts • Crompton • Drinkwater •
Brandy • Thompson • Chester • McGarvey • Coleman •
Hanson
Substitutes: Ingram-Hughes • Mellor • Butterfield

Sunday 4 June 2000
v EXCELSIOR MOUSCRON (Belgium) Second Phase •
Won: 1-0
Ingram-Hanson • Eckersley • Chester • Crompton •
Drinkwater • Thompson • Coleman • Butterfield • Mellor •
McGarvey • **Hanson**
Substitutes: Waggett • Brandy • Roberts

Sunday 4 June 2000
v ROYAL FRANCS BORAINS (Belgium) Ninth/Tenth Place
Play-Off • Won: 5-1
Ingram-Hughes • Eckersley • Chester • Crompton •
Drinkwater • **Thompson** • **Coleman 2** • Butterfield • Mellor •
McGarvey • **Hanson**
*Substitutes: Waggett • **Brandy** • Roberts*

TOURNAMENT SQUAD

Fabian BRANDY
Jacob BUTTERFIELD
James CHESTER
Theodore COLEMAN
Jonathan CROMPTON
Daniel DRINKWATER
Richard ECKERSLEY

Lee HANSON
Dominic INGRAM-HUGHES
Jay McGARVEY
Tom MELLOR
Matthew ROBERTS
Joseph THOMPSON
James WAGGETT

GENERAL INFORMATION

During the football season the Membership & Supporters' Club office hours are as follows:

Monday to Friday: 9.00am – 5.00pm
Home Match Days: 9.00am – kick-off
(and 20 minutes after the game)

The office will be open one hour prior to departure to our away venues.

MEMBERSHIP

Once we deem Membership has reached its capacity for the season, our books will close for the season and no further applications will be accepted. In the main, sales of match tickets for home games are restricted to members. It is therefore important to note that anyone wishing to attend a home game must become a member. Application forms are available upon request.

MEMBERS' PERSONAL ACCIDENT INSURANCE

Under our special personal accident insurance policy with Lloyds Underwriters, all members are insured whilst in attendance and travelling to and from the stadium (until safe return to current place of residence), for all competitive games played by the Manchester United 1st team, both home and away, anywhere in the world.

The following accidental death and bodily injury benefits apply:

1. Death £10,000 (limited to £1,000 for persons under 16 years of age)
2. Total and irrecoverable loss of sight of both eyes £10,000
3. Total and irrecoverable loss of sight in one eye £5,000
4. Loss of two limbs £10,000
5. Loss of one limb £5,000
6. Total and irrecoverable loss of sight in one eye and loss of one limb £10,000
7. Permanent Total Disablement (other than total loss of sight or one or both eyes or loss of limb) £10,000

The above is subject to the policy conditions and exclusions. Further details are available from the Membership Secretary to whom any enquiries should be addressed.

BRANCHES OF THE SUPPORTERS' CLUB

A full list of all our official branches of the supporters club can be found on pages 218 to 224.

Due to the present demand for match tickets we will not allow any new branches to be formed. All enquiries in this respect should be forwarded for the attention of the Membership Secretary.

AWAY TRAVEL

Domestic Games:
All Club Members, which include Private Box holders, Executive Suite & Club Class Members and Season Ticket holders, are automatically enrolled in our Away Travel Club and, as such, are entitled to book coach travel from Old Trafford to all Premiership venues. Full details can be found on the opposite page.

How to make a Booking:

You can book a place on a coach, subject to availability upon personal application at the Membership Office, in which case you must quote your MUFC customer number. Alternatively, you can make a postal application by submitting the relevant payment, a stamped addressed envelope and a covering letter quoting your MUFC customer number. Telephone reservations are also acceptable if making payment by credit/debit card. Cancellations must be made in advance of the day of the game.

Car Park attendants will be on duty should you wish to park your car on one of our car parks before travelling to an away game. This service is offered at no extra charge but we wish to point out that the Club will not be held responsible for any damage or theft from your vehicle.

Members are advised to check match ticket availability before booking a place on a coach. Details can be obtained by telephoning our Ticket & Match Information line on **0161 872 0199**.

MEMBERS' COACH TRAVEL FROM OLD TRAFFORD

Opponents	Executive Coach	Luxury Coach	*Departure Time	**Estimated Return Time to Old Trafford
Arsenal	£20.00	£15.00	8.30 am	9.30 pm
Aston Villa	£14.00	£10.00	11.30 am	7.30 pm
Charlton Athletic	£20.00	£15.00	8.00 am	10.00 pm
Chelsea	£20.00	£15.00	8.30 am	9.30 pm
Coventry City	£14.00	£10.00	11.30 am	7.30 pm
Derby County	£12.00	£9.00	11.00 am	8.00 pm
Everton	£11.00	£8.00	1.00 pm	6.15 pm
Ipswich Town	£21.00	£16.00	8.30 am	10.30 pm
Leeds United	£11.00	£8.00	1.00 pm	6.15 pm
Leicester City	£12.00	£9.00	11.00 am	8.00 pm
Liverpool	£11.00	£8.00	1.00 pm	6.15 pm
Manchester City	No transport arranged for this fixture			
Middlesbrough	£15.00	£11.00	11.00 am	8.00 pm
Newcastle United	£17.00	£13.00	10.30 am	8.30 pm
Southampton	£20.00	£15.00	8.30 am	10.00 pm
Sunderland	£17.00	£13.00	10.30 am	8.30 pm
Tottenham Hotspur	£20.00	£15.00	9.00 am	9.30 pm
West Ham United	£20.00	£15.00	8.30 am	9.30 pm
Wembley Stadium	£22.00	£17.00	8.30 am	10.00 pm

All times based on games with a 3.00pm kick-off

* Departure times are subject to change and it is vital to check the actual time when making your booking

** Return times shown are only estimated and are subject to traffic congestion

EUROPEAN TRAVEL

The Membership Office is also responsible for organising members travel and distribution of match tickets for our European away games. Full details will be made known when available, via all usual channels.

ABERDEEN Branch Secretary George Cowie, 113 Girdleness Road, Torry, Aberdeen AB11 8FB **Tel** 01224 891181 (between 6.00-7.30pm only please) *Departure points* 6.00am Guild Street, Aberdeen; 6.15am by pass, Stonehaven; 7.00am The Kingsway, Dundee.

ABERGELE AND COAST Branch Secretary Eddie Williams, 14 Maes-y-Dre, Abergele, Clwyd, North Wales, LL22 7HW **Tel** 01745 823694 *Departure points* Aber; Llanfairfechen; Penmaen Mawr; Conwy; Llandudno Junction; Colwyn Bay; Abergele; Rhyl; Rhuddlan; Dyserth; Prestatyn; Mostyn; Holywell; Flint; Deeside

ABERYSTWYTH AND DISTRICT Branch Secretary: Alan Evans, 6 Tregerddan, Bow Street, Dyfed, SY24 5AW **Tel** 01970 828117 after 6pm *Departure points* Please contact Branch Secretary

ASHBOURNE Branch Secretary Diane O'Connell, 2 Stanton Road, Ashbourne, Derbyshire, DE6 1SH **Tel** 01335 346105(evenings) *Departure points* 11.45am (4.45pm) Markeaton Roundabout, Derby; 12 noon(5.00pm) Ashbourne Bus Station. Times in brackets denote evening fixtures. Contact branch secretary for details of travel to away fixtures

BARNSLEY Branch Secretary Mick Mitchell, 12 Saxon Crescent, Worsbrough, Barnsley, S70 5PY **Tel** 01226 283 983 *Departure points* 12.30pm (5.30pm) Locke Park Working Mens Club, Park Road, Barnsley via A628 or 2½hours before any other kick-off times

BARROW AND FURNESS Branch Secretary Robert Bayliff, 31 Ashworth Street, Dalton-in-Furness, Cumbria, LA15 8SH **Tel** 01229 465277 **Mobile**: 07788 762936 *Departure points* Barrow, Ramsden Square 9.30am (4.00pm); Dalton 9.45am(4.15pm); Ulverston 10.00am(4.30pm) and A590 route to M6, times in brackets denote evening fixtures

BEDFORDSHIRE Branch Secretary Nigel Denton, 4 Abbey Road, Bedford, MK41 9LG. **Tel** 0410 964329 *Departure points* Bedford Bus Station, pick-up at Milton Keynes 'Coachways', Junction 14, M1

BERWICK-UPON-TWEED Branch Secretary Margaret Walker, 17 Lords Mount, Berwick-Upon-Tweed, Northumberland, TD15 1LY **Tel** 01289 304427 Chairman Raymond Dixon, 92 Shielfield Terrace, Berwick-upon-Tweed **Tel** 01289 308671 SAE please for all enquiries All telephone calls before 9.00pm please *Departure points* Berwick, Belford, Alnwick, Stannington, Washington; Scotch Corner, Leeming Bar and anywhere on the main A1- by arrangement

BIRMINGHAM Branch Secretary Paul Evans, 179 Longbridge Lane, Birmingham B31 4LA
Tel 0121 604 1385 (6.30-9.00pm) *Departure points* Longbridge; Birmingham (Rotunda; New Street); Tennis Courts Public House (A34); Junction 7, M6; Coach fares £10.00 (adults), £5.00 (juniors) Coaches operate for all home games For times please telephone or send a stamped addressed envelope

BLACK COUNTRY The branch attend all home/away games Coach details are as follows
Departure points St Lawrence Tavern, Darlaston 11.00am (4.00pm); Woden Public House, Wednesbury; 11.10am (4.10pm) Friendly Lodge Hotel, J10, M6 11.15am (4.15pm); Wheatsheaf Public House, off J11, M6 11.25am (4.25pm) Times in brackets denote evening fixtures
For further information contact Branch Secretary Ade Steventon **Tel** 0121 531 0826 (6.30- 9.00pm) **Mobile** 07931 714318 (6-9.30pm) or Ken Lawton **Tel** 01902 636393 (6.30-9pm)

BLACKPOOL, PRESTON AND FYLDE Branch Chairman Martin Day **Tel** 01253 891301 For coach bookings contact Travel Secretary Mrs Jean Halliday **Tel** 01772 635887 *Departure points* Cleveleys; Blackpool; St. Annes; Lytham; Freckleton; Preston United members on holiday are very welcome

BRADFORD AND LEEDS Branch Secretary Sally Hampshire, PO Box 87, Cleckheaton, West Yorkshire, BD19 6YN For further details please contact above

BRIDGNORTH AND DISTRICT Branch Secretary Ann Saxby, 30 Pitchford Road, Albrighton, Near Wolverhampton **Tel** 01902 373840
Departure points Ludlow; Bridgnorth; Albrighton; Wolverhampton

BRIDGWATER AND SOUTH WEST Branch Secretary Ray White, 4 Spencer Close, Bridgwater, Somerset, TA6 5SP **Tel** 01278 452186 *Departure points* Taunton; Bridgwater; Weston-Super-Mare; Clevedon, Aztec West (Bristol)

BRIGHTON Branch Secretary Colin Singers, 34 Meadowview Road, Sompting, Lancing, West Sussex **Tel** 01903 761679 *Departure points* 6.30am Worthing Central, 6.40am Shoreham (George Pub); 7.00am Brighton Railway Station; 7.45am Gatwick Airport

BRISTOL, BATH & DISTRICT Branch Secretary Jim Smith, 108 Coriander Drive, Bradley Stoke, Bristol, BS32 0DL **Tel** 0117 979 2459 (5.30-8.30 pm) *Departure points* Coach 1: Keynsham Church 07.45 (12.25); Bath Train Station 08.05 (12.45); Nailsworth 08.50 (13.30); Sainsbury's Stroud 09.00 (13.40); Coach 2: Bristol Temple Meads 08.40 (13.20); Bradley Stoke South 08.55 (13.35); Bradley Stoke North 09.00 (13.40); M5 Junction 14 09.10 (13.50); M5 Junction 13 09.20 (14.00) Coach fares for home matches, all 19 league matches booked before 1st August, luxury coach adult £10.50 jnrs/oaps £7.50; executive coach adult £13.00 jnrs/oaps £9.50; For individual matches, luxury coach adult £12.00, jnrs/oaps £8.50; executive coach adult £14.50, jnrs/oaps £10.50 All coach seats and match tickets are booked and paid for in advance
Times in brackets denote evening fixtures

BURTON-ON-TRENT Branch Secretary Mrs Pat Wright, 45 Foston Avenue, Burton-on-Trent, Staffordshire, DE13 0PL **Tel** 01283 532534 *Departure points* Moira (garage); Swadlincote; Burton (B&Q Lichfield Street); Stoke area

CARLISLE AND DISTRICT Branch Secretary Arnold Heard, 28 Kentmere Grove, Morton Park, Carlisle, Cumbria, CA2 6JD **Tel/Fax** 01228 538262 **Mobile** 0860 782769 *Departure points* For departure times and details on the branch, please contact Branch Secretary

CENTRAL POWYS Branch Secretary Bryn Thomas, 10 Well Lane, Bungalows, Llanidloes, Powys, SY18 6BA **Tel** 01686 412391(H) 01686 413 3200(W) *Departure points* Crossgates 10.30am; Rhayader 10.45am; Llanidloes 11.05am; Newtown 11.25am

CHEPSTOW AND DISTRICT Branch Secretary Anthony Parsons, 56 Treowen Road, Newbridge, Newport, Gwent, NP11 3DN **Tel** 01495 246253 *Departure points* Newbridge, Pontypool, Cwmbran Bus Station; Newport; Coldra Langstone; Magor; Caldicot; Chepstow For departure times and further details contact Branch Secretary

CHESTER AND NORTH WALES Branch Chairman Eddie Mansell, 45 Overlea Drive, Hawarden, Deeside, Clwyd, CH5 3HR **Tel** 01244 520332 Ticket & Travel Secretary Des Wright **Tel** 01244 851464 Branch Secretary Mrs Barbra Hammond, 93 Broughton Hall Road, Broughton, Chester **Tel** 01244 535161 Membership Secretary Mrs Irene Keidel, 3 Springfield Drive, Buckley, Clwyd **Tel** 01244 550943 *Departure points* Oswestry; Ellesmere; Wrexham; Chester; Rhyl; Greenfield; Flint; Connah's Quay; Deeside Leisure Centre; Queensferry; Strawberry Roundabout; Whitby; Ellesmere Port

CLEVELAND Branch Secretary John Higgins, 41 Ashford Avenue, Acklam, Middlesbrough TS5 4QL **Tel** 01642 643112 Treasurer Brian Tose, 2 Cowbar Cottages, Staithes, Cleveland TS13 5DA **Tel** 01947 841372 *Departure points* Please contact Branch Secretary for details

COLWYN BAY AND DISTRICT Branch Secretary Bill Griffiths, Whitefield, 60 Church Road, Rhos-on-Sea, Colwyn Bay, Clwyd, Wales LL28 4YS **Tel** 01492 540240 *Departure points* 10.45am (3.45pm) Alpine Travel coach garage, Builder Street West, Llandudno; 11.00am (4.00pm) Bus Stop, Mostyn Broadway (opposite Asda stores); 11.45am (4.15pm) Labour Club, Llandudno Junction; 11.30am (4.30pm) Guy's Newsagents, Conway Road, Colwyn Bay; 11.35am (4.35pm) Honda Centre, Old Colwyn; 11.40am (4.40pm) Queen's Hotel, Old Colwyn; 11.45am (4.45pm) Fair View Inn, Llandudlas; 11.50am (4.50pm) Slaters Showrooms, Abergele; 12.00noon (5.00pm) Talardy Inn on the Park Hotel, St. Asaph; 12.5pm (5.45pm) Plough Hotel, Aston Hill, Queensferry Times in brackets denote evening fixtures

CORBY Branch Chairman Andy Hobbs, 32 Lower Pastures, Great Oakley, Corby, Northants
Tel 01536 744 838 **Mobile** 07974 571353 Branch Meetings 7.15pm 1st Sunday of the month, Lodge Park Sports Centre, Shetland Way, Corby *Departure points* Co-op Extra Store, Alexandra Road, Corby 8.30am (1.30pm); Co-op Extra Superstore, Northfield Avenue, Kettering 8.40am (1.40pm) Times in brackets denote evening fixtures

CRAWLEY Branch Secretary Steve Whiting, 5 Bolney Court, Bewbush, Crawley, W Sussex
Tel 01293 424552 Ticket & Travel Secretary Gary Hillier, 18 Westway, Three Bridges, Crawley, W Sussex **Mobile** 0976 272725 *Departure Points* Contact Ticket & Travel Secretary

CREWE AND NANTWICH Branch Secretary Andy Ridgway, 38 Murrayfield Drive, Willaston, Nantwich, Cheshire **Tel** 01270 68418 *Departure points* 12.30pm (5.30pm) Nantwich Barony; 12.40pm (5.40pm) Earl of Crewe; 12.50pm (5.50pm) Cross Keys Away travel subject to demand Times in brackets denote evening fixtures

DONCASTER AND DISTRICT Branch Secretary Albert Thompson, 89 Anchorage Lane, Sprotboro, Doncaster, South Yorkshire, DN5 8EB **Tel** 01302 782964 Branch Treasurer Sue Moyles, 217 Warning Tongue Lane, Cantley **Tel** 01302 530422 **Fax** 01482 591708 Branch Chairman Paul Kelly, 58 Oak Grove, Conisbrough DN12 2HN **Tel** 01709 324058 *Departure points* 10.30am (4.30pm) Broadway Dunscroft; 10.40am (4.40pm) Edenthorpe; 10.50am (4.50pm) Waterdale (opposite main library); 11.00am (5.00pm); The Highwayman, Woodlands Times in brackets denote 8.00pm kick-off Meetings held first Sunday of every month (unless there is a home match) in the Wheatley Hotel at 7.00pm

DORSET Branch Secretary Mark Pattison,89 Parkstone Road, Poole, Dorset, BH15 2NZ **Tel** 01202 744348 *Departure points* Poole Train Station 6.15am (10.30am); Banksome (Courts) 6.20am (10.35am); Bournemouth, 6.30am (10.45am); Christchurch (Bargates) 6.45am (11.00am); Ringwood 7.00am (11.15am); Rownham Services 7.15am (11.30am); Chieveley Services 8.30am (12.30pm) Times in brackets denote evening fixtures

DUKINFIELD AND HYDE Branch Secretary Marilyn Chadderton, 12 Brownville Grove, Dukinfield, Cheshire, SK16 5AS **Tel** 0161 338 4892 *Departure points* Details of meetings and travel available from the above or S Jones **Tel** 0161 343 5260

EAST ANGLIA Branch Secretary Mark Donovan, The Street, Holywell Row, Mildenhall, Bury St Edmonds, Suffolk, IP28 8LT **Tel** 01638 717075 **(9.00am-6.00pm)** Details of your local representative can also be obtained by telephoning this number Executive travel available to all home fixtures via the following services:
Service No.1 Clacton; Colchester; Braintree; Great Dunmow; Bishop Stortford
Service No.2 Felixstowe; Nacton; Ipswich; Stowmarket; Bury St. Edmonds
Service No.3 Thetford; Mildenhall; Newmarket; Cambridge; Huntingdon
Service No.4 Lowestoft; Great Yarmouth; Norwich; East Dereham; Kings Lynn
Coaches also operate to all away games for which departure details are dependent on demand and ticket availability

EAST YORKSHIRE Branch Secretary Ian Baxter, 18 Soberhill Drive, Holme Moor, York YO43 4BH **Mobile 0468 821 844** Information for Tickets & Travel from Hull on **0374 775 078** *Departure points* Coach 1: 10.30am (3.30pm) Hull Marina; 10.40am (3.40pm) N. Ferriby; Coach 2:10.30am (3.30pm) Bay Horse, Mkt Weighton; 11.00am (4.00pm) Redbeck Cafe, Howden; 11.15am (4.15pm) Junction 34, M62 Times in brackets denote evening fixtures

ECCLES Branch Secretary Gareth Morris, 11 Brentwood Drive, Monton, Eccles, Manchester, M30 9LP **Tel 0161 281 9435** *Departure point* (Away games only) Rock House Hotel, Peel Green Road, Peel Green, Eccles For departure times please contact Branch Secretary

FEATHERSTONE & DISTRICT Branch Secretary Paul Kingsbury, 11 Hardwick Road, Featherstone, Nr Pontefract, W Yorks WF7 5JA **Tel 01977 793910 Mobile 07971 778161** Treasurer Andrew Dyson, 46 Northfield Drive, Pontefract, W Yorks WF8 2DL **Tel 01977 709561 Mobile 07979 326183** *Departure points* Pontefract Sorting Office 11.30am (4.30pm); Corner Pocket, Featherstone 11.40am (4.40pm); Green Lane, Featherstone 11.45am (4.45pm); Castleford Bus Station 11.55am (4.55pm) Meetings held every fortnight (Mondays) at the Girnhill Lane WMC, Featherstone at 8.00pm Times in brackets denote evening fixtures

GLAMORGAN AND GWENT Branch Secretary Neil Chambers, 201 Malpas Road, Newport, South Wales NP20 5PP Branch Chairman Cameron Erskine **Tel 02920 623705** (10.00am-1.00pm Monday-Friday Answerphone at other times) **Mobile 07585 615546** *Departure points* Skewen; Port Talbot; Bridgend; Cardiff; Newport

GLASGOW Branch Secretary David Sharkey, 45 Lavender Drive, Greenhills, East Kilbride G75 9JH **Tel 01355 902592** (7-11pm) Coach run to all home games *Departure points* 8.00am (1.00pm) Queen Street Station, Glasgow; 8.15am (1.15pm) The Angel, Uddingston; Any M74 Service Stations Times in brackets denote evening fixtures

GLOUCESTER AND CHELTENHAM Branch Secretary Mike Brown, 14 Swanswell Drive, Granleyfields, Cheltenham, GL51 6NA **Tel 01242 232267** (7.30-9.00pm) Coach Bookings Paul Brown, 59 Katherine Close, Churchdown, Gloucester GL3 1PB **Tel/Fax 01452 859553 Mobile 0961 573404 E-mail muscglos@aol.com** *Departure points* 9.15am (2.15pm) Station Road, Gloucester (outside British School of Motoring); 9.25am (2.25pm) Midland Hotel, Cheltenham; 9.30am (2.30pm) Cheltenham Gas Works Times in brackets denote evening fixtures

GRIMSBY AND DISTRICT Branch Secretary Bob England, 61 Shaw Drive, Scartho, Grimsby, DN33 2JB **Tel 01472 752130** Travel Arrangements Craig Collins (Branch Chairman) **Tel 01472 314273**

GUERNSEY Branch Secretary Eddie Martel, Ayia Napa, Rue des Barras, Les Maresqets, Vale, Guernsey, Channel Isles **Tel 01481 46285**

GWYNEDD Branch Secretary Gwyn Hughes, Sibrwd y Don, Tan y Cefn, Llanwnda, Caernarfon, Gwynedd, LL54 7YB **Tel 01286 830073 E-mail Gwyn.Hughes@manutd.com** Ticket Secretary Stephen Jones, Gwynant, Carmel, Caernarfon, Gwynedd LL54 7AA **Tel 07050 380804** *Departure points* Pwllheli; Llanwnda; Caernarfon; Bangor; For departure times, please contact branch secretary

HAMPSHIRE Branch Secretary Roy Debenham, 11 Lindley Gardens, Alresford, Hampshire, SO24 9PU **Tel 01962 734420** Ticket & Coach Secretary Pete Boyd, 23 Weavers Crofts, Melksham Wilts SN12 8BP **Tel 01225 700354** Chairman Paul Marsh, Oaktree Cottage, Commonhill Road, Braisfield, Hants SO51 0QF **Tel 01794 368951** *Departure points* (1) St George's Playing Field, Cosham (Near IBM); (2) Fareham Railway Station; (3) Parkway, Eastleigh Airport; (4) Bullington Cross Pub, Bullington Cross; Cheively Services, Newbury Times vary for weekend/evening matches, check with P Boyd

HARROGATE AND DISTRICT Branch Secretary Michael Heaton, Tel/Fax 01423 780679 Branch Secretary can be contacted on his mobile **Tel 07957 172 002** *Departure points* Coaches leave from Northallerton, Thirsk, Ripon, and also cater for the Nidderdale and Wenslydale areas, Harrogate & Skipton districts For further information regarding the above branch, including pick-up times, please contact the Secretary Transport is provided to all home and away fixtures, which includes European

HASTINGS Branch Secretary Tim Martin, 30 Silvan Road, St Leonards-on-Sea, East Sussex TN38 9RD (NO PERSONAL CALLERS) **Tel 01424 853189** (6.00-8.00pm) **Mobile 0973 656716** (Daytime) **Fax 01424 854989** Rod Beckingham **Tel 01424 443477** (6.00-7.00pm) *Departure points* 5.40am (10.00am) Eastbourne, Tesco's Roundabout; 6.00am (10.20am) Bexhill, Viking Chip Shop; 6.15am (10.30am) Silverhill Traffic lights; 6.40am(10.55 am); Hurst Green, George Pub; 7.00am (11.10am) Pembury, Camden Arms Pub Times in brackets denote evening fixtures For details of travel to away games please contact Branch Secretary

HEREFORD Branch Secretary Norman Elliss, 40 Chichester Close, Abbeyfields, Belmont, Hereford, HR2 7YU **Tel 01432 359923 Fax 01432 342880** *Departure points* 8.30am (2.00pm) Leominster; 9.00am (2.30pm) Bulmers Car Park, Hereford; 9.30am (3.00pm) Ledbury; 9.45am (3.15pm) Malvern Link BP Garage; 10.00am (3.30pm) Oak Apple Pub, Worcester; Times in brackets denote mid-week fixtures

HERTFORDSHIRE Organised travel to home & away games Pick-up points at Hertford, Welwyn, Stevenage, Hitchin and Luton Travel arrangements - contact Mick Prior **Tel 01438 361900** Membership - contact Mick Slack **Tel 01462 622451** Correspondence to Steve Bocking, 64 Westmill Road, Hitchin, Herts SG5 2SD **Tel 01462 622076**

HEYWOOD Branch Secretary Lee Swettenham, 30 Wilton Grove, Heywood, Lancs. OL10 1AZ **Tel 01706 360626 E-mail swetts@btinternet.com** Chairman Dennis Hall, 2 Hartford Avenue, Summit, Heywood, Lancs *Departure Point* 1.00pm (6.00pm midweek) Sullivans Bar, Bridge Street, Heywood

HIGHLANDS & ISLANDS Branch Secretary Ken Glass, The Millers Cottage, Milton, Invergordon, Ross-Shire, IV18 0NQ **Tel 01862 842395** *Departure points* Coach departs 5.30am Farraline Park Bus Station, Inverness For other departure points contact secretary

HYNDBURN & PENDLE Branch Secretary: Alan Haslam, 97 Crabtree Avenue, Edgeside, Waterfoot, Rossendale, BB4 9TB **Tel 01706 831736** *Departure points* Barnoldswick 11.15am (4.45pm); Nelson 11.30am (5.00pm); Burnley 11.45am (5.15pm); Accrington 12.15pm (5.45pm); Haslingden 12.20pm (5.50pm); Rawtenstall 12.30pm (6.00pm) Times in brackets denote evening fixtures

INVICTA REDS (KENT) Branch Secretary Victor Hatherly **Tel 01634 865613** For all information on tickets and travel times please contact Shaun Rogers **Tel 01622 721344** (evenings) **Mobile 0421 458638** Please send correspondence to: Invicta Reds, c/o 'Pop-In' Newsagents, 97 Boundary Road, Ramsgate, Kent, CT11 7NP *Departure points* Ramsgate; Herne Bay; Canterbury; M2 Service Area; Junction 3, M2; Little Chef Services A2 by Cobham; Dartford Tunnel; Junctions 28 and 26, M25

ISLE OF MAN Chairman Graham Barlow, 21 Thirlmere Drive, Onchan, Isle of Man **Tel 01624 661270** Branch Secretary Gill Keown, 5 King Williams Way, Castletown, Isle of Man, IM9 1DH **Tel 01624 823143 E-mail Reddevil@enterprise.net**

JERSEY Branch Secretary Mark Jones, 5 Rosemount Cottages, James Road, St.Saviour, Jersey, Channel Islands **Tel 01534 34786(H) 01534 885885(W)**

Should any members be in Jersey during the football season, the branch shows television games in private club Free food provided, everybody welcome, including children Contact Branch Secretary for details

KEIGHLEY Branch Secretary Kevin Granger, 3 Spring Terrace, Long Lee, Keighley, West Yorkshire, BD21 4SZ **Tel 01535 661862 Mobile 0709 555653 Fax 01535 600564 E-mail k.d.granger@talk21.com** *Departure points* Coach leaves from Keighley Technical College in Cavendish Street then travels to Colne, and joins M65 & M66 to Manchester Contact Branch Secretary for more details

KNUTSFORD Branch Secretary John Butler, 4 Hollingford Place, Knutsford WA16 9DP **Tel/Fax 01565 651360** Meetings most Tuesdays, The Angel Hotel, King Street, Knutsford

LANCASTER AND DISTRICT Branch Secretary Ed Currie, 30 Dorrington Road, Lancaster LA1 4TG **Tel 01524 36797 Mobile 07880 550247** *Departure points* 11.45am (4.45pm) Carnforth Ex Servicemens; 12.00pm (5.00pm) Morecambe Shrimp Roundabout; 12.20pm (5.20pm) Lancaster Dalton Square and A6 route to Broughton Roundabout for M6 Times in brackets denote evening fixtures

LEAMINGTON SPA Branch Secretary Mrs Norma Worton, 23 Cornhill Grove, Kenilworth, Warwickshire, CV8 2QP **Tel 01926 859476 E-mail Norma.Worton@manutd.com** *Departure points* Newbold Terrace, Leamington Spa; Leyes Lane, Kenilworth; London Road, Coventry;

LINCOLN Branch Secretary Steve Stone, 154 Scorer Street, Lincoln, Lincolnshire, LN5 7SX **Tel 01522 885671** *Departure points* Unity Square at 10.00am on Saturday's (3.00pm kick-off) Midweek matches, depart at 3.00pm from Unity Square

LONDON Branch Secretary Ralph Mortimer, 55 Boyne Avenue, Hendon, London, NW4 2JL **Tel 0181 203 1213** (after 6.30pm) *Departure points* Home Games, Coaches depart from following points: Semley Place (alongside Victoria Coach Station 8.00pm (12.30pm); Staples Corner (opposite Courts) 8.30am (1.15pm); Junction 11, M1 (under motorway) 9.00am (1.45pm); Times in brackets denote evening fixtures All coaches need to be reserved in advance by calling Ralph Mortimer **0208 203 1213** after 6.30pm Away Games: A coach will run for all away games, subject to numbers/tickets Please contact Ralph Mortimer for details

LONDON ASSOCIATION Branch Secretary Najib Armanazi, 22 Campden Hill Court, Campden Hill Road, London W8 7HS **Tel 0171 937 3934** Membership Secretary Alison Watt **Tel 01322 558333** (between 7.00 - 9.00pm)

LONDON FAN CLUB Branch Secretary Paul Molloy, 65 Corbylands Road, Sidcup, Kent, DA15 8JQ **Tel 0181 302 5826** Travel Secretary Mike Dobbin, E-mail **info@mulfc65.freeserve.co.uk** *Departure points* Euston Station by service train - meeting point at top of escalator from Tube) Cheap group travel to most home and away games

MACCLESFIELD Branch Secretary Ian Evans, 25 Pickwick Road, Poynton, Cheshire SK12 1LD **Tel 01625 877260** Chairman Neil Cleland Treasurer Rick Holland, 97 Pierce Street, Macclesfield SK11 6EX **Tel 01625 427762** Membership Secretary Neil McCleland **Tel 01625 613183** *Departure points* Home games, meet Macclesfield Rail Station 11.45am (4.45pm midweek fixtures) For away games, please contact branch secretary

MANSFIELD Branch Secretary Peggy Conheeney, 48 West Bank Avenue, Mansfield, Nottinghamshire, NG19 7BP **Tel/Fax 01623 625140** *Departure points* 10.00am (4.00pm) Kirkby Garage; 10.10am (4.10pm) Northern Bridge, Sutton; 10.30am (4.25pm) Mansfield Shoe Co.; 10.40am (4.40pm) Glapwell; 10.50am (4.55pm) Hipper Street School, Chesterfield; 11.15am (5.35pm) Baslow Coach seats should be booked well in advance Away games are dependent on ticket availability Please contact branch secretary Times in brackets denote evening fixtures

MID CHESHIRE Branch Secretary Leo Lastowecki, 5 Townfield Court, Barnton, Northwich, Cheshire, CW8 4U **Tel** 01606 784790 *Departure points* Please contact Branch Secretary

MIDDLETON & DISTRICT Branch Secretary Kevin Booth, 18 Ennerdale Road, Langley, Middleton, Manchester, M24 5RN **Tel** 0161 643 5662 **Mobile** 0798 9790217 Chairman Mike Conroy, 12 Lulworth Road, Middleton, Manchester 24 **Tel** 0161 653 5696 Home Games: Coaches depart Crown Inn, Middleton 1 hour prior to kick-off Away Games: Contact Secretary

MILLOM AND DISTRICT Branch Secretary/Chairman Clive Carter, 47 Settle Street, Millom, Cumbria, LA18 5AR **Tel** 01229 773565 Treasurer Malcom French, 4 Willowside Park, Haverigg, Cumbria, LA18 4PT **Tel** 01229 774850 Assistant Treasurer Paul Knott, 80 Market Street, Millom, Cumbria **Tel** 01229 772826

NORTH DEVON Branch Secretary Dave Rogan, Leys Cottage, Hilltop, Fremington, Nr Barnstaple, EX31 3BL **Tel/Fax** 01271 328280 *Departure points* Please contact Branch Secretary

NORTH EAST Branch Secretary John Burgess, 10 Streatlam Close, Stainton, Barnard Castle, Co Durham, DL12 8RQ **Tel** 01833 695200 *Departure points* Central Station, Newcastle 8.30am (1.00pm); A19/A690 Roundabout 8.50am (1.20pm); 8.50am (1.20pm) Peterlee Roundabout 9.00am (1.30pm); Hartlepool Baths 9.15am (1.45pm); Owton Lodge, Hartlepool 9.20am (1.50pm); The Swan, Billingham 9.30am (2.00pm); Sappers Corner 9.40am (2.10pm); Darlington Bus Station 10.00am (2.30pm); Scotch Corner Roundabout 10.10am (2.40pm); Leeming Bar Services A1 10.20am (2.50pm).

NORTH MANCHESTER Branch Secretary Graham May, 25 Walker Road, Chadderton, OL9 8DB **Tel** 0161 681 6149 **Mobile** 0850 133418 Coaches to all home & away games Fortnightly meetings at Leggatts Wine Bar, Oldham Road, Failsworth For all details contact Graham May **0973 128809** (Secretary), Garry Chapman **0161 795 0581**, Dixie **0161 682 3331**

NORTH POWYS Branch Secretary Glyn T Davies, 7 Tan-y-Mur, Montgomery, Powys, SY15 6PR **Tel** 01686 668841 Treasurer Mrs B Elesbury, 1 Llys Maldwyn, Caerhowel, Montgomery, Powys **Tel** 01686 668709 *Departure points* Newtown Back Lane Coach Station 10.30am (4.00pm); Welshpool Spar Car Park 11.00am (4.30pm); Oswestry Mile End Shell Service Station (Little Chef) 11.15am (5.00pm); Wrexham Rhosllewyn 11.30am (5.15pm); Chester/R/about 11.40am (5.30pm) Times in brackets denote evening fixtures For all information on tickets and travel, contact Branch Secretary For areas of Branch, contact your reps or direct to Secretary Seven weeks notice must be given when ordering tickets Night games bus leaves at 4.00pm

NORTH STAFFORDSHIRE Branch Secretary Peter Hall, Cheddleton Heath House, Cheddleton Heath Road, Leek ST13 7DX **Tel** 01538 360364 *Departure points* 12.30pm (5.15pm) Leek Bus Station Times in brackets denote evening fixtures

NORTH YORKSHIRE Branch Secretary Miss Jacky Potter, c/o MUSC N. Yorkshire, PO Box 480, York YO24 3ZW **Tel**/Fax 01904 787291 (6.00-8.00pm) **Mobile** 07980 854042 **E-mail** musc@jaks.freeserve.co.uk *Departure points* Executive coaches to all home games from Whitby, Scarborough, Malton and York, booking in advance is required Please phone secretary for further details

NOTTINGHAM Branch Secretary Wayne Roe **Tel** 01773 510784 (home Travel) **E-mail** wainy@aol.com **Martyn Meek Tel** 01773 768424 (away travel) *Departure points* 10.00am (3.00pm) Nottingham; 10.30am (3.30pm) Ilkeston; 10.45am (3.45pm) Eastwood; 11.00am (4.00pm) Junction 28, M1 Times in brackets denote evening fixtures

OLDHAM Branch Secretary Dave Cone, 67 Nelson Way, Washbrook, Chadderton, Lancashire, OL9 8NL **Tel** 0161 626 9734 **Mobile** 07973 939255 Chairman Martyn Lucas, 1 Wickentree Holt, Norden, Rochdale OL12 7PQ **Tel** 01706 355728 Meeting every Tuesday night 7.30-9.00pm at Horton Arms, 1 Ward Street, off Middleton Road, Chadderton, Oldham Match Travel Coach to all home matches; Mid-week - leaves at 6.00pm; Weekend 3.00pm k.o. - leaves at 1.00pm; Weekend 4.00pm k.o. - leaves at 1.30pm; Away Travel - subject to receiving match tickets

OXFORD, BANBURY AND DISTRICT Branch Secretary Mick Thorne, "'The Paddock", 111 Eynsham Road, Botley, Oxford OX2 9BY **Tel** 01865 864924 (6.00-8.00pm Monday-Friday only) **Fax** 01865 864924 (Anytime) *Departure points* McLeans Coach Yard, Witney 8.00am (2.00pm); Botley Road Park-n-Ride, Oxford 8.30am (2.30pm); Plough Inn, Bicester 8.45am (2.45pm); Bus Station, Banbury 9.00am (3.00pm) Times in brackets denote evening fixtures Mid-week European matches, coaches depart 30 minutes earlier Coach fare for home games adults £11.00, Junior & OAP's £8.00 All coach seats must be booked in advance Away travel, including European, subject to match tickets New members welcome Large sae for copy of branch review

PETERBOROUGH AND DISTRICT Branch Secretary Andrew Dobney, 3 Northgate, West Pinchbeck, Spalding, Lincs, PE11 3TB **Tel** 01775 640743 *Departure points* Spalding Bus Station 9.00am (1.30pm); Peterborough, Key Theatre 9.45am (2.15pm); Grantham, Foston Services 10.30am (3.00pm) Times in brackets denote evening fixtures

PLYMOUTH Branch Secretary Dave Price, 34 Princess Avenue, Plymstock, Plymouth PL9 9EP **Tel** 01752 482049 or Branch Information Line 01579 348497 *Departure Points* 6.30am (11.00am) Tamar Bridge; 6.45am (11.15am) Bretonside; 7.00am (11.30am) Plympton; 7.15am (11.45am) Ivybridge; 7.30am (12 noon) South Brent (London Inn); 7.50am (12.20pm) Exeter Services Times in brackets denote evening fixtures

PONTYPRIDD Branch Secretary Lawrence Badman, 11 Laura Street, Treforest, Pontypridd, Mid Glamorgan, South Wales, CF37 1NW **Tel** 01443 406894 *Departure points* For coach departure and pick-up points please contact Branch Secretary

REDDITCH Branch Secretary Mark Richardson, 90 Alcester Road, Hollywood, Worcestershire, B47 5NS **Tel/Fax** 0121 246 0237 *Departure points* Redditch & Bromsgrove

ROCHDALE Branch Chairman Paul Mulligan, 54 Norden Road, Bamford, Rochdale, Lancs OL11 5PN **Tel** 01706 368909 Regular coach service to home games

RUGBY AND NUNEATON Branch Secretary Greg Pugh, 63 Catesby Road, Rugby, Warwickshire CV22 5JL **Tel** 01788 567900 Chairman Mick Moore, 143 Marston Lane, Attleborough, Nuneaton, Warwickshire **Tel** 01203 343 868 *Departure points* St Thomas Cross Pub, Rugby; McDonalds Junction 2, M6, Coventry; Council House, Coton Road, Nuneaton Departure times vary according to kick-off

RUNCORN AND WIDNES Branch Secretary Elizabeth Scott, 39 Park Road, Runcorn, Cheshire, WA7 4SS

SCUNTHORPE Branch Secretary Pat Davies **Tel** 01724 851359 Chairman Guy Davies **Tel** 01724 851359 Transport Manager Tony Fish **Tel** 01724 341029

SHEFFIELD & ROTHERHAM Branch Secretary Roger Everitt, 27 South Street, Kimberworth, Rotherham, South Yorkshire, S61 1ER **Tel** 01709 563613 Coach Travel available to all home games *Departure points* Saturdays: Rotherham (Nellie Denes) 11.00am; Sheffield (Midland Railway Station) 11.20am; Stockbridge 11.50am; Midweek games: Rotherham (Nellie Denes) 4.30pm; Meadowhall Coach Park 4.45pm Kick-off times vary Sat/Sun, please contact Branch Secretary

SHOEBURYNESS, SOUTH END AND DISTRICT Branch Secretary Bob Lambert, 23 Royal Oak Drive, Wickford, Essex, SS11 8NT **Tel** 01268 560168 Chairman Gary Black **Tel** 01702 219072
Departure points 7.00am Cambridge Hotel, Shoeburyness; 7.15am Bell Public House, A127; 7.20am Rayleigh Weir; 7.30am McDonalds Burger Bar, A127; 7.40am Fortune of War Public House, A127; 8.00am Brentwood High Street; 8.05am Little Chef, Brentwood By-pass
Additional pick-ups by arrangement with branch secretary All coach seats should be booked in advance Ring for details of midweek fixtures

SHREWSBURY Branch Secretary Martyn Hunt, 50 Whitehart, Reabrook, Shrewsbury, SY3 7TE **Tel** 01743 350397 Chirk Secretary Mike Davies **Tel** 01743 350390 *Departure points* Reabrook Island; Abbey Church; Monkmoor Inn; Heathgates Island; Harlescott Inn; Hand Hotel, Chirk 3.00 & 4.00pm kick-off: Depart Reabrook 10.30am; 7.30 & 8.00pm kick-off:Depart Reabrook 3.00pm;

SOUTH ELMSALL & DISTRICT Branch Secretary Bill Fieldsend, 72 Cambridge St, Moorthorpe, South Elmsall, Pontefract, West Yorkshire, WF9 2AR **Tel** 01977 648358 **Mobile** 07818 245954
Treasurer Mark Bossons **Tel** 01977 650316 Meetings held every Tuesday at Pretoria WMC, South Elmsall *Departure points* 11.45am (4.30pm) Hemsworth Market; 11.50am (4.40pm) Mill Lane; 12 noon (5.00pm) Pretoria WMC Times in brackets denote evening fixtures

SOUTHPORT Branch Secretary Robert Stephenson, 143 Heysham Road, Southport, Merseyside, PR9 7ED **Tel** 01704 220685 Weekly meetings held Tuesday evening at The Mount Pleasant Hotel, Manchester Road *Departure point* The Mount Pleasant Hotel, Manchester Road, Southport, picking-up en route

STALYBRIDGE Branch Secretary Walt Petrenko **Mobile** 07788 491977 Chairman S Hepburn, **Tel** 0161 344 2328 Treasurer R A Wild **Tel** 0161 338 7277 Membership Secretary A Baxter
Tel 01457 838 764 Away Travel Nigel Barrett **Mobile** 0802 799482 Home Travel B Williamson **Tel** 0161 338 6832 *Departure points* Branch is based at The Pineapple, 18 Kenworthy Street, Stalybridge Landlord Addy Dearnaley **Tel** 0161 338 2542 Home coach leaves from The Pineapple 1½ hours before kick-off Away coaches are arranged when applicable per game, coaches run most games

STOKE-ON-TRENT Branch Secretary Geoff Boughey, 63 Shrewsbury Drive, Newcastle, Staffordshire, ST5 7RQ **Tel/Fax** 01782 561680 (home) **Mobile** 0468 561680 **E-mail** geoffboughey@cwcom.net *Departure points* 12.00noon (5.00pm) Hanley Bus Station; 12.10pm (5.10pm) School Street, Newcastle; 12.15pm (5.15pm) Little Chef A34; 12.30pm (5.30pm) The Millstone Pub, Butt Lane Times in brackets denote evening fixtures Branch meetings every Monday night Contact Branch Secretary for details

STOURBRIDGE & KIDDERMINSTER Branch Secretary, Robert Banks, 7 Croftwood Road, Wollescote, Stourbridge, West Midlands DY9 7EU **Tel** 01384 826636 *Departure Points* Contact Branch Secretary for departure points and times

SURREY Branch Secretary Mrs Maureen Asker, 80 Cheam Road, Ewell, Surrey, KT17 1QF **Tel** 0208 393 4763 *Departure point* Coach departs Ewell West Station 7.45am

SWANSEA Branch Secretary Dave Squibb, 156 Cecil Street, Manselton, Swansea, SA5 8QJ **Tel** 01792 641981 **E-mail** david.squibb@manutd.com *Departure points* Swansea (via Heads of Valleys Road); Neath; Hirwaun; Merthyr; Tredegar; Ebbw Vale; Brynmawr; Abergavenny; Monmouth

SWINDON Branch Secretary Martin Rendle, 19 Cornfield Road, Devizes, Wiltshire, SN10 3BA **Tel** 01380 728358 (between 8.00pm-10.00pm Monday to Friday) *Departure points* Kingsdown Inn; Stratton St Margaret; Swindon

TELFORD Branch Secretary Sal Laher, 4 Hollyoak Grove, Lakeside, Priorslee, Telford, TF2 9GE **Tel 01952 299224** Members' and committee meetings held on the first Thursday of every month at Champion Jockey, Donnington from 7.30pm *Departure points* Saturday (3pm kick-off) 10.30am Cuckoo Oak, Madeley; 10.40am Heath Hill, Dawley; 10.50am Bucks Head, Wellington; 11.00am Dakengates; 11.10am Bridge, Donnington; 11.20am Newport. Midweek (8.00pm kick-off) departure starts 4.30pm with ten minutes later for each of the above locations. Contact Branch Secretary for membership and further details

TORBAY Branch Secretary Vernon Savage, 5 Courtland Road, Shiphay, Torquay, Devon TQ2 6JU **Tel 01803 616139** *Departure points* 7.00am Upper Cockington Lane, Torquay; 7.20am Newton Abbot Railway Station; 7.30am Kingsteignton Fountain; 7.45am Countess Wear Roundabout, Exeter; Taunton 8.15am; Other departure times by arrangement with the Branch Secretary Midweek coach departure times, add 5 hours to above times

UTTOXETER & DISTRICT Branch Secretary Peter Quirk, The Smithfield Hotel, 37 High Street, Uttoxeter, Staffs, ST14 7HN **Tel/Fax 01889 562682** Branch Chairman Ray Phillips **Tel 01889 567323**

WALSALL Branch Secretary Ian Robottom, 157 Somerfield Road, Bloxwich, Walsall WS3 2EN **Tel 01922 861746** *Departure points* 10.50am (4.15pm) Junction 9 (M6); 11.15am (4.50pm) Bell Pub, Bloxwich; 11.30am (5.15pm) Roman Way Hotel, A5 Cannock; 11.50am (5.35pm) Dovecote Pub, Stone Road, Stafford

WARRINGTON Branch Secretary Su Buckley, 4 Vaudrey Drive, Woolston, Warrington, Cheshire, WA1 4HG **Tel 01925 816966** *Departure points* Blackburn Arms 1.00pm (6.00pm); Churchills 1.10pm (6.10pm); Chevvies 1.15pm (6.15pm); Highway Man/Kingsway 1.20pm (6.20pm); Rope 'n' Anchor 1.25pm (6.25pm); Times in brackets denote evening fixtures

WELLINGBOROUGH Branch Secretary Paul Walpole, 7 Cowgill Close, Cherry Lodge, Northampton NN3 8PB **Tel/Fax 01604 787612** *Departure points* Shoe Factory, Irchester Road, Rushden 8.30am (1.30pm); Doc Martins Shoe Factory, Irchester 8.35am (1.35pm); The Cuckoo Public House, Woolaston 8.45am (1.45pm); Police Station, Wellingborough 8.55am (1.55pm); Duke of York Public House, Wellingborough 9.00am (2.00pm); Trumpet Public House, Northampton 9.10am (2.10pm); Abington Park Bus Stop, Northampton 9.15 am (2.15pm); Campbell Square, Northampton 9.20am (2.20pm); Mill Lane Layby (opposite Cock Hotel Public House), Kingsthorpe 9.25am (2.25pm); Top of Bants Lane (opposite Timken), Dugton 9.30am (2.30pm);

WEST CUMBRIA Branch Secretary Robert Wilson, 23 Calder Drive, Moorclose, Workington, Cumbria CA14 3NZ **Tel 01900 870211 Mobile 0370 837634 E-mail robertwilson3@btinternet.com** *Departure points* Coach 1 departs: Egremont 9.45am (3.15pm); Cleator Moor 10am (3.30pm); Whitehaven 10.15am (3.45pm); Distington 10.20am (3.50pm); Cockermouth 10.35am (4.05pm) Coach 2 departs: Salterbeck 9.45am (3.15pm); Harrington Road 9.50am (3.20pm); Workington 10am (3.30pm); Station Inn 10.10am (3.40pm); Netherhall Cr 10.12am (3.42pm); Netherton 10.15am (3.45pm); Dearham 10.20am (3.50pm) Times in brackets denotes 8pm kick-off, contact branch secretary for other kick-off times

WEST DEVON Branch Secretary Mrs R M Bolt, 16 Moorview, North Tawton, Devon, EX20 2HW **Tel 01837 82682** (all enquiries) *Departure points* North Tawton; Crediton; Exeter

WESTMORLAND Branch Secretary Dennis Alderson, 71 Calder Drive, Kendal, Cumbria, LA9 6LR **Tel 01539 728248 Mobile 0973 965373** *Departure points* Ambleside; Windermere; Staveley, Kendal and Forton Services For departure times and further details, please contact Branch Secretary

WORKSOP Branch Secretary Mick Askew, 20 Park Street, Worksop, Nottinghamshire **Tel 01909 486194**

YEOVIL Branch Secretary Richard Chapman-Cox, 34 Crofton Avenue, Yeovil, Somerset, BA21 4DL **Tel 01935 478285 Mobile 07930 505349 E-mail richard.chapman-cox@manutd.com** *Departure points* Please contact Branch Secretary

MANCHESTER UNITED DISABLED SUPPORTERS' ASSOCIATION – (MUDSA) Branch Secretary Phil Downs, M.U.D.S.A., PO Box 141, South D.O., M20 5BA **Tel 0161 434 1989 Fax 0161 445 5221 E-mail phil.downs@cwcom.net**

IRISH BRANCHES

ANTRIM TOWN Branch Secretary Alex Mould, 14 Donegore Drive, Parkhall, Antrim, Northern Ireland, BT41 1EB **Mobile 07899 818623** Chairman William Cameron, 92 Donegore Drive, Parkhall, Antrim, N Ireland **Tel 02894 461634** Club meetings held every other Thursday in the Top of the Town Bar, Antrim All members must be registered with Manchester United's official membership scheme

ARKLOW Branch Secretary James Cullen, 52 South Green, Arklow, Co Wicklow, Eire **Tel 087 2327859** or **0402 39816** All trips arranged via local committee members Pick-ups Waterford to Dublin Anyone interested in joining, please contact the Secretary

BALLYCASTLE Branch Secretary Sean Fleming, Glenshesk Bar, 76 Castle Street, Ballycastle, Co Antrim, Northern Ireland, BT54 6AR **Tel 028 20 762322** Branch Chairman Derek McKendry

BALLYMONEY Branch Secretary Malachy McAleese, 17 Eastburn Drive, Ballymoney, Co Antrim, Northern Ireland, BT53 6PJ **Tel 028 276 67623 Mobile 07850 345812 E-mail musc@eastburndrive.freeserve.co.uk** Chairman Gerry McAleese, 11 Greenville Avenue, Ballymoney, Co Antrim, Northern Ireland **Tel 028 276 65446** *Departure point* Ballymoney United Social Club, Grove Road, Ballymena; Belfast Harbour or Belfast International Airport; Meetings: Last Thursday of every month, Ballymoney United Social Club, Castle Street, Ballymoney **Tel 028 276 66054** New Members always welcome

BANBRIDGE Branch Secretary James Loney, 83 McGreavy Park, Derrymacash, Lurgan, Northern Ireland **Tel 028 38322723 Mobile 07901 833076** Chairman Kevin Nelson, 10 Ballynamoney Park, Derrymacash, Lurgan, N Irelan **Tel 028 38344232** *Departure Points* 6.00am Corner House, Derrymacash; 6.10am Terra Travel, Lurgan; 6.20am Downslire, Banbridge Town Centre - Saturday & Sunday matches, times stay the same

BANGOR Branch Secretary Gary Wilsdon, 4 Bexley Road, Bangor, Co Down, BT19 7TS **Tel 028 91 458485 E-mail gary.wilsdon@virgin.net** Branch Meetings Every other Monday 8.00pm at the Imperial Bar, Central Avenue, Bangor

BELFAST REDS Branch Secretary John Bond, 53 Hillhead Crescent, Belfast, Northern Ireland, BT11 9FS **Tel 028 90 627861**

BUNDORAN Branch Secretary Danny Tighe, "United Cottage", The Rock, Bundoran, Co Donegal, Eire **Tel/Fax 072 42080 Mobile 086 859 7718** *Departure point* The Holyrood Hotel and additional pick-up points en route to Dublin Port All bookings to be made through Branch Secretary only Bookings should be made well in advance as travel arrangements have to be made New members are welcome

CARLINGFORD LOUTH Branch Secretary Harry Harold, Mountain Park, Carlingford, Co Louth, Ireland **Tel 042 73379**

CARLOW Branch Secretary Michael Lawlor, Trafford House, 20 New Oak Estate, Carlow, Ireland **Tel 0503 43759 Mobile 086 8950030** (Mon-Friday 7.00-9.00pm only) Treasurer William Carroll **Mobile 086 8593062** (Mon-Fri 9.00am-5.00pm only)

CARRICKFERGUS Branch Secretary Gary Callaghan, 3 Red Fort Park, Carrickfergus, Co Antrim, Northern Ireland, BT38 9EW **Tel 028 93 355362 Fax 028 93 369995 E-mail aca@globalnet.co.uk** The branch holds their meetings fortnightly on a Monday evening at 8.00pm in the Quality Hotel, Carrickfergus New members are welcome, especially Family and Juniors The branch presently has a membership of 165 and organises trips to Old Trafford for all home games They also travel to away matches including European whenever possible

CARRYDUFF Branch Secretary John White, 'Stretford End', 4 Baronscourt Glen, Carryduff, Co Down, Northern Ireland, BT8 8RF **Tel 028 90 812377 E-mail whitedevil@nireland.com** Chairman John Dempsey **Tel/Fax 028 90 814823 E-mail john.dempsey@dnet.co.uk** Vice-Chairman Wilson Steele **Tel 028 94 464987** *Departure point* The branch organise coach trips to Old Trafford for every home game from The Royal Ascot, Carryduff and The Grand Opera House, Belfast Branch meetings are held every week. No alcohol and no other club colours are permitted on the coach. Junior members particularly welcome as we are a family orientated branch. Branch Membership exceeds 400 and ALL members must be registered with Manchester United's Official Membership Scheme. The Branch owns a number of Season Tickets, which are used on trips

CASTLEDAWSON Branch Secretary Niall Wright, 22 Park View, Castledawson, Co Londonderry, Northern Ireland **Tel 028 79 468779**

CASTLEPOLLARD Branch Secretary Anne Foley, Coole, Mullingar, Co Westmeath, Ireland **Tel/Fax 00 353 044 61613 E-mail muscpollard@hotmail.com** *Departure points* The Square, Castlepollard Additional pick-up points by arrangement with Branch Secretary. Branch meetings on 3rd Monday of every month. Notification of additional meetings by 'newsletter'

CASTLEWELLAN Branch Secretary Seamus Owens, 18 Mourne Gardens, Dublin Road, Castlewellan, Co Down, Northern Ireland, BT31 9BY **Tel 028 437 78137 Fax 028 437 70762 Mobile 07714 756 455** Chairman Tony Corr **Tel 028 437 22885** Treasurer Michael Burns **Tel 028 437 78665**

CITY OF DERRY Branch Secretary Mark Thompson, 210 Hillcrest, Kilfennan, Londonderry, Northern Ireland, BT47 6GF **Tel 028 7134 6537 E-mail mthompson@freeuk.com** Meetings: First Tuesday of every month at the Upstairs Downstairs Bar, Dungiven Road, Londonderry at 8.30pm

CLARA Branch Secretary Michael Kenny, River Street, Clara, Co Offaly, Ireland

COLERAINE Branch Secretary Noel Adair, 106 Lisnablaugh Road, Harper's Hill, Coleraine, Co Derry, Northern Ireland **Tel 01265 57744**

COOKSTOWN Branch Secretary Geoffrey Wilson, 10 Cookstown Road, Moneymore, Co Londonderry, Northern Ireland, BT45 7QF **Tel 028 86748625 Mobile 07833 945847** Meeting: First Monday of every month at Royal Hotel, Cookstown - 9.00pm All members must be registered with Manchester United's official membership scheme

CORK AREA Branch Secretary Paul Kearney, Beech Road, Passage West, Co Cork, Republic of Ireland **Tel 021 841190**

COUNTY CAVAN Chairman Owen Farrelly **Tel** 046 42184 Secretary (joint): Richard Leddy **Tel** 046 42209 Secretary (joint): Jimmy Murray **Tel** 046 42501 Meetings: Third Monday of each month in Jimmy's Bar, Main St, Mullagh

COUNTY LONGFORD Branch Secretary Seamus Gill, 17 Springlawn, Longford, Republic of Ireland **Tel** 043 47848 **Fax** 043 41655 Chairman Harry Ryan, 58 Teffia Park, Longford, Co. Longford Treasurer Noel Daly, 18 Shannonvale, Longford, Co Longford

COUNTY MONAGHAN Branch Secretary Seamus Gallagher **Tel** 047 57232 Chairman Gerard Treanor **Tel** 087 57232 Meetings fortnightly Bellevue Tavern, Dublin Street, Monaghan **Tel** 047 84311 **Fax** 047 83265

COUNTY ROSCOMMON Branch Secretary Noel Scally, Cashel, Boyle, Co Roscommon, Ireland **Tel** 079 64995 Chairman Seamus Sweeney, Croghan, Coyle, Co. Roscommon **Tel** 079 68061 President: George Tiernan, 8 Termon Road, Boyle, Co Roscommon **Tel** 079 62930

COUNTY TIPPERARY Branch Secretary Mrs Kathleen Hogan, 45 Canon Hayes Park, Tipperary, Republic of Ireland **Tel** 062 51042

COUNTY WATERFORD Branch Secretary Mrs Helen Grant, "Old Trafford", Ballinamuck, Dungarvan, Co Waterford **Tel/Fax** 058 44219 Chairman Oliver Drummy, 8 Cloneety Tce., Dungarvan, Co. Waterford **Tel** 058 42365 Vice-Chairman Pat Grant, "Old Trafford", Ballinamuck, Dungarvan, Co Waterford, Ireland **Tel/Fax** 058 44219 Treasurer Judy Connors, 26 Hillview Drive, Dungarvan, Co Waterford Membership Secretary Ann Houlihan, Feddans Cross, Rathgormac

CRAIGAVON Branch Secretary Eamon Atkinson, 8 Rowan Park, Tullygally Road, Craigavon, Co Armagh, Northern Ireland, BT65 5AY **Tel** 028 38 343870 Chairperson James Nolan **Tel** 028 38 341434 Treasurer Susan Atkinson *Departure Points* Lurgan Town Centre; Tullygally Road, Craigavon; Mayfair Centre, Portadown; Tandragee & Banbridge

DONEGAL Branch Secretary Liam Friel, Kiltoal, Convoy, Lifford, Co Donegal **Tel** 087 6736967 Chairman Paddy Delap, West Hill, Letterkenny, Co Donegal **Tel/Fax** 074 22240 Treasurer Paul Dolan, Knockbrack, Letterkenny, Co Donegal **Tel** 087 2865504 Meeting held at Club Rooms, Rossbracken *Departure point* O'Boyces, Letterkenny Pick-up points as arranged with travel organiser, Tony Murray, Gortlee, Letterkenny, Co Donegal **Tel** 074 24111

DOWNPATRICK Branch Secretary Terry Holland, 20 Racecourse Road, Downpatrick, Co Down, Northern Ireland **Tel/Fax** 028 44 616467 **Mobile** 07712 622242

DUNDALK Chairman Michael McCourt, Secretary Joan Kirk, Assistant Secretary Arthur Carron, Treasurer Mary Laverty, Ticket & Travel Dickie O'Hanrahan, Committee Members Ollie Kelly, Gery Dullaghan

DUNGANNON Branch Secretary Ian Hall, 'Silveridge', 229 Killyman Road, Dungannon, Co Tyrone, Northern Ireland, BT71 6RS **Tel** 028 87 723085 **(h) Tel:** 028 87 752255 **(w) Mobile** 07787 124765 Meetings every 2 weeks (all year) at 30 Church Street, Dungannon For details on membership, meetings, and trips contact branch secretary or Keith Houston on 028 87 722735 or Lawrence McKinley 07867 941163

ENNIS Branch Secretary Seamus Hughes, 'Old Trafford', Quin, Ennis, Co Clare, Republic of Ireland **Tel** 065 68 20282 **Mobile** 086 239 3975 Branch Chairman Eamon Murphy, Knockboy, Ballynacally, Co Clare, Ireland **Tel** 065 68 28105 Meetings held at Roslevan Arms, Tulla Road, Ennis

FERMANAGH Branch Secretary Gabriel Maguire, 80 Glenwood Gardens, Enniskillen, BT74 5LT **Tel** 028 66 325 950 **Mobile** 07788 421739 Chairman Eric Brown, 166 Main Street, Lisnaskea Treasurer Raymond McBrien, Ardlougher Road, Irvinestown Meetings held in Charlie's Lounge, Enniskillen

FIRST BALLYCLARE Branch Secretary Alan Munce, 7 Merion Park, Ballyclare, Co Antrim, Northern Ireland, BT39 9XD **Tel** 028 93 324126

FIRST NORTH DOWN Branch Secretary Robert Quee, "Stretford Ender", 67 Springhill Road, Bangor West, Co Down, Northern Ireland, BT20 3PD 1st North Down meet at the Ballykillaire Sports Complex on the Old Belfast Road, Bangor on the 2nd Tuesday of each month at 8pm New members are welcome, phone 028 91 453094 or Bob Quee 07790 761 828

FIRST PORTAFERRY Branch Secretary David Peacock, 5 Loughshore Road, Portaferry, Northern Ireland, BT22 1PD **Tel** 028 427 28420/28646 **Fax** 028 427 29834 Chair Tony Cleary Treasurer Hugh Conlon Branch meetings held 1st Tuesday every month @ 9.00pm at McNamara's, High Street, Portaferry

FOYLE Branch Secretary Martin Harkin, 2 Harvest Meadows, Dunlade Road, Greysteel, Co Derry, Northern Ireland, BT47 3BG Meeting point Ulsterbus Club, Bishop Street, Derry City Travel Arrangements Meet Ulsterbus at midnight, boat at 0250 on matchday Hotel Comfort Friendly, Hyde Road Return boat 1430, arrive Ulsterbus Club 2030

GALWAY Branch Secretary Patsy Devlin, 37 Gortgreine, Rahoon, Galway, Ireland **Tel** 00 353 091 582634 **Fax** 00 353 91 582634 (1) Meetings held monthly in Currans Hotel, Eyre Square
(2) All live TV games at Brennans Bar, New Docks (3) Membership open all year round

GLENOWEN Branch Secretary Jim Turner, 4 Dermot Hill Drive, Belfast, Northern Ireland BT12 7GG **Tel** 02890 242682 **Mobile** 07990 848 961 (day) **E-mail** Jimmy.Turner@tesco.net

IVEAGH YOUTH Branch Secretary Russell Allen, 2 Iveagh Crescent, Belfast, Northern Ireland, BT12 6AW **Tel** 028 90 542651 (office) 028 90 329621 (home) Assistant Branch Secretary Brendan McBride, 3 Gransha Park, Belfast BT11 8AT **Tel** 028 90 522400 (work) 028 90 203171 (home)

IRELAND (DUBLIN) Branch Secretary Eddie Gibbons, 19 Cherry Orchard Crescent, Ballyfermont, Dublin 10 **Tel** 01 626 9759 **Fax** 01 6236388 Membership Secretary Michael O'Toole, 49 Briarwood Lawn, Mulmuddart, Dublin 15 **Tel** 01 821 5702

KILKENNY Branch Secretary John Joe Ryan **Tel** 056 6565827 (day) 056 65136 (after 6.00pm) **Fax** 056 64043 Branch Chairman Pat Murray **Tel** 056 71772

KILLALOE Branch Secretary Michael Flynn, 611 Cross Road, Killaloe, Co Clare, Ireland **Tel** 061 376031

KILLARNEY Branch Secretary Frank Roberts, St Margaret's Road, Killarney, Co Kerry, Republic of Ireland Chairman Bill Keefe Treasurer Denis Spillane Meetings held on the first Wednesday of every month at which future trips are organised

LAGAN Branch Secretary Errol Hall, 11 Arthur Park, Newtownabby, N Ireland BT36 7EL **Tel** 028 90 861949

LAOIS Branch Secretary Denis Moran, Newpark, Portlaoise, Co Laois, Ireland **Tel** 0502 22681

LARNE Branch Secretary Brian Haveron, 69 Croft Manor, Ballygally, Larne, Co Antrim BT40 2RU **Tel** 028 28 261197 (day) 028 28 583027 (night) **Mobile** 0385 388959 Branch Chairman John Hylands, 43 Olderfleet Road, Larne, Co Antrim BT40 1AS **Tel** 028 28 277888 Meetings: Every Monday night 8.00pm at the St. John's Masonic Club Rooms, Mill Brae, Larne We are a family orientated branch

LIMERICK Branch Secretary Dennis O'Sullivan, 14 Rossa Avenue, Mulgrave Street, Limerick, Republic of Ireland **Tel** 061 311502 **Mobile** 086 8435828

LISBURN Branch Secretary Colin Scott, 7 Barban Hill, Dromore, Co Down, Northern Ireland, BT25 1PR **Tel** 028 92 699608 **Mobile** 07808 532951 **E-mail** lisburnmusc@gcs-internet.com
The Branch meets each Tuesday night at 8.30pm at the Club Rooms on Sackville Street. To join the Branch you must be an official member of Manchester United. The branch travel to all games, league and European, and some away. Anyone interested in joining, families and kids welcome, please contact the branch secretary

LISTOWEL Branch Secretary Aiden O'Connor, 55 Pytha Fold Road, Withington, Manchester M20 4UR **Tel** 0161 434 4713 Assistant Secretary David O'Brien, Bedford, Listowel, Co Kerry Ireland **Tel** 068 22250

LURGAN Branch Secretary John Furphy, 123 Drumbeg North, Craigavon, Co Armagh, N Ireland BT65 5AE **Tel** 028 38 341842

MAYO Branch Secretary Seamus Moran, Belclare, Westport, Co Mayo, Ireland **Tel** 00 353 982 7533 (h) 00 353 985 5202 **Mobile** 00 353 872 417966 **Fax** 00 353 982 8874 Chairperson Liam Connell, 70 Knockaphunta, Castlebar, Co Mayo, Ireland Treasurer T J Gannon, 4 The Paddock, Castlebar Road, Westport, Co Mayo, Ireland PRO Kieran Mongey, Blackfort, Castlebar, Co Mayo, Ireland

MEATH Branch Secretary Colm McManus, 46 Beechlawn, Kells, Co Meath, Republic of Ireland **Tel** 046 49831 Pick-up points for travel to Old Trafford: Jack's Railway Bar, Kells; Fairgreen, Naven

NEWRY Branch Secretary Brendan McConville, 14 Willow Grove, Newry, Co Down, Northern Ireland, BT34 1JH **Tel** 028 30 266996 Chairman Jeffrey Clements Meetings: - First Tuesday of each month at the Club Rooms, Newry

NEWTOWNARDS Branch Secretary Leo Cafolla, 11 Strangford Gate Drive, Newtownards, Co Down, Northern Ireland, BT23 8ZW **Tel** 07710 820300 **Fax** 028 91 811822
Meeting every other Monday 7.30pm at Nixx Sport's Bar, Newtownards Junior Branch also

NORTH BELFAST Branch Secretary Robert Savage, 59 Hollybrook Manor, Glenganely, Belfast, Northern Ireland, BT36 7XR **Tel** 028 90 832270
Our meetings are held every second Sunday of the month in the Shamrock Social Club

OMAGH Branch Secretary Brendan McLaughlin, 4 Pinefield Court, Killyclougher, Omagh, Co Tyrone, Northern Ireland, BT79 7YT **Tel** 028 82 250025 **Mobile** 077 10 366 486

PORTADOWN Branch Secretary Harold Beck, 23 Kernan Grove, Portadown, Co Armagh, BT63 5RX **Tel** 028 3 833 6877 **Mobile** 07703 360423

PORTAVOGIE Branch Secretary Robert McMaster, 6 New Road, Portavogie, Co Down BT22 1EN

PORTRUSH Branch Secretary James Friel, 15-17 Causway Street, Portrush, Northern Ireland

PORTSTEWART Branch Secretary Ryan McLaughlin, 45 Drumavalley, Bellarena, Limavady, Co. Derry, Northern Ireland BT49 0LT **Tel** 028 777 50281 after 6.00pm Club Meetings held every second Wednesday of the month at 7.30pm, Anchor Bar, Portstewart

ROSTREVOR Branch Chairman John Parr, 16 Drumreagh Park, Rostrevor BT34 3DU Tel 028 417 39797 Branch Secretary Roger Morgan, 23 Ardfield Crescent, Warrenpoint, Co Down Tel 028 417 54783 Treasurer John Franklin, 14 Rosswood Park, Rostrevor, Co Down BT34 3DZ Tel 028 417 38906 Ass. Secretary M Rea, 8 The Square, Rostrevor, Co. Down Tel 028 417 39808 Club President Paul Braham

SION MILLS Branch Secretary Jim Hunter, 122 Melmount, Sion Mills, Co Tyrone, Northern Ireland, BT82 9EU Tel 028816 58226 (h) 02882 252491 (w)

SLIGO Branch Chairman Eddie Gray, 27 Cartron Heights, Sligo, Republic of Ireland Tel 071 44387 Branch Secretary Martin Feeney, 40 Cartron Bay, Sligo, Republic of Ireland Tel 071 71272

SOUTH BELFAST Branch Secretary James Copeland, 17 Oakhurst Avenue, Blacks Road, Belfast BT10 0PD Tel 02890 615184 or 01232 871231 Mobile 0467 271648 Chairman Danny Nolan Vice-Chairman Michael Murphy Treasurer James McLaughlin Departure Point Balmoral Hotel, Blacks Road

STEWARTSTOWN Branch Secretary Robert O'Neill, 6 Castle Farm Road, Stewartstown, Co Tyrone, Northern Ireland

STRABANE Branch Secretary Gerry Donnelly, 27 Dublin Road, Strabane, Co Tyrone, Northern Ireland, BT82 9EA Tel 02871 883376

TALLAGHT (CO DUBLIN) Branch Secretary Jimmy Pluck, 32 Kilcarrig Cresent, Fettercairn, Tallaght, Co Dublin 24, Republic of Ireland Tel/Fax 4597045

TIPPERARY TOWN Branch Secretary John Ryan, 19 Marian Terrace, Tipperary Town, Co Tipperary, Republic of Ireland Tel 086 8831456 (24 hours) Fax 086 8934635 (24 hours).

TOWER ARDS Branch Secretary Stephen Rowley Tel 028 91 810457 (h) 028 90 432014 (b) Meetings held every second Sunday in the Tower Inn, Mill Street, Newtownards

TRALEE Branch Secretary Johnny Switzer, Dromtacker, Tralee, Co Kerry, Republic of Ireland Tel 066 7124787

WARRENPOINT Branch Secretary Pat Treanor, 31 Oakland Grove, Warrenpoint Tel 028 417 73921 Mobile 07775 968595 Chairmain John Bird, 23 Greendale Crescent, Rostrevor, Co Down Tel: 028 417 3837 Treasurer Leo Tohill, 46 Carmen Park, Warrenpoint, Co Down Tel 028 417 72453 Club web site address is http://www.muwp/manutd.htm Club based at Cearnogs Bar, The Square, Warrenpoint, Co Down, N Ireland Tel 028 417 53429 Branch meets last Friday of every month at 8.00pm

WEST BELFAST Branch Secretary John McAllister, 25 Broadway, Belfast BT12 6AS Tel 028 90 329423 Fax 0870 0637348 E-mail hoyt@lineone.net Branch Chairman George McCabe, 21 Beechmount Street, Belfast, BT12 7NG Treasurer Mr G Burns Committee Mr Liam Curran, Mr Mark Mallon, Mr Michael Curran Meetings held fortnightly on Tuesday evening in "The Red Devil Bar", Falls Road, Belfast For information contact Branch Secretary

OVERSEAS BRANCHES

BELGIUM Chairman Peter Bauwens, Merellaan 52, 9060 Zelzate, Belgium Tel/Fax 00 32 934 40578 Branch Secretary Bjørn Tack Tel/Fax 00 32 934 40578

CANADA Manchester United Supporters Club, 12 St Clair Avenue East, PO Box 69057, Toronto, Ontario, M4T 3AI, Canada E-mail chairman@muscc.com Fax 00 1 416 480 0501 FAO: Maureen Website www.muscc.com

CYPRUS Branch President Ronis Soteriades, P.O.Box 51365, 3504 Limassol, Cyprus Tel 05 337690 Fax 05 388652

GERMAN FRIENDS Branch President Marco Hornfeck, Silberstein 36, 95179 Geroldsgrün, Germany Tel 09267 8111

GERMAN KREFELD REDS Branch Secretary Andrew Marsh, Innsbrucker Str, 47807 Krefeld, Germany Tel/Fax 02151 392908 Chairman Stuart Dykes Tel 02151 477917 Fax 02151 435168 E-mail stuart.dykes@ta-online.de

GERMAN REDS Branch Secretary Thomas Rochel, Lessingstr 23, D-39108 Magdeburg, Germany Tel 00 49 391 733 8275 Fax 00 49 391 7313127 E-mail th.rochel@t-online.de

GIBRALTAR Manchester United Supporters Gibraltar Branch, PO Box 22, Gibraltar Tel 350 76846 Fax 350 71608 Mobile 587 05000 Branch Chairman Clive A Moberley Branch Secretary Gerald Laguea

HOLLAND Branch Chairman Ron Snellen, PO Box 33742, 2503 BA Den Haag, Holland Tel 00 31 70 329 8602 Fax 00 31 70 367 2247 Internet www.dutch-mancunians.nl E-mail dennisvandervin@hetnet.nl

HONG KONG 12B Shun Ho Tower, 24-30 Ice House Street, Central, Hong Kong Tel 00 852 2869 1993 Fax 00 852 2869 4312 Branch Secretary/Treasurer Rick Adkinson Chairman Mark Saunders

ICELAND Branch Secretary Bubbi Avesson, Studningsmannaklubbur, Manchester United á Íslandi, PO Box 12170, 132 Reykjavik, Iceland

LUXEMBOURG Branch Secretary Steve Kaiser Tel 00 352 4301 33073 (w) 00 352 340265 (H)

MALTA Quarries Square, Msida MSD 03, Malta Tel 00 356 22351 Fax 00 356 231902 E-mail: musc@maltanet.net.mt Website www.maltazone.com/hosted/mufc Branch President: John Buttigieg

MAURITIUS Branch Secretary Yacoob Atchia, Flamingo Pool House, Remeno Street, Rose Hill, Mauritius, Indian Ocean Tel 464 7382/454 7761/454 3570/464 7750 Fax 454 7839 E-mail abyss.manutd@intnet.mu Chairman Swallay Banhoo Tel 464 4450 (h) Treasurer Naniel Baichoo Tel 454 3570 (w) 465 0387 (h)

NEW SOUTH WALES Chairperson Steve Griffiths Vice-Chairperson Tony Redman Treasurer Jeanette Frost Secretary John Panaretto Founders Fred & Ann Pollitt Branch Address P.O.Box 693, Sutherland, New South Wales 1499, Australia Tel/Fax 00 61 2 982 29781 Website http://manutd-nsw.one.net.au/index.htm

NEW ZEALAND Branch Chairman Brian Wood, 55 Pine Street, Mount Eden, Auckland, New Zealand Secretary Gillian Goodinson, 20 Sandown Road, Rothesay Bay, Auckland, New Zealand

SCANDANAVIA Branch Secretary Per H Larsen, PO Box 4003 Dreggen, N-5835 Bergan, Norway Tel +47 5530 2770 (Mon - Fri 08.00-16.00) Fax +47 5596 2033 E-Mail muscsb@united.no

SOUTH AUSTRALIA PO Box 276, Ingle Farm, South Australia 5098 Fax 08 82816731 Branch Secretary Mick Griffiths Tel 08 82644499 Branch Chairman Chris Golder Tel 08 82630602 Vice-Chairma John Harrison Tel 08 82603413 Treasurer Charlie Kelly Tel 08 82628245 Meetings are held at the Para Hills Soccer Club, Bridge Road, Para Hills, SA. The Manchester United Supporters Amateur League Soccer team train and play at Para Hills Soccer Club.

SWISS DEVILS Branch Secretary Marc Tanner, Dorfstrasse 30d, 5430 Wettingen, Switzerland Tel (00 41 56) 426 94 80 Website www.swissdevils.ch E-mail vonisan@yahoo.co.uk

TOKYO Branch Secretary Hiroki Miyaji, 2-24-10 Minami-Ayoma, Minato-ku, Tokyo, Japan Tel +81 3 3470 3441 English Information Stephen Ryan Tel +81 3 3380 8441 E-mail best-oz@kk.iij4u.or.jp

U.S.A. Branch Secretary Peter Holland, MUSC USA Branch HQ, 139 West Neck Road, Huntingdon, N.Y. 11743, U.S.A. Tel 00 1 516 547 5500 (day) Fax 00 1 516 547 6800 (day) Tel/Fax 00 1 516 261 7314 (evening) E-mail muscusa@datacapture.com (day) muscusa@muscusa.com (evening) Web Site www.muscusa.com Webmaster jpkell@ix.netcom.com

VICTORIAN AUSTRALIA President Kieran Dunleavy, PO Box 1199, Camberwell, 3124 Victoria Tel/Fax 9 804 0244 Web Page Http://www.strug.com.au-sidcol E-mail muscovic@vicnet.net.au

WESTERN AUSTRALIA Branch Chairman Graham Wyche, 19 Frobisher Avenue, Sorrento 6020, Perth, Western Australia Tel/Fax (08) 9 447 1144; Mobile 0417 903 101 E-mail freobook@omen.com.au

YOUR CHANCE

TO SAVE  £5

ON THESE OFFICIAL
AUTOBIOGRAPHIES!

Andy Cole: The Autobiography
Andy Cole with Peter Fitton
ISBN: 0 233 99737 7

Dwight Yorke: The Official Biography
Hunter Davies
ISBN: 0 233 99759 8

Simply order either of the books shown and save
£5 off the published price of £14.99.

They are yours for only £9.99 each!

Phone 0870 900 2050 quoting reference AD05 to order copies.

Postage and packaging is free.